SAGE Readings
for Introductory Sociology

Kimberly McGann
Nazareth College

Los Angeles | London | New Delhi
Singapore | Washington DC | Boston

Los Angeles | London | New Delhi
Singapore | Washington DC | Boston

FOR INFORMATION:

SAGE Publications, Inc.
2455 Teller Road
Thousand Oaks, California 91320
E-mail: order@sagepub.com

SAGE Publications Ltd.
1 Oliver's Yard
55 City Road
London, EC1Y 1SP
United Kingdom

SAGE Publications India Pvt. Ltd.
B 1/I 1 Mohan Cooperative Industrial Area
Mathura Road, New Delhi 110 044
India

SAGE Publications Asia-Pacific Pte. Ltd.
3 Church Street
#10-04 Samsung Hub
Singapore 049483

Printed in the United States of America

Cataloging-in-publication data is available for this title from the Library of Congress.

ISBN 978-1-4833-7869-5

This book is printed on acid-free paper.

Acquisitions Editor: Jeff Lasser
Editorial Assistant: Alexandra Croell
Production Editor: Kelly DeRosa
Copy Editor: Marié Murray
Typesetter: Hurix Systems Pvt. Ltd.
Proofreader: Dennis W. Webb
Cover Designer: Anupama Krishnan
Marketing Manager: Erica DeLuca

15 16 17 18 19 10 9 8 7 6 5 4 3 2 1

SAGE was founded in 1965 by Sara Miller McCune to support the dissemination of usable knowledge by publishing innovative and high-quality research and teaching content. Today, we publish more than 750 journals, including those of more than 300 learned societies, more than 800 new books per year, and a growing range of library products including archives, data, case studies, reports, conference highlights, and video. SAGE remains majority-owned by our founder, and after Sara's lifetime will become owned by a charitable trust that secures our continued independence.

Los Angeles | London | Washington DC | New Delhi | Singapore | Boston

SAGE Readings
for Introductory Sociology

Table of Contents

Part III: Constructing Deviance and Normality

Part IV: Gender

Part V: Race

Part VI: Social Class

Theme/Topic Alternative Table of Contents

Preface

⟩⟩ WHERE DID THIS BOOK COME FROM?

In 1994, I was a sophomore in college standing in line to register for my junior year. (Yes, we still had to stand in line in those days, although there was someone with a computer to enter our class choices at the front of the line!) I was very excited to finally have an early enough registration slot that I would be able to get into several classes I had been closed out of in previous semesters. But when I got to the front of the line I discovered that I couldn't register until I declared a major, something I had not yet done. I asked if I had to decide right then and was told no but that I would have go to the end of the line when I came back! Unwilling to lose my place, I hemmed and hawed a bit and finally blurted, "Well, those sociology classes look like the most interesting ones, so put me down for that." It turned out to be an excellent, if haphazard choice, and I eventually went on to earn my PhD in sociology.

Given this true story, I obviously didn't go through childhood dreaming of being a sociologist when I grew up. I wound up in my first sociology course as an innocent bystander of the liberal arts requirements at my school, and this is one of the most common ways students wind up in an introduction to sociology course. And many, like me, are intrigued and choose to take more courses, major or minor, or even go on to graduate school and earn PhDs. Regardless of how you wound up enrolled in your sociology class, this set of readings was put together for you. This volume contains readings that have withstood the scrutiny of not just enthusiastic future sociology majors but also many a skeptical, sleepy, distracted college student over the past 10 years; they have been used in introduction to sociology courses at a community college, large and small state universities, and at a private liberal arts institution. Those selected for inclusion in this volume are here not just because they are good representatives of the key concepts in sociology but also because they present arguments and ideas that are relevant to the day-to-day lives of college students and have, in my experience, sparked lively discussions and much interest in class.

\\\\ WHAT'S IN THIS BOOK?

Sociology is a broad discipline whose boundaries are defined less by subject and more by perspective. This volume gathers in one place some of the classic readings in sociology, as well as contemporary articles that examine common sociological themes in an engaging and accessible fashion. This range is reflected here in readings covering topics from power, politics, and poverty to why there's always a line for the women's restroom, how Viagra transformed impotence to erectile dysfunction, and strategies college students use to normalize cheating. You'll find a range of readings that deal with big-picture (what sociologists call macrolevel) issues and also readings that examine the nitty-gritty microlevel details of social life and interaction.

\\\\ HOW SHOULD I READ THIS BOOK?

This book was designed to be appropriate for use either in conjunction with a traditional textbook or as a stand-alone text for an introduction to sociology course. Whether your instructor has assigned this book as a supplement or your only text, there are additional materials included to help you get the most from each article. Each reading has a brief introduction that places it in perspective for you and suggests an approach to reading the piece. There are also discussion questions and/or activities to accompany each piece that may be used as the basis of class discussion by your teacher or simply as thought-provoking exercises for you to do on your own. The writing styles of the readings vary widely, and you will likely find many of the pieces accessible and enjoyable to read. However, there are some that are likely to present more of a challenge, and I encourage you not to give up on these! Think of writing like wrapping paper: Just because you don't think it's attractive or it's hard to take apart doesn't mean that what's inside isn't really enjoyable! All these articles have something important and interesting to say about the social world we live in. Just as we shouldn't judge a book by its cover, I encourage you not to judge an article's ideas by its writing style!

⫶⫶ I LIKE THIS! WHAT DO I DO NOW?

If you find yourself intrigued with some of the ideas you encounter in this book, you might consider majoring or minoring in sociology if you aren't already. Many students over the years have found a sociological perspective to be a compelling, useful, and meaningful way to understand the world around them but are unsure what exactly to do with those skills and ideas once they graduate. Your professor and the chair of the sociology department should be your first stop. They will have a good idea of the types of jobs that majors and minors from your school have found. The American Sociological Association also has an excellent set of resources for those interested in using a sociology major or minor on the job market. Just visit asanet.org and type *sociology major* into the search box (or visit directly at http://www.asanet.org/students/resources_majors.cfm).

Finally, remember that you don't have to major or minor in sociology to put the ideas from these readings to work in your own life and the world around you. A sociological perspective is a valuable tool for understanding how the context of the social world has consequences (good and bad) for what happens to individuals. Not only can this help you make informed decisions about your own life choices, but you'll be able to see how social forces also influence your life chances and plan accordingly.

⫶⫶ ACKNOWLEDGMENTS

I was lucky enough to have Donileen Loseke and Spencer Cahill introduce me to sociology at Skidmore College when I was an undergraduate, and I am still grateful for their dedication and talent as both sociologists and teachers. My experiences with them set the standard that I still aspire to as a teacher and scholar.

Contrary to popular belief, one does not magically age out of writer's block, fits of procrastination, or self-doubt. Rebecca Plante at Ithaca College has been unfailingly helpful and supportive about all aspects of this project, and I'm grateful for the time she has taken out of her own already too busy publishing schedule to lend an ear. Rachel Bailey Jones has also provided years of moral support and enviable scholarly output that convinced me this project was indeed doable. Our school, Nazareth College, also facilitated this project by granting me a sabbatical, which allowed me to take on this project without fear of not having time to finish.

I'd like to thank Jeff Lasser at SAGE Publications for taking a chance on a new author and for having a wonderfully collaborative and straightforward approach to this process. This has been a thoroughly enjoyable project to work on.

Finally, I am most grateful to all of the students who have taken introduction to sociology with me over the past 10 or more years. Their insights and feedback have vastly improved my teaching, and I have learned as much from them as they have from me. Their goodwill and willingness to put up with (and occasionally embrace) my wacky analogies, stick figure drawings, and bad jokes always amazes me. College students are interesting people at an interesting time in their lives, and I feel lucky to have a job that lets me be a part of that.

1

The Sociological Imagination

The Promise

C. Wright Mills

Students often enroll in an introduction to sociology course without having any idea what sociology is. Oftentimes, the course description sounded interesting or the class fulfilled a requirement or a friend recommended the class. And sometimes, students leave class at the end of the semester having learned a great deal about poverty, social norms, culture, race, and gender but perhaps still a little fuzzy on what makes sociology "sociology." This is not just understandable, but it also should be of no great surprise given that many of the topics that sociologists study are also studied by other disciplines. Social workers and economists also study the distribution of wealth and the effects of poverty. Psychologists are interested in how social norms affect people's behavior. Anthropologists study culture. Historians look at how gender roles and race relations have changed over time. If there's so much overlap in what different disciplines study, what is it that makes sociology unique as discipline?

The answer lies not in what *sociologists study, but in* how *they study the world around them. This unique sociological perspective is described in this classic piece by C. Wright Mills. He uses the term* sociological imagination *to describe a way of studying the world that connects what happens to individuals to larger social, cultural, political, and economic forces. Or as he puts it, "Neither the life of an individual nor the history of a society can be understood without understanding both" (p. 3). What Mills is arguing is that sociology provides a perspective that lets people see how what happens to them is influenced by events, policies, and interactions that make up the social structure of a society. It's important to note that he's not at all arguing that we as individuals have no autonomy and that our own individual actions and efforts don't matter in what happens to us. Instead, he's urging us to be aware of the social and historical context in which our lives unfold and to think about how those social and historical forces shape our individual life chances. (Life chances are the odds that some opportunity or obstacle will present itself to you.) To give one example—college students who graduated between 2008 and 2014 are much more likely to be unemployed or underemployed than students who graduated before 2008. Why might this be? From an individual perspective, we might argue that these particular students are less motivated or not as smart or qualified as those who graduated before 2008. Perhaps they just didn't try as hard to get jobs. These are all individual-level explanations, and none of them explain why these graduates were so much less likely to find good jobs. But if we employ Mills's sociological imagination, it immediately becomes clear that the number of jobs available in the U.S. economy shrank drastically in 2008 due to the financial crisis. It certainly mattered for students graduating in that time period if they were smart, qualified, and motivated to find a job. But it also mattered that there weren't enough jobs in the economy for all the qualified candidates. This is an example of linking what's happening at the social and historical level (the economy shrank and had fewer jobs available) to what happens to individuals (the 2008—2014 cohort of college graduates were less likely to find good jobs.) This is the underpinning of sociological imagination, and it is this way of thinking about the world that defines sociology.*

As you read this article, think about what aspects of your life are shaped by where and when you are living. The sociological imagination is the underpinning of sociology as a discipline, but it's also incredibly useful in understanding how and why life unfolds the way it does for you and those around you. Once you start to be able to see the connections between what happens to individuals and larger social forces, you're well on your way to having a better understanding of the social world and being able to see the world from a sociological perspective.

Nowadays men often feel that their private lives are a series of traps. They sense that within their everyday worlds, they cannot overcome their troubles, and in this feeling, they are often quite correct: What ordinary men are directly aware of and what they try to do are bounded by the private orbits in which they live; their visions and their powers are limited to the close-up scenes of job, family, neighborhood; in other milieux, they move vicariously and remain spectators. And the more aware they become, however vaguely, of ambitions and of threats which transcend their immediate locales, the more trapped they seem to feel.

Underlying this sense of being trapped are seemingly impersonal changes in the very structure of continent-wide societies. The facts of contemporary history are also facts about the success and the failure of individual men and women. When a society is industrialized, a peasant becomes a worker; a feudal lord is liquidated or becomes a businessman. When classes rise or fall, a man is employed or unemployed; when the rate of investment goes up or down, a man takes new heart or goes broke. When wars happen, an insurance salesman becomes a rocket launcher; a store clerk, a radar man; a wife lives alone; a child grows up without a father. Neither the life of an individual nor the history of a society can be understood without understanding both.

Yet men do not usually define the troubles they endure in terms of historical change and institutional contradiction. The well-being they enjoy, they do not usually impute to the big ups and downs of the societies in which they live. Seldom aware of the intricate connection between the patterns of their own lives and the course of world history, ordinary men do not usually know what this connection means for the kinds of men they are becoming and for the kinds of history-making in which they might take part. They do not possess the quality of mind essential to grasp the interplay of man and society, of biography and history, of self and world. They cannot cope with their personal troubles in such ways as to control the structural transformations that usually lie behind them.

What they need, and what they feel they need, is a quality of mind that will help them to use information and to develop reason in order to achieve lucid summations of what is going on in the world and of what may be happening within themselves. It is this quality, I am going to contend, that journalists and scholars, artists and publics, scientists and editors are coming to expect of what may be called the sociological imagination.

 1

The sociological imagination enables its possessor to understand the larger historical scene in terms of its meaning for the inner life and the external career of a variety of individuals. It enables him to take into account how individuals, in the welter of their daily experience, often become falsely conscious of their social positions. Within that welter, the framework of modern society is sought, and within that framework the psychologies of a variety of men and women are formulated. By such means the personal uneasiness of individuals is focused upon explicit troubles and the indifference of publics is transformed into involvement with public issues.

The first fruit of this imagination—and the first lesson of the social science that embodies it—is the idea that the individual can understand his own experience and gauge his own fate only by locating himself within his period, that he can know his own chances in life only by becoming aware of those of all individuals in his circumstances. In many ways it is a terrible lesson; in many ways a magnificent one. We do not know the limits of man's capacities for supreme effort or willing degradation, for agony or glee, for pleasurable brutality or the sweetness of reason. But in our time we have come to know that the limits of 'human nature' are frighteningly broad. We have come to know that every individual lives, from one generation to the next, in some society; that he lives out a biography, and that he lives it out within some historical sequence. By the fact of his living he contributes, however minutely, to the shaping of this society and to the course of its history, even as he is made by society and by its historical push and shove.

The sociological imagination enables us to grasp history and biography and the relations between the two within society. That is its task and its promise. To recognize this task and this promise is the mark of the classic social analyst It is characteristic of Herbert Spencer—turgid, polysyllabic, comprehensive; of E. A. Ross—graceful, muckraking, upright; of Auguste Comte and Emile Durkheim; of the intricate and subtle Karl Mannheim. It is the quality of all that is intellectually excellent in Karl Marx; it is the clue to Thorstein Veblen's brilliant and ironic insight, to Joseph Schumpeter's many-sided constructions of reality; it is the basis of the psychological sweep of W. E. H. Lecky no less than of the profundity and clarity of Max Weber. And it is the signal of what is best in contemporary studies of man and society.

No social study that does not come back to the problems of biography, of history and of their intersections within a society has completed its intellectual journey. Whatever the specific problems of the classic social analysts, however limited or however broad the features of social reality they have examined, those who have been imaginatively aware of the promise of their work have consistently asked three sorts of questions:

(1) What is the structure of this particular society as a whole? What are its essential components, and how are they related to one another? How does it differ from other varieties of social order? Within it, what is the meaning of any particular feature for its continuance and for its change?

(2) Where does this society stand in human history? What are the mechanics by which it is changing? What is its place within and its meaning for the development of

humanity as a whole? How does any particular feature we are examining affect, and how is it affected by, the historical period in which it moves? And this period—what are its essential features? How does it differ from other periods? What are its characteristic ways of history-making?

(3) What varieties of men and women now prevail in this society and in this period? And what varieties are coming to prevail? In what ways are they selected and formed, liberated and repressed, made sensitive and blunted? What kinds of 'human nature' are revealed in the conduct and character we observe in this society in this period? And what is the meaning for 'human nature' of each and every feature of the society we are examining?

Whether the point of interest is a great power state or a minor literary mood, a family, a prison, a creed—these are the kinds of questions the best social analysts have asked. They are the intellectual pivots of classic studies of man in society—and they are the questions inevitably raised by any mind possessing the sociological imagination. For that imagination is the capacity to shift from one perspective to another—from the political to the psychological from examination of a single family to comparative assessment of the national budgets of the world; from the theological school to the military establishment; from considerations of an oil industry to studies of contemporary poetry. It is the capacity to range from the most impersonal and remote transformations to the most intimate features of the human self—and to see the relations between the two. Back of its use there is always the urge to know the social and historical meaning of the individual in the society and in the period in which he has his quality and his being.

That, in brief, is why it is by means of the sociological imagination that men now hope to grasp what is going on in the world, and to understand what is happening in themselves as minute points of the intersections of biography and history within society. In large part contemporary man's self-conscious view of himself as at least an outsider, if not a permanent stranger, rests upon an absorbed realization of social relativity and of the transformative power of history. The sociological imagination is the most fruitful form of this self-consciousness. By its use men whose mentalities have swept only a series of limited orbits often come to feel as if suddenly awakened in a house with which they had only supposed themselves to be familiar. Correctly or incorrectly, they often come to feel that they can now provide themselves with adequate summations, cohesive assessments, comprehensive orientations. Older decisions that once appeared sound now seem to them products of a mind unaccountably dense. Their capacity for astonishment is made lively again. They acquire a new way of thinking, they experience a transvaluation of values: in a word, by their reflection and by their sensibility, they realize the cultural meaning of the social sciences.

⃥ 2

Perhaps the most fruitful distinction with which the sociological imagination works is between 'the personal troubles of milieu' and 'the public issues of social structure.' This distinction is an essential tool of the sociological imagination and a feature of all classic work in social science.

Troubles occur within the character of the individual and within the range of his immediate relations with others; they have to do with his self and with those limited areas of social life of which he is directly and personally aware. Accordingly, the statement and the resolution of troubles properly lie within the individual as a biographical entity and within the scope of his immediate milieu—the social setting that is directly open to his personal experience and to some extent his willful activity. A trouble is a private matter: values cherished by an individual are felt by him to be threatened.

Issues have to do with matters that transcend these local environments of the individual and the range of his inner life They have to do with the organization of many such milieux into the institutions of an historical society as a whole, with the ways in which various milieux overlap and interpenetrate to form the larger structure of social and historical life. An issue is a public matter: some value cherished by publics is felt to be threatened. Often there is a debate about what that value really is and about what it is that really threatens it. This debate is often without focus if only because it is the very nature of an issue, unlike even widespread trouble, that it cannot very well be defined in terms of the immediate and everyday environments of ordinary men. An issue, in fact, often involves a crisis in institutional arrangements, and often too it involves what Marxists call 'contradictions' or 'antagonisms.'

In these terms, consider unemployment. When, in a city of 100,000, only one man is unemployed, that is his personal trouble, and for its relief we properly look to the character of the man, his skills, and his immediate opportunities. But when in a nation of 50 million employees, 15 million men are unemployed, that is an issue, and we may not hope to find its solution within the range of opportunities open to any one individual. The very structure of opportunities has collapsed. Both the correct statement of the problem and the range of possible solutions require us to consider the economic and political institutions of the society, and not merely the personal situation and character of a scatter of individuals.

Consider war. The personal problem of war, when it occurs, may be how to survive it or how to die in it with honor; how to make money out of it; how to climb into the higher safety of the military apparatus; or how to contribute to the war's termination. In short, according to one's values, to find a set of milieux and within it to survive the war or make one's death in it meaningful. But the structural issues of war have to do with its causes; with what types of men it throws up into command; with its effects upon economic and political, family and religious institutions, with the unorganized irresponsibility of a world of nation-states.

Consider marriage. Inside a marriage a man and a woman may experience personal troubles, but when the divorce rate during the first four years of marriage is 250 out of every 1,000 attempts, this is an indication of a structural issue having to do with the institutions of marriage and the family and other institutions that bear upon them.

In so far as an economy is so arranged that slumps occur, the problem of unemployment becomes incapable of personal solution. In so far as war is inherent in the nation-state system and in the uneven industrialization of the world, the ordinary individual in his restricted milieu will be powerless—with or without psychiatric aid—to solve the troubles this system or lack of system imposes upon him. In so far as the family as an institution turns women into darling little slaves and men into their chief providers and unweaned dependents, the problem of a satisfactory marriage remains incapable of purely private solution.

What we experience in various and specific milieux, I have noted, is often caused by structural changes. Accordingly, to understand the changes of many personal milieux we are required to look beyond them. And the number and variety of such structural changes increase as the institutions within which we live become more embracing and more intricately connected with one another. To be aware of the idea of social structure and to use it with sensibility is to be capable of tracing such linkages among a great variety of milieux. To be able to do that is to possess the sociological imagination.

DISCUSSION QUESTIONS

1. Make a list of three to four important goals you would like to accomplish sometime in the future. What larger social forces will either facilitate your achieving these goals or make them more difficult to attain?

2. How do you think your life would be different if you had been born 75 years ago? What do you think would have been different about your childhood? Your diet and exercise habits? Your life expectancy? Your educational opportunities? Your career choices? Your fashion sense?

3. Friendship seems like a natural, freely chosen relationship that is based entirely on individual preferences. People who meet and enjoy each other's

company often become friends. How do larger social forces influence our "choice" of friends? Does when and where you grow up affect who you might become friends with? Does your gender, race, or social class? What role do you think technology and social media might play in how people go about getting and maintaining friendships?

2

Invitation to Sociology

A Humanistic Perspective

Peter L. Berger

In the previous piece, C. Wright Mills provided a description of one of the broadest defining features of sociology as a discipline, the sociological imagination. In this article, Peter Berger adds more detail and depth to our understanding of what sociology is as a discipline and what it means to be a sociologist. He notes wryly at the beginning of this piece, "there are very few jokes about sociologists" (p. 10). Although this article was written well before the invention of the Internet, a quick Google search today will confirm his observation. For example, there are 196,000 sociologist jokes compared to almost 9 million psychologist jokes. He uses this observation as a jumping off point to talk about how little the general public knows about sociology and to address the typical (and largely incorrect) assumptions about what sociology is and what kinds of people choose to become sociologists. It's not just a variation on social work (or vice versa), nor are the tools of sociological thinking only useful to those who wish to make the world a better place. And while he notes that statistics often play a role in sociological inquiry, it is the broader commitment to scientific standards of data, objectivity, and logic that make sociology a science.

Think for a moment, before you continue reading, about whether you've ever taken a particular interest in some aspect of the world around you that is usually taken for granted. Why are we so irritated with the people who cut in line at the grocery store or sit in our seat halfway through the semester? What does the wild popularity of reality television say about our culture? Why do men's sports teams have cheerleaders, but women's teams do not? Why are some people seemingly unable to follow the unwritten rules of conversational turn taking? Why do people often eat lunch with people of their own race? A central characteristic of a sociologist is curiosity and eagerness to carefully and systematically study the social world, either from a macrolevel (for example, studying how world peace can be achieved), a microlevel (such as how romantic partners use text messaging), or both. Does this sound like it might be you?

There are very few jokes about sociologists. This is frustrating for the sociologists, especially if they compare themselves with their more favored second cousins, the psychologists, who have pretty much taken over that sector of American humor that used to be occupied by clergymen. A psychologist, introduced as such at a party, at once finds himself the object of considerable attention and uncomfortable mirth. A sociologist in the same circumstance is likely to meet with no more of a reaction than if he had been announced as an insurance salesman. He will have to win his attention the hard way, just like everyone else. This is annoying and unfair, but it may also be instructive. The dearth of jokes about sociologists indicates, of course, that they are not as much part of the popular imagination as psychologists have become. But it probably also indicates that there is a certain ambiguity in the images that people do have of them. It may thus be a good starting point for our considerations to take a closer look at some of these images.

If one asks undergraduate students why they are taking sociology as a major, one often gets the reply, "because I like to work with people." If one then goes on to ask such students about their occupational future, as they envisage it, one often hears that they intend to go into social work. Of this more in a moment. Other answers are more vague and general, but all indicate that the student in question would rather deal with people than with things. Occupations mentioned in this connection include personnel work, human relations in industry, public relations, advertising, community planning or religious work of the unordained variety. The common assumption is that in all these lines of endeavor one might "do something for people," "help people," "do work that is useful for the community." The image of the sociologist involved here could be described as a secularized version of the liberal Protestant ministry, with the YMCA secretary perhaps furnishing the connecting link between sacred and profane benevolence. Sociology is seen as an up-to-date variation on the classic American theme of "uplift." The sociologist is understood as one professionally concerned with edifying activities on behalf of individuals and of the community at large.

One of these days a great American novel will have to be written on the savage disappointment this sort of motivation is bound to suffer in most of the occupations just mentioned. There is moving pathos in the fate of these likers of people who go into personnel work and come up for the first time against the human realities of a strike that they must fight on one side of the savagely drawn battle lines, or who go into public relations and discover just what it is that they are expected to put over in what experts in the field have called "the engineering of consent," or who go into community agencies to begin a brutal education in the politics of real estate speculation. But our concern here is not with the despoiling of innocence. It is rather with a particular image of the sociologist, an image that is inaccurate and misleading.

It is, of course, true that some Boy Scout types have become sociologists. It is also true that a benevolent interest in people could be the biographical starting point for sociological studies. But it is important to point out that a malevolent and misanthropic outlook could serve just as well. Sociological insights are valuable to anyone concerned with action in society. But this action need not be particularly humanitarian. Some American sociologists today are employed by governmental agencies seeking to plan more livable communities for the nation. Other American sociologists are employed by governmental agencies concerned with wiping communities of hostile nations off the map, if and when the necessity should arise. Whatever the moral implications of these respective activities may be, there is no reason why interesting sociological studies could not be carried on in both. Similarly, criminology, as a special field within sociology, has uncovered valuable information about processes of crime in modern society. This information is equally valuable for those seeking to fight crime as it would be for those interested in promoting it. The fact that more criminologists have been employed by the police than by gangsters can be ascribed to the ethical bias of the criminologists themselves, the public relations of the police and perhaps the lack of scientific sophistication of the gangsters. It has nothing to do with the character of the information itself. In sum, "working with people" can mean getting them out of slums or getting them into jail, selling them propaganda or robbing them of their money (be it legally or illegally), making them produce better automobiles or making them better bomber pilots. As an image of the sociologist, then, the phrase leaves something to be desired, even though it may serve to describe at least the initial impulse as a result of which some people turn to the study of sociology.

Some additional comments are called for in connection with a closely related image of the sociologist as a sort of theoretician for social work. This image is understandable in view of the development of sociology in America. At least one of the roots of American sociology is to be found in the worries of social workers confronted with the massive problems following in the wake of the industrial revolution—the rapid growth of cities and of slums within them, mass immigration, mass movements of people, the disruption of traditional ways of life and the resulting disorientation of individuals caught in these processes. Much sociological research has been spurred by this sort of concern. And so it is still quite customary for undergraduate students planning to go into social work to major in sociology.

Actually, American social work has been far more influenced by psychology than by sociology in the development of its "theory." Very probably this fact is not unrelated to what was previously said about the relative status of sociology and psychology in the popular imagination. Social workers have had to fight an uphill battle for a long time to be recognized as "professionals," and to get the prestige, power and (not least) pay that such recognition entails. Looking around for a "professional" model to emulate, they found that of the psychiatrist to be the most natural. And so contemporary social workers receive their "clients" in an office, conduct fifty-minute "clinical interviews" with them, record the interviews in quadruplicate and discuss them with a hierarchy of "supervisors." Having adopted the outward paraphernalia of the psychiatrist, they naturally also adopted his ideology. Thus contemporary American social-work "theory" consists very largely of a somewhat bowdlerized version of psychoanalytic psychology, a sort of poor man's Freudianism that serves to legitimate the social worker's claim to help people in a "scientific" way. We are not interested here in investigating the "scientific" validity of this synthetic doctrine. Our point is that not only does it have very little to do with sociology, but it is marked, indeed, by a singular obtuseness with regard to social reality. The identification of sociology with social work in the minds of many people is somewhat a phenomenon of "cultural lag," dating from the period when as yet pre- "professional" social workers dealt with poverty rather than with libidinal frustration, and did so without the benefit of a dictaphone.

But even if American social work had not jumped on the bandwagon of popular psychologism the image of the sociologist as the social worker's theoretical mentor would be misleading. Social work, whatever its theoretical rationalization, is a certain *practice* in society. Sociology is not a practice, but an *attempt to understand*. Certainly this understanding may have use for the practitioner. For that matter, we would contend that a more profound grasp of sociology would be of great use to the social worker and that such grasp would obviate the necessity of his descending into the mythological depths of the "subconscious" to explain matters that are typically quite conscious, much more simple and, indeed, *social* in nature. But there is nothing inherent in the sociological enterprise of trying to understand society that necessarily leads to this practice, or to any other. Sociological understanding can be recommended to social workers, but also to salesmen, nurses, evangelists and politicians—in fact, to anyone whose goals involve the manipulation of men, for whatever purpose and with whatever moral justification.

This conception of the sociological enterprise is implied in the classic statement by Max Weber, one of the most important figures in the development of the field, to the effect that sociology is "value-free." Since it will be necessary to return to this a number of times later, it may be well to explicate it a little further at this point. Certainly the statement does *not* mean that the sociologist has or should have no values. In any case, it is just about impossible for a human being to exist without any values at all, though, of course, there can be tremendous variation in the values one may hold. The sociologist will normally have many values as a citizen, a private person, a member of a religious group or as an adherent of some other association of people. But within the limits of his activities as a sociologist there is one fundamental value only—that of scientific integrity. Even there, of course, the sociologist, being human, will have to reckon with his convictions, emotions and prejudices. But it is part of his intellectual training that he tries to understand and control these as *bias* that ought to be eliminated, as far as possible, from his work. It goes without saying that this is not always easy to do, but it is not impossible. The sociologist tries to see what is there. He may have hopes or fears concerning what he may find. But he will try to see regardless of his hopes or fears. It is thus an act of pure perception, as pure as humanly limited means allow, toward which sociology strives.

It is gratifying from certain value positions (including some of this writer's) that sociological insights have served in a number of instances to improve the lot of groups of human beings by uncovering morally shocking conditions or by clearing away collective illusions or by showing that socially desired results could be obtained in more humane fashion. One might point, for example, to some applications of sociological knowledge in the penological practice of Western countries. Or one might cite the use made of sociological studies in the Supreme Court decision of 1954 on racial segregation in the public schools. Or one could look at the applications of other sociological studies to the humane planning of urban redevelopment. Certainly the sociologist who is morally and politically sensitive will derive gratification from such instances. But, once more, it will be well to keep in mind that what is at issue here is not sociological understanding as such but certain applications of this understanding. It is not difficult to see how the same understanding could be applied with opposite intentions. Thus the sociological understanding of the dynamics of racial prejudice can be applied effectively by those promoting intragroup hatred as well as by those wanting to spread tolerance. And the sociological understanding of the nature of human solidarity can be employed in the service of both totalitarian and democratic regimes. It is sobering to realize that the same processes that generate consensus can be manipulated by a social group worker in a summer camp in the Adirondacks and by a Communist brainwasher in a prisoner camp in China. One may readily grant that the sociologist can sometimes be called upon to give advice when it comes to changing certain social conditions deemed undesirable. But the image of the sociologist as social reformer suffers from the same confusion as the image of him as social worker.

If these images of the sociologist all have an element of "cultural lag" about them, we can now turn to some other images that are of more recent date and refer themselves to more recent developments in the discipline. One such image is that of the sociologist as a gatherer of statistics about human behavior. The sociologist is here seen essentially as an aide-de-camp to an IBM machine. He goes out with a questionnaire, interviews people selected at random, then goes home, enters his tabulations onto innumerable punch cards, which are then fed into a machine. In all of this, of course, he is supported by a large staff and a very large budget. Included in this image is the implication that the results of all this effort are picayune, a pedantic restatement of what everybody knows anyway. As one observer remarked pithily, a sociologist is a fellow who spends $100,000 to find his way to a house of ill repute.

This image of the sociologist has been strengthened in the public mind by the activities of many agencies that might well be called parasociological, mainly agencies concerned with public opinion and market trends. The pollster has become a well-known figure in American life, inopportuning people about their views from foreign policy to toilet paper. Since the methods used in the pollster business bear close resemblance to sociological research, the growth of this image of the sociologist is understandable. The Kinsey studies of American sexual behavior have probably greatly augmented the impact of this image. The fundamental sociological question, whether concerned with premarital petting or with Republican votes or with the incidence of gang knifings, is always presumed to be "how often?" or "how many?" Incidentally the very few jokes current about sociologists usually relate to this statistical image (which jokes had better be left to the imagination of the reader).

Statistical data by themselves do not make sociology. They become sociology only when they are sociologically interpreted, put within a theoretical frame of reference that is sociological. Simple counting, or even correlating different items that one counts, is not sociology. There is almost no sociology in the Kinsey reports. This does not mean that the data in these studies are not true or that they cannot be relevant to sociological understanding. They are, taken by themselves, raw materials that can be used in sociological interpretation. The interpretation, however, must be broader than the data themselves. So the sociologist cannot arrest himself at the frequency tables of premarital petting or extramarital pederasty.

These enumerations are meaningful to him only in terms of their much broader implications for an understanding of institutions and values in our society. To arrive at such understanding the sociologist will often have to apply statistical techniques, especially when he is dealing with the mass phenomena of modern social life. But sociology consists of statistics as little as philology consists of conjugating irregular verbs or chemistry of making nasty smells in test tubes.

Sociology has, from its beginnings, understood itself as a science. There has been much controversy about the precise meaning of this self-definition. For instance, German sociologists have emphasized the difference between the social and the natural sciences much more strongly than their French or American colleagues. But the allegiance of sociologists to the scientific ethos has meant everywhere a willingness to be bound by certain scientific canons of procedure. If the sociologist remains faithful to his calling, his statements must be arrived at through the observation of certain rules of evidence that allow others to check on or to repeat or to develop his findings further. It is this scientific discipline that often supplies the motive for reading a sociological work as against, say, a novel on the same topic that might describe matters in much more impressive and convincing language. As sociologists tried to develop their scientific rules of evidence, they were compelled to reflect upon methodological problems. This is why methodology is a necessary and valid part of the sociological enterprise.

Finally, we would look at an image of the sociologist not so much in his professional role as in his being, supposedly, a certain kind of person. This is the image of the sociologist as a detached, sardonic observer, and a cold manipulator of men. Where this image prevails, it may represent an ironic triumph of the sociologist's own efforts to be accepted as a genuine scientist. The sociologist here becomes the self-appointed superior man, standing off from the warm vitality of common existence, finding his satisfactions not in living but in coolly appraising the lives of others, filing them away in little categories, and thus presumably missing the real significance of what he is observing. Further, there is the notion that, when he involves himself in social processes at all, the sociologist does so as an uncommitted technician, putting his manipulative skills at the disposal of the powers that be.

This last image is probably not very widely held. It is mainly held by people concerned for political reasons with actual or possible misuses of sociology in modern societies. There is not very much to say about this image by way of refutation. As a general portrait of the contemporary sociologist it is certainly a gross distortion. It fits very few individuals that anyone is likely to meet in this country today. The problem of the political role of the social scientist is, nevertheless, a very genuine one. For instance, the employment of sociologists by certain branches of industry and government raises moral questions that ought to be faced more widely than they have been so far. These are, however, moral questions that concern all men in positions of responsibility in modern society. The image of the sociologist as an observer without compassion and a manipulator without conscience need not detain us further here. By and large, history produces very few Talleyrands. As for contemporary sociologists, most of them would lack the emotional equipment for such a role, even if they should aspire to it in moments of feverish fantasy.

How then are we to conceive of the sociologist? In discussing the various images of him that abound in the popular mind we have already brought out certain elements that would have to go into our conception. We can now put them together. In doing so, we shall construct what sociologists themselves call an "ideal type." This means that what we delineate will not be found in reality in its pure form. Instead, one will find approximations to it and deviations from it, in varying degrees. Nor is it to be understood as an empirical average. We would not even claim that all individuals who now call themselves sociologists will recognize themselves without reservations in our conception, nor would we dispute the right of those who do not so recognize themselves to use the appellation. Our business is not excommunication. We would, however, contend that our "ideal type" corresponds to the self-conception of most sociologists in the mainstream of the discipline, both historically (at least in this century) and today.

The sociologist, then, is someone concerned with understanding society in a disciplined way. The nature of this discipline is scientific. This means that what the sociologist finds and says about the social phenomena he studies occurs within a certain rather strictly defined frame of reference. One of the main characteristics of this scientific frame of reference is that operations are bound by certain rules of evidence. As a scientist, the sociologist tries to be objective, to control his personal preferences and prejudices, to perceive clearly rather than to judge normatively. This restraint, of course, does not embrace the totality of the sociologist's existence as human being, but is limited to his operations *qua* sociologist. Nor does the sociologist claim that his frame of reference is the only one within which society can be looked at. For that matter, very few scientists in any field would claim today that one should look at the world only scientifically. The botanist looking at a daffodil has no reason to dispute the right of the poet to look at the same object in a very different manner. There are many ways of playing. The point is not that one denies other people's games but that one is clear about the rules of one's own. The game of the sociologist, then, uses scientific rules. As a result, the sociologist must be clear in his own mind as to the meaning of these rules. That is, he must concern himself with methodological questions. Methodology does not constitute his goal. The latter, let us recall once more, is the attempt to understand society. Methodology helps in reaching this goal. In order to understand society, or that segment of it that he is studying at the moment, the sociologist will use a variety of means. Among these are statistical techniques. Statistics can be very useful in answering certain sociological questions. But statistics does not constitute sociology. As a scientist, the sociologist will have to be concerned with the exact significance of the terms he is using. That is, he will have to be careful about terminology. This does not have to mean that he must invent a new language of his own, but it does mean that he cannot naively use the language of everyday discourse. Finally, the interest of the sociologist is primarily theoretical. That is, he is interested in understanding for its own sake. He may be aware of or even concerned with the practical applicability and consequences of his findings, but at that point he leaves the sociological frame of reference as such and moves into realms of values, beliefs and ideas that he shares with other men who are not sociologists.

We daresay that this conception of the sociologist would meet with very wide consensus within the discipline today. But we would like to go a little bit further here and ask a somewhat more personal (and therefore, no doubt, more controversial) question. We would like to ask not only what it is that the sociologist is doing but also what it is that drives him to it. Or, to use the phrase Max Weber used in a similar connection, we want to inquire a little into the nature of the sociologist's demon. In doing so, we shall evoke an image that is not so much ideal-typical in the above sense but more confessional in the sense of personal commitment. Again, we are not interested in excommunicating anyone. The game of sociology goes on in a spacious playground. We are just describing a little more closely those we would like to tempt to join our game.

We would say then that the sociologist (that is, the one we would really like to invite to our game) is a person intensively, endlessly, shamelessly interested in the doings of men. His natural habitat is all the human gathering places of the world, wherever men come together. The sociologist may be interested in many other things. But his consuming interest remains in the world of men, their institutions, their history, their passions. And since he is interested in men, nothing that men do can be altogether tedious for him. He will naturally be interested in the events that engage men's ultimate beliefs, their moments of tragedy and grandeur and ecstasy. But he will also be fascinated by the common place, the everyday. He will know reverence, but this reverence will not prevent him from wanting to see and to understand. He may sometimes feel revulsion or contempt. But this also will not deter him from wanting to have his questions answered. The sociologist, in his quest for understanding, moves through the world of men without respect for the usual lines of demarcation. Nobility and degradation, power and obscurity, intelligence and folly—these are equally *interesting* to him, however unequal they may be in his personal values or tastes. Thus his questions may lead him to all possible levels of society, the best and the least known places, the most respected and the most despised. And, if he is a good sociologist, he will find himself in all these places because his own questions have so taken possession of him that he has little choice but to seek for answers.

To be sure, sociology is an individual pastime in the sense that it interests some men and bores others. Some like to observe human beings, others to experiment with mice. The world is big enough to hold all kinds and there is no logical priority for one interest as against another. But the word "pastime" is weak in describing what we mean. Sociology is more like a passion. The sociological perspective is more like a demon that possesses one, that drives one compellingly, again and again, to the questions that are its own. An introduction to sociology is, therefore, an invitation to a very special kind of passion.

◈ DISCUSSION QUESTIONS

1. After reading Berger's article, how might you respond to a friend who mistakes sociology for social work?

2. The tools of sociological thinking can be used just as easily for promoting social evil as social good. Think of an example of a sociological research topic or technique that could be used to promote either good or harm in society.

3. What responsibility do you think sociologists should have in trying to make the world a better place? Should sociologists strive to be detached observers of the social world and studiously avoid making policy recommendations or getting involved in solving social problems? Or do you think they should balance doing scientific research with advocating for solutions to social problems?

3

The Rest Room and Equal Opportunity

Harvey Molotch

Social structure can be defined as organized patterns of relationships that allow people to form societies and live together. It's these social structures that Mills, in The Sociological Imagination, *argues have a profound effect on shaping the lives of individuals. Social structures don't just shape obvious things like education, jobs, income, health, and so on. Social structures also shape the way we interact with each other and how the details of our daily lives are organized and experienced. For example, it's a common sight at sporting events, concerts, airports, and most other places people congregate in any significant number, to see women waiting in line to use the restroom. This is generally attributed to women's propensity to use the bathroom as a place to socialize, fussily fix their appearance, or take their time in answering nature's call. On the surface, who has to wait to relieve themselves and who doesn't seems like a fairly unscholarly topic for study. For one thing, we generally avoid even talking about most natural bodily functions (as I'm doing in this introduction by using euphemisms and more scientific language). But this seemingly mundane detail of daily life provides a telling example of sociological imagination in general and of what sociologists mean when they refer to social structure in particular.*

It's important to remember that looking at the influence of social structures is not an argument that people don't have individual agency or that what happens to us is completely determined by social structure. Social structures shape rather than determine our behaviors and life chances. A good analogy for social structure might be the paths available for you to walk on at a park that you visit with a friend. As you get out and start walking on the wide, clearly marked trail from the parking lot, you and your friend start chatting. Odds are that if you are busy enjoying your conversation with your friend, you'll meander on the main trail until you get to some type of junction that forces you to decide which way to go. That doesn't mean that you're not free to pay attention to the smaller, less clearly marked side trails you pass along the way. You certainly could decide to go on those instead, but the main path suggests a route that you're likely to follow, especially if you're not paying attention. Social structure works the same way. It suggests the trajectory of our life chances the same way that a wide, clear path shapes (but does not determine) the route we take on a walk through the woods. We're always free to "trailblaze" whether on a walk or in life, but it tends to take extra attention, effort, and time.

As you read Molotch's article, pay attention to how he describes the various ways that social structures all but ensure that most women will have waiting in line at the restroom will become a regular feature of going out in public for them. Why does he think we should care about this seemingly trivial aspect of public life?

At the risk of appearing disrespectful, let me say that the best way to understand equal opportunity is to use the public toilet. Sometimes a gross approach can best clarify a subtle issue. Through the example of how society is organized to provide men and women with the capacity to relieve themselves, we can understand what it takes, as a more general matter, to provide members of different social groups with authentic equal opportunity.

In many public buildings, the amount of floor area dedicated for the men's room and the women's room is the same. The prevailing public bathroom doctrine in the U.S. is one of segregation among the genders, but with equality the guiding ideology. In some jurisdictions, this square footage equality is enshrined in law. Such an arrangement follows the dictum that equality can be achieved only by policies that are "gender-blind" (or "color-blind" or "ethnic-blind") in the allocation of a public resource. To give less to women (or blacks or Hispanics) would be discrimination; to give more would be "reverse discrimination."[1] Women and men have the same proportion of a building to use as rest rooms. Presumably this should provide members of both genders with equal opportunity for dealing with their bodily needs in a timely and convenient way.

The trouble with this sort of equality is that, being blind, it fails to recognize differences between men as a group and women as a group. These differences are not amenable to easy change. Part of women's demand for bathrooms can not exist for men because only women menstruate. Women make trips to the rest room to secure hygienic and socially appropriate adaptations to this physical fact. And because men's physiology suits them for the use of urinals, a large number of men can be serviced by a relatively small physical space. Women in our society use toilets to urinate, and toilets require a larger area than urinals. By creating men's and women's rooms of the same size, society guarantees that *individual* women will be worse off than individual men. By distributing a resource equally, an unequal result is structurally guaranteed.

The consequences are easily visible at intermission time whenever men and women congregate in theater lobbies. When the house is full, the women form a waiting line in front of the bathroom while the men do their business without delay. Women experience discomfort and are excluded from conversations that occur under more salutary conditions elsewhere in the lobby. If toward the rear of the line, women may experience anxiety that they will miss the curtain rise. Indeed, they may arrive too late to be seated for the opening scene, dance routine, or orchestral movement. Their late arrival is easily taken by others (particularly men) as evidence of characterological slowness or preoccupation with primping and powder room gossip. All these difficulties are built into the structure of the situation. Equality of square feet to the genders delivers women special burdens of physical discomfort, social disadvantage, psychological anxiety, compromised access to the full product (the performance), and public ridicule.

An obvious solution, one I'll call the "liberal" policy, is to make women's rooms larger than men's. Women's bathrooms need to be big enough to get women in and out as quickly as men's bathrooms get men in and out. No more and no less. A little applied sociological research in various types of settings would establish the appropriate ratios needed to accomplish such gender equality.

An alternative solution, one I'll call "conservative," would be for women to change the way they do things, rather than for society to change the structuring of rest room space. There is no need to overturn the principle of equality of square footage among the genders. Instead, women need to use their allotted square footage more efficiently. If women truly want to relieve themselves as efficiently as men, they can take some initiative. Options do exist short of biological alteration.

While women may not be capable of adapting to urinals, they could relieve themselves by squatting over a common trough. This would save some space—perhaps enough to achieve efficiency parity with men. Women are not physically bound to use up so many square feet. It is a cultural issue, and in this case the problem derives from a faulty element of women's culture. It is not physiologically given that each woman should have her own cubicle, much less her own toilet, or that she should sit rather than squat.

This joins the issue well. Should women be forced to change or should the burden be placed on men who may have to give up some of their own square footage so that women might have more? The response from the liberal camp is that even if women's spatial needs are cultural, these needs should be recognized and indulged. Cultural notions of privacy and modes of using toilets were not arrived at by women in isolation from men. Men's conceptions of "decency"—at least as much as women's—encourage women to be physically modest and demure. Men's recurring violence toward women encourages bathroom segregation in the first instance because segregation makes it easier for potential assailants to be spotted as "out of place." Providing women with latched cubicles provides a further bit of security in a world made less secure by men. Thus, prescriptions of dignity and protections from assault come from the common culture produced by women and men. Whatever their origins, these cultural imperatives have become a real force and are sustained by continuing pressures on women's lives. Until this common culture is itself transformed, U.S. women can not become as efficient as Tiwi women in their capacity to urinate in public settings, regardless of the efficiency advantages. On the other hand, altering the spatial allocations for men's and women's bathrooms is relatively simple and inexpensive.

It becomes harder to be a liberal as the weight of cultural imperative seems to lighten. Suppose, for example, that *a part* of the reason for the line in front of the ladies' room is, in fact, a tendency for women to primp longer than men or to gossip among one another at the sinks (although the lines in front of *toilet stalls* would belie such an assumption). Should vanity and sociability be subsidized at the expense of the larger community? But here again, the culture that men and women have produced in common becomes relevant. Perhaps women "take a powder" to escape the oppression of men, using the rest rooms as a refuge from social conditions imposed by the dominant gender? Perhaps the need to look lovely, every moment and in every way, is created by men's need to display a public companion whose make-up is flawless, whose head has every hair in place, and whose body is perfectly scented. Women are driven to decorate themselves as men's commodities and the consequence is bathroom demand. Should men pay for this "service" through sacrificing their own square footage or should women adjust by waiting in line and climbing all over one another for a patch of the vanity mirror?

Again it turns on who should change what. The conservative answer might be for women to give up primping, but that would fly in the face of the demand (also championed by conservatives) that women's cultural role is to be beautiful for their men. Although not because they wished to increase rest room efficiency, radical feminists have argued that women should ease up on their beauty treatments, precisely because it ratifies their subservience to men and deflects them from success in occupational and other realms. But again the liberal view holds appeal: at least until the transition to feminism, the *existing cultural arrangement* necessitates an asymmetric distribution of space to provide equality of opportunity among the genders.

As the issues become subtle, reasonable people come to disagree on who should do what and what community expense should be incurred to achieve parity. Such controversy stems from the effort to provide equal opportunity for individuals by taking into account differences among groups. The same problem arises no matter what the issue and no matter what the group. If people commonly get their job leads by word-of-mouth through friends and neighbors, then black people—excluded from the neighborhoods of employers and of those employed in expanding job sectors—will be at labor market disadvantage. Black people's chronically higher unemployment rate stands as evidence of disadvantage: their longer queue for jobs is analogous to the longer line in front of the women's rest room. Blacks can be told to work harder, to use their meager resources more efficiently, to rearrange their lives and cultures to better their job qualifications. Alternatively, their present plight can be understood as *structural*—stemming from a history of enslavement, Jim Crow segregation, and white prejudice that now results in concrete arrangements that hinder individual life changes. One must be color-sighted, rather than color-blind, to deal with these differences. But this is no reverse racism: it rests on perception of social structural locations, not upon inherent inferiority attributed to group membership. Such government mandated policies as open job-searches, ethnic hiring targets, and preference for minority vendors and subcontractors can counteract structural biases that hold down opportunities of women, blacks, and other minorities. Affirmative action programs should be conceived as compensatory efforts to overcome such structured disadvantage (although the legal interpretation of the statutes is usually drawn more narrowly).[2]

Equality is not a matter of arithmetic division, but of social accounting. Figuring out what is equal treatment necessitates—in every instance—a sociological analysis of exactly how it is that structures operate on people's lives. Besides rejecting the conservatives' penchant for blaming the victim, liberal policies need a concrete analytic basis that goes beyond goodhearted sympathy for the downtrodden. As in the rest room case, we need to specify how current patterns of "equal" treatment of groups yield unequal opportunities to individuals. We then should determine exactly what it would take (e.g., square feet to gender ratios) to redress the inequality.

Besides careful analysis, equality also involves a decision as to who is going to change and in what way. These decisions will often take from some and give to others. Thus we have the two-pronged essence of action on behalf of equal opportunity: sociological analysis and political struggle.

☒ DISCUSSION QUESTIONS

1. What are the social structural influences that Molotch argues all but ensure that most women, much of the time, will have to wait in line?

2. What are the two definitions of equality in restroom access that Molotch uses?

3. What are the two options Molotch proposes for remedying women having to wait in line to use the restroom?

4. Why does Molotch think it matters if women have to wait in line to use the restroom?

5. Find someone who is a different gender than you and compare your experiences in accessing restrooms. Ask people who are not the same gender how, if at all, they plan or make accommodations to ensure they will be able to relieve themselves when they need to. Have they ever missed something important to them because they were waiting in line for the restroom?

☒ REFERENCES

Binion, Gayle. "Affirmative Action Reconsidered: Justification, Objectives, Myths and Misconceptions." *Women & Politics.* 7, 1 Spring 1987, pp. 43-62.

Glazer, Nathan, 1975, Affirmative Discrimination: Ethnic Inequality and Public Policy, New York: Basic Books.

☒ NOTES

1. Government acts that provide unequal resources in the name of progressive reform have been denounced in just such terms. See Glazer (1975) for a strong instance.

2. Affirmative action is ordinarily justified as redress for past or present discrimination, rather than necessary actions to bring about future parity. See Binion (1987) for a forceful argument that the proper rationale for affirmative action is *integration* of excluded groups "into the social, political, and economic systems" (Binion, 1987:58).

4

An Introduction to McDonaldization

George Ritzer

If you ask someone what discipline sociology is most similar to, the common answers are anthropology, psychology, or social work. And certainly sociology does have quite a bit in common with these disciplines, as well as many others. But if you think about this question a bit differently and instead look not at what is being studied but why *and* how *the studying is being done, it turns out that sociology has the greatest overlap with physics.*

Physics? You might be scratching your head at that—and on the surface it does seem a bit strange. After all, the physicists are the folks trying to find out how the universe came into existence (a really big macrolevel question) all the way down to quantum physics, which studies the tiniest particles that make up the universe, several layers smaller than even atoms (a very microlevel question). But what sociology and physics have in common are their general goals and the types of challenges they face in doing research. Physicists are interested in understanding the rules and principles that govern the physical *world. They develop theories that can explain why the components of the physical world act the way they do. Sociologists are interested in doing the same thing, except they are looking for the rules and principles that govern the* social *world. And just as physicists look at both a macro and microlevel for this understanding, so do sociologists. Physicists also often encounter the same problem sociologists sometimes face in tying together data and test hypotheses—the data aren't always there. Just as some subatomic particles are extremely difficult to find and observe, many types of people aren't very forthcoming about making themselves available for researchers (e.g., how do you study all the child molesters who haven't been caught yet?).*

Ritzer, George. (2007). *The mcdonaldization of society* (5th ed.). Thousand Oaks, CA: SAGE Publications, Inc.

In this article, Ritzer introduces the concept of McDonaldization (and yes, he is referring to the home of the Big Mac!). McDonaldization is a good example of a general rule or principle that a sociologist developed to try to understand why the social world works the way it does. Ritzer argues that the characteristics of the fast-food industry are increasingly seeping into more and more of the social structures that shape even the minutest aspects of our lives. As you read, think about what social structures that affect you have some or all of the characteristics of McDonaldization that Ritzer describes.

Ray Kroc (1902–1984), the genius behind the franchising of McDonald's restaurants, was a man with big ideas and grand ambitions. But even Kroc could not have anticipated the astounding impact of his creation. McDonald's is the basis of one of the most influential developments in contemporary society. Its reverberations extend far beyond its point of origin in the United States and in the fast-food business. It has influenced a wide range of undertakings, indeed the way of life, of a significant portion of the world. And having rebounded from some well-publicized economic difficulties, that impact is likely to expand at an accelerating rate in the early 21st century.

However, this is not a book about McDonald's, or even about the fast-food business, although both will be discussed frequently throughout these pages. I devote all this attention to McDonald's (as well as to the industry of which it is a part and that it played such a key role in spawning) because it serves here as the major example of, and the paradigm for, a wide-ranging process I call McDonaldization—that is,

the process by which the principles of the fast-food restaurant are coming to dominate more and more sectors of American society as well as of the rest of the world.

McDonaldization has shown every sign of being an inexorable process, sweeping through seemingly impervious institutions (e.g., religion) and regions (European nations such as France) of the world.

\\\ THE DIMENSIONS OF MCDONALDIZATION

Why has the McDonald's model proven so irresistible? Eating fast food at McDonald's has certainly become a "sign" that, among other things, one is in tune with the contemporary lifestyle. There is also a kind of magic or enchantment associated with such food and its settings. The focus here, however, is on the four alluring dimensions that lie at the heart of the success of this model and, more generally, of McDonaldization. In short, McDonald's has succeeded because it offers consumers, workers, and managers efficiency, calculability, predictability, and control. Chapters 3 through 6 will be devoted to each of these aspects, but it is important to at least mention them at this point.

Efficiency

One important element of the success of McDonald's is *efficiency*, or the optimum method for getting from one point to another. For consumers, McDonald's (its drive-through is a good example) offers the best available way to get from being hungry to being full. The fast-food model offers, or at least appears to offer, an efficient method for satisfying many other needs, as well. Woody Allen's orgasmatron offered an efficient method for getting people from quiescence to sexual gratification. Other institutions fashioned on the McDonald's model offer similar efficiency in exercising, losing weight, lubricating cars, getting new glasses or contacts, or completing income tax forms. Like their customers, workers in McDonaldized systems function efficiently by following the steps in a predesigned process.

Calculability

Calculability emphasizes the quantitative aspects of products sold (portion size, cost) and services offered (the time it takes to get the product). In McDonaldized systems, quantity has become equivalent to quality; a lot of something, or the quick delivery of it, means it must be good. As two observers of contemporary American culture put it, "As a culture, we tend to believe deeply that in general 'bigger is better.'" People can quantify things and feel that they are getting a lot of food for what appears to be a nominal sum of money (best exemplified by the McDonald's current "Dollar Menu," which played a key role in recent years in leading McDonald's out of its doldrums and to steadily increasing sales). In a recent Denny's ad, a man says, "I'm going to eat too much, but I'm never going to pay too much." This calculation does not take into account an important point, however: The high profit margin of fast-food chains indicates that the owners, not the consumers, get the best deal.

People also calculate how much time it will take to drive to McDonald's, be served the food, eat it, and return home; they then compare that interval to the time required to prepare food at home. They often conclude, rightly or wrongly, that a trip to the fast-food restaurant will take less time than eating at home. This sort of calculation particularly supports home delivery franchises such as Domino's, as well as other chains that emphasize saving time. A notable example of time savings in another sort of chain is LensCrafters, which promises people "Glasses fast, glasses in one hour." H&M is known for its "fast fashion."

Some McDonaldized institutions combine the emphases on time and money. Domino's promises pizza delivery in half an hour, or the pizza is free. Pizza Hut will serve a personal pan pizza in 5 minutes, or it, too, will be free.

Workers in McDonaldized systems also emphasize the quantitative rather than the qualitative aspects of their work. Since the quality of the work is allowed to vary little, workers focus on things such as how quickly tasks can be accomplished. In a situation analogous to that of the customer, workers are expected to do a lot of work, very quickly, for low pay.

Predictability

McDonald's also offers *predictability*, the assurance that products and services will be the same over time and in all locales. The Egg McMuffin in New York will be, for all intents and purposes, identical to those in Chicago and Los Angeles. Also, those eaten next week or next year will be identical to those eaten today. Customers take great comfort in knowing that McDonald's offers no surprises. People know that the next Egg McMuffin they eat will not be awful, although it will not be exceptionally delicious, either. The success of the McDonald's model suggests that many people have come to prefer a world in which there are few surprises. "This is strange," notes a British observer "considering [McDonald's is] the product of a culture which honours individualism above all."

The workers in McDonaldized systems also behave in predictable ways. They follow corporate rules as well as the dictates of their managers. In many cases, what they do, and even what they say, is highly predictable.

Control

The fourth element in the success of McDonald's, *control,* is exerted over the people who enter the world of McDonald's. Lines, limited menus, few options, and uncomfortable seats all lead diners to do what management wishes them to do—eat quickly and leave. Furthermore, the drive-through (in some cases, walk-through) window invites diners to leave before they eat. In the Domino's model, customers never enter in the first place.

The people who work in McDonaldized organizations are also controlled to a high degree, usually more blatantly and directly than customers. They are trained to do a limited number of things in precisely the way they are told to do them. This control is reinforced by the technologies used and the way the organization is set up to bolster this control. Managers and inspectors make sure that workers toe the line.

〰 A CRITIQUE OF McDONALDIZATION: THE IRRATIONALITY OF RATIONALITY

McDonaldization offers powerful advantages. In fact, efficiency, predictability, calculability, and control through nonhuman technology (that is, technology that controls people rather than being controlled by them) can be thought of as not only the basic components of a rational system but also as powerful advantages of such a system. However, rational systems inevitably spawn irrationalities. The downside of McDonaldization will be dealt with most systematically under the heading of the irrationality of rationality; in fact, paradoxically, the irrationality of rationality can be thought of as the fifth dimension of McDonaldization (see Chapter 7).

Criticism, in fact, can be applied to all facets of the McDonaldizing world. As just one example, at the opening of Euro Disney, a French politician said that it will "bombard France with uprooted creations that are to culture what fast food is to gastronomy." Although McDonaldization offers many advantages (explained later in this chapter), this book will focus on the great costs and enormous risks of McDonaldization. McDonald's and other purveyors of the fast-food model spend billions of dollars each year detailing the benefits of their system. Critics of the system, however, have few outlets for their ideas. For example, no one sponsors commercials between Saturday-morning cartoons warning children of the dangers associated with fast-food restaurants.

Nonetheless, a legitimate question may be raised about this critique of McDonaldization: Is it animated by a romanticization of the past, an impossible desire to return to a world that no longer exists? Some critics do base their critiques on nostalgia for a time when life was slower and offered more surprises, when at least some people (those who were better off economically) were freer, and when one was more likely to deal with a human being than a robot or a computer. Although they have a point, these critics have undoubtedly exaggerated the positive aspects of a world without McDonald's, and they have certainly tended to forget the liabilities associated with earlier eras. As an example of the latter, take the following anecdote about a visit to a pizzeria in Havana, Cuba, which in some respects is decades behind the United States:

> The pizza's not much to rave about—they scrimp on tomato sauce, and the dough is mushy.
>
> It was about 7:30 P.M., and as usual the place was standing-room-only, with people two deep jostling for a stool to come open and a waiting line spilling out onto the sidewalk.
>
> The menu is similarly Spartan. . . . To drink, there is tap water. That's it— no toppings, no soda, no beer, no coffee, no salt, no pepper. And no special orders.
>
> A very few people are eating. Most are waiting. . . . Fingers are drumming, flies are buzzing, the clock is ticking. The waiter wears a watch around his belt loop, but he hardly needs it; time is evidently not his chief concern. After a while, tempers begin to fray.
>
> But right now, it's 8:45 P.M. at the pizzeria, I've been waiting an hour and a quarter for two small pies.

Few would prefer such a restaurant to the fast, friendly, diverse offerings of, say, Pizza Hut. More important, however, critics who revere the past do not seem to realize that we are not returning to such a world. In fact, fast-food restaurants have begun to appear even in Havana (and many more are likely after the death of Fidel Castro). The increase in the number of people crowding the planet, the acceleration of technological change, the increasing pace of life—all this and more make it impossible to go back to the world, if it ever existed, of home-cooked meals, traditional restaurant dinners, high-quality foods, meals loaded with surprises, and restaurants run by chefs free to express their creativity.

It is more valid to critique McDonaldization from the perspective of a conceivable future. Unfettered by the constraints of McDonaldized systems, but using the technological advances made possible by them, people could have the potential to be far more thoughtful, skillful, creative, and well-rounded than they are now. In short, if the world was less McDonaldized, people would be better able to live up to their human potential.

We must look at McDonaldization as both "enabling" and "constraining." McDonaldized systems enable us to do many things we were not able to do in the past; however, these systems also keep us from doing things we otherwise would do. McDonaldization is a "double-edged" phenomenon. We must not lose sight of that fact, even though this book will focus on the constraints associated with McDonaldization—its "dark side."

ILLUSTRATING THE DIMENSIONS OF MCDONALDIZATION: THE CASE OF IKEA

An interesting example of McDonaldization, especially since it has its roots in Sweden rather than the United States, is Ikea. Its popularity stems from the fact that it offers at very low prices trendy furniture based on well-known Swedish designs. It has a large and devoted clientele throughout the world. What is interesting about Ikea from the point of view of this book is how well it fits the dimensions of McDonaldization. The similarities go beyond that, however. For example, just as with the opening of a new McDonald's, there is great anticipation over the opening of the first Ikea in a particular location. Just the rumor that one was to open in Dayton, Ohio, led to the following statement: "We here in Dayton are peeing our collective pants waiting for the Ikea announcement." Ikea is also a global phenomenon—it is now in 34 countries (including China and Japan) and sells in those countries both its signature products as well as those more adapted to local tastes and interests.

In terms of *efficiency*, Ikea offers one-stop furniture shopping with an extraordinary range of furniture. In general, there is no waiting for one's purchases, since a huge warehouse is attached to each store (one often enters through the warehouse), with large numbers of virtually everything in stock.

Much of the efficiency at Ikea stems from the fact that customers are expected to do a lot of the work:

- Unlike McDonald's, there are relatively few Ikea's in any given area; thus, customers most often spend many hours driving great distances to get to a store. This is known as the "Ikea road trip."

- On entry, customers are expected to take a map to guide themselves through the huge and purposely maze-like store (Ikea hopes, like Las Vegas casinos, that customers will get "lost" in the maze and wander for hours, spending money as they go). There are no employees to guide anyone, but there are arrows painted on the floor that customers can follow on their own.

- Also upon entry, customers are expected to grab a pencil and an order form and to write down the shelf and bin numbers for the larger items they wish to purchase; a yellow shopping bag is to be picked up on entry for smaller items. There are few employees and little in the way of help available as customers wander through the stores. Customers can switch from a shopping bag to a shopping cart after leaving the showroom and entering the marketplace, where they can pick up other smaller items.

- If customers eat in the cafeteria, they are expected to clean their tables after eating. There is even this helpful sign: "Why should I clean my own table? At Ikea, cleaning your own table at the end of your meal is one of the reasons you paid less at the start."

- Most of the furniture sold is unassembled in flat packages, and customers are expected to load most of the items (except the largest) into their cars themselves. After they get home, they must break down (and dispose) of the packaging and then put their furniture together; the only tool supposedly required is an Allen wrench.

- If the furniture does not fit into your car, you can rent a truck on site to transport it home or have it delivered, although the cost tends to be high, especially relative to the price paid for the furniture.

- To get a catalog, customers often sign up online.

Calculability is at the heart of Ikea, especially the idea that what is offered is at a very low price. Like a McDonald's "Dollar Menu," one can get a lot of furniture—a roomful, even a houseful—at bargain prices. As with value meals, customers feel they are getting value for their money. (There is even a large cafeteria offering low-priced food, including the chain's signature Swedish meatballs and 99-cent breakfasts.) However, as is always the case in McDonaldized settings, low price generally means that the quality is inferior, and it is often the case that Ikea products fall apart in relatively short order. Ikea also emphasizes the huge size of its stores, which often approach 300,000 square feet or about four to five football fields. This mammoth size leads the consumer to believe that there will be a lot of furniture offered (and there is) and that, given the store's reputation, most of it will be highly affordable.

Of course, there is great *predictability* about any given Ikea—large parking lots, a supervised children's play area (where Ikea provides personnel, but only because supervised children give parents more time and peace of mind to shop and spend), the masses of inexpensive, Swedish-design furniture, exit through the warehouse and the checkout counters, boxes to take home with furniture requiring assembly, and so on.

An Ikea is a highly *controlled* environment, mainly in the sense that the maze-like structure of the store virtually forces the consumer to traverse the entire place and to see virtually everything it has to offer. If one tries to take a path other than that set by Ikea, one is likely to become lost and disoriented. There seems to be no way out that does not lead to the checkout counter, where you pay for your purchases.

There are a variety of *irrationalities* associated with the rationality of Ikea, most notably the poor quality of most of its products. Although the furniture is purportedly easy to assemble, many are more likely to think of it as "impossible-to-assemble." Then there are the often long hours required to get to an Ikea, to wander through it, to drive back home, and then to assemble the purchases.

⟨⟨ DISCUSSION QUESTIONS

1. What are the four dimensions of McDonaldization that Ritzer describes? Try to develop an acronym or other mnemonic to remember each dimension and what it means.

2. What does Ritzer mean by the "irrationality of rationality"? Why does he say that it should really be considered a fifth dimension of McDonaldization?

3. Try applying the principles of McDonaldization to education. How are K–12 schools and colleges increasingly becoming McDonaldized?

4. What are the upsides to McDonaldization? Should we always assume it's a bad thing? Are there any social structures or aspects of social life that you think either shouldn't or couldn't be McDonaldized?

5

Damned Lies and Statistics

Untangling Numbers from the Media, Politicians, and Activists

Joel Best

One of the greatest changes in recent history is the exponential increase in the amount of information available to each of us. The growth of the World Wide Web and ever-increasing Internet connectivity gives us access to almost unfathomable amounts of information right at our fingertips. Journalists, activists, social commentators, and researchers are all eager to take advantage of new ways to reach audiences and to use statistics to lend credibility to their stories, opinions, and research. In this article, Joel Best illuminates some of ways that statistics are commonly misused or misinterpreted. He argues that it is a combination of innumeracy *(the mathematical equivalent of illiteracy) and* mutant statistics *(incorrect statistics that are widely propagated) that causes us to believe things about the world that simply are not (and sometimes cannot be) true. Statistics tend to be accepted at face value, particularly if provided by an expert or reputable source, but Best warns us that we should be on the lookout for a whole host of common mistakes, sometimes unintentional and sometimes not, when we turn to numbers to understand the social world. As you read, think about whether you can recall any statistics that you've heard of that sound like they might not be as accurate as they seemed at the time.*

T he dissertation prospectus began by quoting a statistic—a "grabber" meant to capture the reader's attention. (A dissertation prospectus is a lenthy proposal for a research project leading to a Ph.D. degree—the ultimate credential for a would-be scholar.) The Graduate Student who wrote this prospectus* undoubtedly wanted to seem scholarly to the professors who would read it; they would be supervising the proposed research. And what could be more scholarly than a nice, authoritative statistic, quoted from a professional journal in the Student's field?

So the prospectus began with this (carefully footnoted) quotation: "Every year since 1950, the number of American children gunned down has doubled." I had been invited to serve on the Student's dissertation committee. When I read the quotation, I assumed the Student had made an error in copying it. I went to the library and looked up the article the Student had cited. There, in the journal's 1995 volume, was exactly the same sentence: "Every year since 1950, the number of American children gunned down has doubled."

This quotation is my nomination for a dubious distinction: I think it may be the worst—that is, the most inaccurate—social statistic ever.

What makes this statistic so bad? Just for the sake of argument, let's assume that the "number of American children gunned down" in 1950 was one. If the number doubled each year, there must have been two children gunned down in 1951, four in 1952, eight in 1953, and so on. By 1960, the number would have been 1,024. By 1965, it would have been 32,768 (in 1965, the FBI identified only 9,960 criminal homicides in the entire country, including adult as well as child victims). In 1970, the number would have passed one million; in 1980, *one billion* (more than four times the total U.S. population in that year). Only three years later, in 1983, the number of American children gunned down would have been 8.6 billion (about twice the Earth's population at the time). Another milestone would have been passed in 1987, when the number of gunned-down American children (137 billion) would have surpassed the best estimates for the total human population throughout history (110 billion). By 1995, when the article was published, the annual number of victims would have been over 35 *trillion*—a really big number, of a magnitude you rarely encounter outside economics or astronomy.

Thus my nomination: estimating the number of American child gunshot victims in 1995 at 35 trillion must be as far off—as hilariously, wildly wrong—as a social statistic can be. (If anyone spots a more inaccurate social statistic, I'd love to hear about it.)

---

*For reasons that will become obvious, I have decided not to name the Graduate Student, the Author, or the Journal Editor. They made mistakes, but the mistakes they made were, as this book will show, all too common.

Where did the article's Author get this statistic? I wrote the Author, who responded that the statistic came from the Children's Defense Fund (the CDF is a well-known advocacy group for children). The CDF's *The State of America's Children Yearbook*—1994 does state: "The number of American children killed each year by guns has doubled since 1950." Note the difference in the wording— the CDF claimed there were twice as many deaths in 1994 as in 1950; the article's Author reworded that claim and created a very different meaning.

It is worth examining the history of this statistic. It began with the CDF noting that child gunshot deaths doubled from 1950 to 1994. This is not quite as dramatic an increase as it might seem. Remember that the U.S. population also rose throughout this period; in fact, it grew about 73 percent—or nearly double. Therefore, we might expect all sorts of things—including the number of child gunshot deaths—to increase, to nearly double just because the population grew. Before we can decide whether twice as many deaths indicates that things are getting worse, we'd have to know more.* The CDF statistic raises other issues as well: Where did the statistic come from? Who counts child gun-shot deaths, and how? What do they mean by a "child" (some CDF statistics about violence include everyone under age 25)? What do they mean "killed by guns" (gunshot death statistics often include suicides and accidents, as well as homicides)? But people rarely ask questions of this sort when they encounter statistics. Most of the time, most people simply *accept statistics without question.*

Certainly, the article's Author didn't ask many probing, critical questions about the CDF's claim. Impressed by the statistic, the Author *repeated* it—well, meant to repeat it. Instead, by rewording the CDF's claim, the Author created a *mutant statistic,* one garbled almost beyond recognition.

But people treat mutant statistics just as they do other statistics—that is, they usually accept even the most implausible claims without question

Statistics, then, have a bad reputation. We suspect that statistics may be wrong, that people who use statistics may be "lying"—trying to manipulate us by using numbers to some-how distort the truth. Yet, at the same time, we need statistics; we depend upon them to summarize and clarify the nature of our complex society. This is particularly true when we talk about social problems. Debates about social problems routinely raise questions that demand statistical answers: Is the problem widespread? How many people—and which people—does it affect? Is it getting worse? What does it cost society? What will it cost to deal with it? Convincing answers to such questions demand evidence, and that usually means numbers, measurements, statistics.

---

*For instance, since only child victims are at issue, a careful analysis would control for the relative sizes of the child population in the two years. We are ought to have assurances that the methods of counting child gunshot victims did not change overtime, and so on.

But can't you prove anything with statistics? It depends on what "prove" means. If we want to know, say, how many children are "gunned down" each year, we can't simply guess—puck a number from thin air: one hundred, one thousand, ten thousand, 35 trillion, whatever. Obviously, there's no reason to consider an arbitrary guess "proof" of anything. However, it might be possible for someone—using records kept by police departments or hospital emergency rooms or coroner—to keep track of children who have been shot; compiling careful, complete records might give us a fairly accurate idea of the number of gunned-down children. If that number seems accurate enough, we might consider it very strong evidence—or proof.

The solution to the problem of bad statistics is not to ignore all statistics, or to assume that every number is false. Some statistics are bad, but others are pretty good, and we need statistics—good statistics—to talk sensibly about social problems. The solution, then, is not to give up on statistics, but to become better judges of the numbers we encounter. We need to think critically about statistics—at least critically enough to suspect that the number of children gunned down hasn't been doubling each year since 1950.

Social statistics describe society, but they are also products of our social arrangements. The people who bring social statistics to our attention have reasons for doing so; they inevitably want something, just as reporter and the other media figures who repeat and publicize statistics have their own goals. Statistics are tools, used for particular purposes. Thinking critically about statistics requires understanding their place in society.

While we may be more suspicious of statistics presented by people with whom we disagree—people who favor different political parties or have different beliefs—bad statistics are used to promote all sorts of causes. Bad statistics come from conservatives on the political right and liberals on the left, from wealthy corporations and powerful government agencies, and from advocates of the poor and the powerless.

※ MUTANT STATISTICS

Methods for Mangling Numbers

Not all statistics start out bad, but any statistic can be made worse. Numbers—even good numbers—can be misunderstood or misinterpreted. Their meanings can be stretched, twisted, distorted, or mangled. These alterations create what we can call *mutant statistics*—distorted versions of the original figures.

Many mutant statistics have their roots in innumeracy. Remember that innumeracy—difficulties grasping the meanings of numbers and calculations—is widespread. The general public may be innumerate, but often the advocates promoting social problems are not any better. They may become confused about a number's precise meaning; they may misunderstand how the problem has been defined, how it has been measured, or what sort of sampling has been used. At the same time, their commitment to their cause and their enthusiasm for promoting the problem ("After all, it's a big problem!") may lead them to "improve" the statistic, to make the numbers seem more dramatic, even more compelling. Some mutant statistics may be products of advocates' cynicism, of their deliberate attempts to distort information in order to make their claims more convincing; this seems particularly likely when mutation occurs at the hands of large institutions that twist information into the form most favorable to their vested interests. But mutation can also be a product of sincere, albeit muddled interpretations by innumerate advocates.

Once someone utters a mutant statistic, there is a good chance that those who hear it will accept it and repeat it. Innumerate advocates influence their audiences: the media repeat mutant statistics; and the public accepts—or at least does not challenge—whatever numbers the media present. A political leader or a respected commentator may hear a statistic and repeat it, making the number seem even more credible. As statistics gain wide circulation, number laundering occurs. The figures become harder to challenge because everyone has heard them, everyone assumes the numbers must be correct. Particularly when numbers reinforce our beliefs, prejudices, or interests ("Of course that's true!"), we take figures as facts, without subjecting them to criticism.

Once created, *mutant statistics have a good chance of spreading and enduring*. But how and why does mutation occur? This chapter explores four common ways of creating mutant numbers. It begins with the most basic errors—making inappropriate *generalizations* from a statistic. It then turns to *transformations*—taking a number that means one thing and interpreting it to mean something completely different. The third section concerns *confusion*—transformations that involve misunderstanding the meaning of more complicated statistics. Finally, we'll consider *compound errors*—the ways in which bad statistics can be linked to form chains of error. In these four ways, bad statistics not only take on lives of their own, but they do increasing damage as they persist.

Generalization: Elementary Forms of Error

Generalization is an essential step in statistical reasoning. We rarely are able to count all the cases of some social problem. Instead, we collect some evidence, usually from a sample, and generalize from it to the larger problem. The process of generalization involves the basic processes discussed in chapter 2: the problem must be defined, and a means of measurement and a sample must be chosen.

These are elementary steps in social research. The basic principles are known: definitions and measures need to be clear and reasonable; samples should be representative. But even the most basic principles can be violated and, surprisingly often, no one notices when this happens. Mutant statistics—based on flawed definitions, poor measurements, or bad samples—emerge, and often receive a surprising amount of attention.

Questionable Definitions

Consider the flurry of media coverage about an "epidemic" of fires in African American churches in the South in 1996. Various advocates charged that the fires were the work of a racist conspiracy. Their claims recalled the history of racial terrorism in the South; black churches had often been targets of arson or bombing. Perhaps because 1996 was an election year, politicians—both Democrats (including President Clinton and Vice President Gore) and Republicans— denounced the fires, as did both the liberal National Council of Churches and the conservative Christian Coalition. Virtually everyone spoke out against the wave of arson.

Activists (such as the antiracist Center for Democratic Renewal) tried to document the increased number of fires; they produced lists of church arsons and statistics about the number of suspicious fires as evidence that the problem was serious. However, investigations, first by journalists and later by a federal task force, called these claims into question. While there were certainly some instances in which whites burned black churches out of racist motives, there was no evidence that a conspiracy linked the various fires. Moreover, the definition of a suspicious church fire proved to be unclear; the activists' lists included fires at churches with mostly white congregations, fires known to have been set by blacks, or by teenage vandals, or by mentally disturbed individuals, and fires set in order to collect insurance. And, when journalists checked the records of the fire insurance industry, they discovered not only that the number of fires in 1996 was not unusually high, but that church arsons had been generally declining since at least 1980. The federal task force ultimately failed to find any evidence of either an epidemic of fires or a conspiracy, although the press gave the task force report little coverage and advocates denounced the study's findings.

In short, statistics attempting to demonstrate the existence of an epidemic of church arsons lacked a clear definition of what ought to count as a racially motivated church fire. Nor did advocates define how many fires it would take to constitute an "epidemic" (although it would presumably be some number above the normal annual total of church fires). The absence of any clear definitions made it difficult to assess the evidence. The advocates who offered lists of fires (and asserted that each blaze was evidence of a racist conspiracy) may have been convinced, but those who tried to identify cases using some sort of clear definition failed to find any evidence that the epidemic even existed.

Inadequate Measurement

Clear, precise definitions are not enough. Whatever is defined must also be measured, and meaningless measurements will produce meaningless statistics. For instance, consider recent federal efforts to count hate crimes (crimes motivated by racial, religious, or other prejudice).

In response to growing concern about hate crimes, the federal government began collecting hate-crime statistics. The Federal Bureau of Investigation invited local law enforcement agencies to submit annual reports on hate crimes within their jurisdictions and, beginning in 1991, the bureau began issuing national hate-crime statistics.

Although the FBI had collected data on the incidence of crime from local agencies for decades, counting hate crimes posed special problems. When police record a reported crime—say, a robbery—it is a relatively straightforward process: usually the victim comes forward and tells of being forced to surrender money to the robber; these facts let the police classify the crime as a robbery. But identifying a hate crime requires something more: an assessment of the criminal's *motive*. A robbery might be a hate crime—*if* prejudice motivates the robber—but the crimes committed by robbers with other motives are not hate crimes. There are real disagreements about how to define and measure hate crimes. Not surprisingly, some activists favor broad, inclusive standards that will avoid false negatives; some feminists, for example, argue that rapes automatically should be considered hate crimes (on the grounds that all rape is motivated by gender prejudice).But local officials (who may be reluctant to publicize tensions within their communities) may favor much narrower standards, so that a cross-burning on an African American family's lawn may be classified as a "teenage prank," rather than a hate crime, depending on how police assess the offenders' motives.

While the recordkeeping may improve over time, the hate-crime statistics reported during the program's early years were nearly worthless. The organizational practices for recording hate crimes obviously varied widely among jurisdictions, making meaningful comparisons impossible. Moreover, it should be noted that, as reporting does improve, the numbers of reported hate crimes will almost certainly increase. That is, incidents that previously would not have been counted as hate crimes will be counted, and successive annual reports will show the incidence of hate crime rising. It may be years before measurement becomes sufficiently standardized to permit meaningful comparisons among jurisdictions, or from year to year. Measurement is always important, but this example illustrates why new statistical measures should be handled with special caution.

Bad Samples

Chapter 2 emphasized the importance of generalizing from representative samples. This is a basic principle, but one that is easily lost. For example, consider a study subtitled "A Survey of 917,410 Images, Descriptions, Short Stories, and Animations Downloaded 8.5 Million Times by Consumers in Over 2000 Cities in Forty Countries, Provinces, and Territories." An undergraduate student published this research in 1995 in a law review; he reported that 83.5 percent of the downloaded images were pornographic. In 1995, the Internet was still a novel phenomenon; people worried that children were frequent users, and that parents did not understand the Internet well enough to protect their children from questionable content. Claims that an extensive research project revealed that a substantial majority of Internet traffic involved pornography generated considerable concern. The huge scope of the study—917,410 images downloaded 8.5 million times—implied that it must be exhaustive.

But, of course, a large sample is not necessarily a good sample. In this case, the researcher did not collect a representative sample of Internet traffic. Rather, he examined postings to only 17 of some 32 Usenet groups that carried image files. Phrased differently, his findings showed that pornographic images accounted for only about 3 percent of Usenet traffic, while Usenet accounted for only about an eighth of the traffic on the entire Internet. In short, the sample of images was drawn from precisely that portion of the Internet where pornographic images were concentrated; it was anything but a representative sample. An alternative way to summarize the study's findings was that only 0.5 percent of Internet traffic involved pornographic images—a markedly lower (and less dramatic) figure than 83.5 percent. This example reminds us that mistaking a large sample for a representative sample can be a serious error.

Transformation: Changing the Meaning of Statistics

Another common form of mutant statistic involves transforming a number's meaning. Usually, this involves someone who tries to repeat a number, but manages to say something different. This chapter's introduction offers an example: recall that 150,000 people with anorexia became 150,000 deaths from anorexia. Of course, not all transformations are as obvious as equating having a disease with dying from it. Often transformations involve more subtle misunderstandings or logical leaps.

Consider the evolution of one critic's estimate that "six percent of America's 52,000 [Roman Catholic] priests are at some point in their adult lives sexually preoccupied with minors." This estimate originated with a psychologist and former priest who treated disturbed clergy and derived the figure from his observations. It was, in short, an educated guess. Still, his claim was often repeated (it was undoubtedly the only statistic available) and, in the process, transformed in at least four important ways. First, some of those who repeated the figure forgot that it was an estimate, and referred to the number as though it were a well-established fact—presumably a finding from a survey of priests. Second, while the psychologist's estimate was based on a sample of priests who had sought psychological treatment (and therefore might well be especially likely to have experienced inappropriate attractions to young people), he generalized to all priests. Third, although the original estimate referred to sexual *attraction,* rather than actual behavior, those who repeated the number often suggested that 6 percent of all priests had had sexual contacts with young people. Fourth, those young people became redefined as "children"; critics charged that 6 percent of priests were pedophiles ("pedophiles" are adults who have sex with prepubescent children). Although the original estimate in fact suggested that twice as many priests were attracted to adolescents as to younger children, this subtlety was lost. Thus, an estimate that perhaps 6 percent of priests in treatment were at some point sexually attracted to young people was transformed into the fact that 6 percent of all priests had had sex with children. Not everyone who repeated the statistic made all four transformations, but the number's original meaning soon became lost in a chorus of claims linking "pedophile priests" to the 6 percent figure.

This example suggests that a single statistic can be transformed in several ways, that it is impossible to predict all the ways a number might be misunderstood and given an entirely new meaning. While it may be especially easy to transform estimates and guesses (because the language of guessing is often vague), even more precisely defined statistics can undergo transformation.

Transformations involve shifts in meaning; advocates convert a statistic about X into a statistic about Y. This is an obvious error. Sometimes transformations are inadvertent; they reflect nothing more than sloppy, imprecise language. In such cases, people try to repeat a statistic, but they accidentally reword a claim in a way that creates a whole new meaning. Of course, other transformations may be deliberate efforts to mislead in order to advance the advocates' cause.

Certainly *transformations often "improve" a claim by making it more dramatic:* the number of anorexics becomes a body count; priests attracted to adolescents become priests having sex with children; homicides of unknown circumstances become serial killings. Such statistics get repeated precisely because they are dramatic, compelling numbers. A transformation that makes a statistic seem less dramatic is likely to be forgotten, but a more dramatic number stands a good chance of being repeated. It is a statistical version of Gresham's Law: *bad statistics drive out good ones.*

Transformation only requires that one person misunderstand a statistic and repeat the number in a way that gives it a new meaning. Once that new meaning—the mutant statistic—is available, many of the ways people may respond to it—accepting it, repeating it, or simply not challenging it—help maintain the error. Even if someone recognizes the mistake and calls attention to it, the error is likely to live on, uncorrected in many people's minds.

Confusion: Garbling Complex Statistics

The examples we've discussed so far in this chapter involve misunderstanding relatively simple, straightforward statistics. But some statistics get mangled because they seem too difficult to grasp, and therefore they are easily confused.

Consider *Workforce 2000*, a 1987 report, commissioned by the U.S. Department of Labor, that projected changes in the American workforce. The population in the workforce is gradually changing for several reasons: most important, a growing proportion of women work, so females account for a growing percentage of workers; in addition, the percentage of workers who are nonwhites is growing (this reflects several developments, including immigration patterns and ethnic differences in birth rates). The combined effect of these changes is gradually to reduce the proportion of white males in the workforce: in 1988 (roughly when *Workforce 2000* appeared), white males accounted for 47.9 percent of all workers; and the report projected that, by 2000, this percentage would fall to 44.8 percent.

However, rather than describing the change in such easily understood terms, the authors of *Workforce 2000* chose to speak of "net additions to the workforce" (see Table 2). What did this term mean? Very simply, the report made predictions about the populations of workers that would enter and leave the workforce (because of death, retirement, and so on) between 1988 and 2000. For example, the authors estimated that 13.5 million white males would join the workforce and 11.3 million would leave during those years. The difference—2.2 million—would be white males' "net addition to the workforce." Because the numbers of female and non-white workers are growing faster than those of white males, white males made up a relatively small share—less than 15 percent—of the anticipated total net addition to the workforce.

Rather than describing the gradual decline in white males' proportion of the workforce in terms of a straightforward percentage (47.9 percent in 1988, falling to 44.8 percent in 2000), the authors of *Workforce 2000* chose to use a more obscure measure (net additions to the workforce). That was an unfortunate choice, because it invited confusion. In fact, it even confused the people who prepared the report. *Workforce 2000* came with an "executive summary"—a brief introduction

Table 2. Projected Net Additions to the Workforce by Ethnicity and Sex, 1988–2000

Worker Category	Projected Net Additions[a]	Percentage
Non-Hispanic white males	2,265,000	11.6
Non-Hispanic white females	6,939,000	35.6
Hispanic males	2,877,000	14.8
Hispanic females	2,464,000	12.7
Black males	1,302,000	6.7
Black females	1,754,000	9.0
Asian & other males	950,000	4.9
Asian & other females	910,000	4.7
Total	19,461,000	100.0

Source: Howard N. Fullerton, "New Labor Force Projections, Spanning 1988 to 2000," *Monthly Labor Review* 112 (November 1989): 3–11 (Table 7).

Note: The data used in this table are similar to, but not precisely the same as those used to prepare Workforce 2000. Therefore, some of the figures are close to—but not precisely the same as—those quoted from the report.

[a] Projected net additions is a total—the number of workers expected to enter the workforce, minus the number expected to leave through death, retirement, and so on.

summarizing the report's key points for those too busy to read the entire document. The *Executive Summary to Workforce 2000* mangled the report's findings by claiming: "Only 15 percent of the new entrants to the labor force over the next 13 years will be native white males, compared to 47 percent in that category today." That sentence was wrong for two reasons: first, it confused *net additions* to the labor force (expected to be roughly 15 percent white males) with all *new entrants* to the labor force (white males were expected to be about 32 percent of all those entering the labor force); and, second, it made a meaningless comparison between the percentage of white males among net workforce entrants and white males' percentage in the existing labor force (roughly 47 percent). The statistical comparison seemed dramatic, but it was pointless.

Unfortunately, the dramatic number captured people's attention. The press fixed on the decline in white male workers as the report's major finding, and they began to repeat the error. Officials at the Department of Labor tried to clarify the confusion, but the mutant statistic predictably took on a life of its own. Politicians, labor and business leaders, and activists all warned that the workplace was about to undergo a sudden change, that white males—historically the typical, the most common category of workers—were an endangered species. The mangled statistic was itself remangled; for example, one official testified before Congress: "By the year 2000, nearly 65% of the total workforce will be women," yet no one asked how or why that might occur. Claims about the vanishing white male worker flourished.

It is easy to see why people repeated these claims; the notion that white males would soon become a small proportion of all workers offered support for very different political ideologies. Liberals saw the coming change as proof that more needed to be done to help women and minorities—who, after all, would be the workers of the future. Liberal proposals based on *Workforce 2000* called for expanded job training for nontraditional (that is, nonwhite or female) workers, additional programs to educate management and workers about the need for diversity in the workplace, and so on. In contrast, conservatives viewed the changing workforce as further evidence that immigration, feminism, and other developments threatened traditional social arrangements. In response to claims that white male workers were disappearing, a wide range of people found it easier to agree ("We knew it! We told you so!") than to ask critical questions about the statistical claims.

The reaction to *Workforce 2000* teaches a disturbing lesson: *complex statistics are prime candidates for mutation.* Not that the statistics in *Workforce 2000* were all that complex—they weren't. But the meaning of "net additions to the workforce" was not obvious, and when people tried to put it in simpler language—such as "new workers"—they mangled the concept. The report's authors made a poor choice when they chose to highlight statistics about net additions; they invited the confusion that followed. They ought to have realized that most people would not grasp this relatively complicated idea. (*Never overestimate the understanding of an innumerate public.*) And, of course, the people who interpreted the report (beginning with the authors of the executive summary!), instead of repeating the statistic, unintentionally mangled it to produce figures with new, wildly distorted meanings. Thus, a correct-but-difficult-to-understand statistic became an easy-to-understand-but-completely-wrong number.

Compound Errors: Creating Chains of Bad Statistics

I have suggested that bad statistics often take on a life of their own. Rarely criticized, they gain widespread acceptance, and they are repeated over and over. Each repetition makes the number seem more credible—after all, everyone agrees that that's the correct figure. And, of course, bad statistics can become worse through mutation: through misuse or misunderstanding, the number becomes further distorted. But that's not the end of the process. Bad statistics can have additional ramifications when they become the basis for calculating still more statistics.

We can think about this process as compounding errors into a chain of bad statistics: one questionable number becomes the basis for a second statistic that is, in turn, flawed; and the process can continue as the second bad number leads to a third, and so on—each number a link in a chain of errors.

Consider, for example, some of the uses to which the Kinsey Reports have been put. During the 1930s and 1940s, the biologist Alfred Kinsey and his colleagues conducted lengthy interviews with several thousand people about their sexual experiences. These interviews became the basis for two books: *Sexual Behavior in the Human Male* (1948) and *Sexual Behavior in the Human Female* (1953), popularly known as the "Kinsey Reports." The books challenged the polite fiction that most sex was confined to marriage; they revealed that many people had experience with a wide range of sexual behaviors, such as masturbation and premarital sex. However, the Kinsey data could not provide accurate estimates for the incidence of different sexual behaviors. While the thousands of interviews constituted a large sample, that sample was not representative, let alone random. The sample contained a much higher proportion of college-educated people than the general population and, in an effort to explore a broad range of sexual experiences, Kinsey deliberately arranged interviews with a substantial number of active homosexuals, as well as with many individuals who had been imprisoned. Nonetheless, commentators sometimes treat the Kinsey findings as though they offer an authoritative, representative portrait of the American population. For example, gay and lesbian activists sometimes argue that one-tenth of the population is homosexual, and they refer to the Kinsey Reports to support this claim.

Rather than define heterosexual and homosexual as a simple dichotomy, the Kinsey Reports described a continuum that ranged from individuals who had never had a homosexual experience, to those who had some incidental homosexual experiences, and so on through those whose sexual experiences had been exclusively homosexual. Still, the male report estimated that "10 per cent of the males are more or less exclusively homosexual . . . for at least three years between the ages of 16 and 55." (Later surveys, based on more representative samples, have concluded that the one-in-ten estimate exaggerated the amount of homosexuality; typically, they find that 3–6 percent of males [and a lower percentage of females] have had significant homosexual experience at some point in their lives [usually in adolescence or early adulthood], and that the incidence of homosexuality among adults is lower—between 1 and 3 percent.) However, gay and lesbian activists often dispute these lower estimates; they prefer the one-in-ten figure because it suggests that homosexuals are a substantial minority group, roughly equal in number to African Americans—too large to be ignored. Thus, the 10 percent figure lives on, and it is often used in calculating other, new statistics about gays and lesbians.

Consider, for example, claims that one-third of teen suicides—or roughly 1,500 deaths per year—involve gay or lesbian adolescents. Gay activists invoked this statistic to portray the hardships gay and lesbian youth confront; it suggests that stigma and social isolation are severe enough to drive many adolescents to kill themselves.

But how could anyone hope to measure gay teen suicides accurately? Many gays and lesbians try to conceal their sexual orientation, and certainly some teenagers might feel driven to suicide because keeping that secret was becoming a burden. But, given this secrecy, how could anyone know just which teenagers who commit suicide are gay or lesbian? Coroners, after all, do not record sexual orientation on death certificates.

So how did advocates arrive at the statistic that one-third of teenagers who kill themselves are homosexual? The answer is that they constructed a chain of bad statistics. They began with the familiar, Kinsey-based claim that one-tenth of the population—including, presumably, one-tenth of teenagers—homosexual. Roughly 4,500 teenage deaths are attributed to suicide each year; on average, then, 10 percent of those—450 suicides—should involve gay or lesbian teens. (Note that we have already incorporated our first dubious statistic—derived from Kinsey's questionable sample—that 10 percent of the population is gay or lesbian.)

Next, advocates drew upon various studies that suggested that homosexuals attempted suicide at a rate two to three times higher than heterosexuals. Note that this figure presumes knowledge about the rates of an often secretive behavior in two populations—one itself often hidden. Multiplying 10 percent (the estimated proportion of homosexuals in the population) by 3 (a suicide rate estimated to be three times higher than that of heterosexuals) led to an estimate that gays and lesbians accounted for 30 percent of suicides—and this figure was in turn rounded up to one-third.[*] Thus, one-third of 4,500 teen suicides—1,500 deaths—involve gay or lesbian youths.

Notice how the final figure depends on the advocates' assumptions. If the proportion of homosexuals among all teenagers is estimated at 3 percent, or 6 percent, the number of gay teen suicides falls. If the rate at which homosexual teens commit suicide is only twice that of heterosexuals, the number falls. (For example, if we instead assume that 3 percent of the adolescent population is gay or lesbian, and that their suicide rate is twice that of heterosexuals, homosexuals would account

---

[*]There is another innumerate error hidden here. Even if 10 percent of the population is homosexual, and their suicide rate is three times that of heterosexuals, homosexuals should account for only one-quarter—not one-third—of suicides. Let Z be the suicide rate for heterosexuals; if: (.1 [the proportion of the population that is homosexual] x 3Z) + (.9 [the proportion of the population that is heterosexual] x Z) = 4,500 (the total number of teen suicides), then: (.1 x 3Z) = 1,125 = one-quarter of 4,500.

for less than 6 percent of all teen suicides.) The final figure depends completely on the assumptions used to make the calculations.

This example offers two important lessons. The first is a reminder that bad statistics can live on. Most social scientists consider Kinsey's 10 percent estimate for homosexuality too high; more recent, more reliable studies have consistently produced lower estimates. Yet some gay and lesbian activists continue to cite the higher figure—precisely because it is the largest available number. In turn, 10 percent often figures into other calculations—not just about gay teen suicides, but also regarding the number of gay voters, the size of the gay population at risk of AIDS, and so on.

The second lesson is perhaps harder to learn. Any claim about the number of gay teen suicides should set off alarm bells. Given the difficulties in learning which deaths are suicides and which teenagers are gay, it obviously would be hard to learn the number of gay teen suicides. It is not unreasonable to ask how the advocates arrived at that number, and which assumptions lay behind their calculations. Those assumptions may be perfectly defensible, but they deserve to be examined. But, of course, such examinations are the exception, not the rule. Once offered, a statistic—such as the claim that gays and lesbians account for one-third of all teen suicides—tends to be repeated, to circulate widely, without confronting questions about its validity.

Compound errors can begin with any of the standard sorts of bad statistics—a guess, a poor sample, an inadvertent transformation, perhaps confusion over the meaning of a complex statistic. People inevitably want to put statistics to use, to explore a number's implications. An estimate for the number of homeless persons can help us predict the costs of social services for the homeless, just as an estimate of the proportion of the population that is homosexual lets us predict the number of gay and lesbian teenagers who may attempt suicide. But, when the original numbers are bad—and we have already explored some of the many ways bad numbers can come into circulation—compound errors can result. Assessing such statistics requires another level of critical thinking: one must ask both how advocates produced the statistic at hand (1,500 gay teen suicides), and whether they based their calculations on earlier numbers that are themselves questionable (e.g., 10 percent of the population is homosexual). The strengths and weaknesses of those original numbers should affect our confidence in the second-generation statistics.

\\\ CHARACTERISTICS OF GOOD STATISTICS

There is much criticism about the production of bad statistics through guessing, dubious definitions, questionable measurement, and poor sampling. At this point, you may be wondering whether all statistics are bad, nothing more than "damned lies." Are there any good statistics? How can we tell the good numbers from the bad?

The problems identified in this chapter suggest some standards that good statistics meet. First, *good statistics are based on more than guessing.* The most basic question about any statistic is: How did someone arrive at this number? All statistics are imperfect, but some flaws are worse than others. Obviously, we should not place too much confidence in guesses (even educated guesses). Watch for the danger signs of guessing: Do the people offering the statistic have a bias—do they want to show that the problem is common (or rare)? Is the statistic a big, round number? Does the statistic describe an unfamiliar, hidden social problem that probably has a large dark figure (if so, how did the advocates manage to come up with their numbers)?

Second, *good statistics are based on clear, reasonable definitions.* Remember, every statistic has to define its subject. Those definitions ought to be clear and made public. An example—particularly a dramatic, disturbing example, a horror story, a worst case—is not a definition. Anyone presenting a statistic describing a social problem should be able and willing to explain the definition used to create the statistic. Definitions usually are broad: they encompass kinds of cases very different from (and usually less serious than) the examples. We need to ask: How broad? What does the definition include? Again, ask yourself whether the people offering the statistic favor broad (or narrow) definitions, and why. Consider whether their definition might exclude too many false negatives or include too many false positives.

Third, *good statistics are based on clear, reasonable measures.* Again, every statistic involves some sort of measurement; while all measures are imperfect, not all flaws are equally serious. People offering a statistic should be able and willing to explain how they measured the social problem, and their choices should seem reasonable. If the people offering the statistic have some sort of bias (in favor of big—or small—numbers), that bias may be reflected in the way they've measured the problem. For example, they may have worded survey questions to encourage certain responses, or they may interpret responses in peculiar ways. Be suspicious of statistics based on hidden measurements, and consider how measurement choices might shape statistics.

Finally, *good statistics are based on good samples.* Clear, reasonable definitions and clear, reasonable measurements are not enough. Almost all statistics generalize from a sample of cases to a larger population, and the methods of selecting that sample should be explained. Good samples are representative of that larger population; ideally, this means the sample has been selected at random. Watch out for statistics based on small, non-random, convenience samples; such samples are easier and cheaper to study, but they are a poor basis for sweeping generalizations. Ask yourself how the sample chosen might skew the resulting statistics

One sign of good statistics is that we're given more than a number; we're told something about the definitions, measurement and sampling behind the figure—about how the number emerged. When that information remains concealed, we have every reason to be skeptical.

﹤ DISCUSSION QUESTIONS

1. The statistic that each year half of all marriages end in divorce routinely makes the rounds in the media. Using the same logic that Best applied to the example of how many children are gunned down each year, explain why this divorce statistic is really a *mutant statistic.*

2. Why do you think statistics add such an air of credibility and authenticity to claims? Why don't we treat people's nonnumerical observations the same way?

3. Peruse any news outlet that you are familiar with and try to find an example of three statics that sound like they might be problematic. Which of Best's characteristics of mutant statistics do you think is at work with each?

4. If you met someone who promised that he or she could double your chances of winning the Powerball lottery for only $10, should you pay that person the money? Assume that he or she really would double your chances. Why or why not?

6

Body Ritual Among the Nacirema

Horace Miner

In this article, anthropologist Horace Miner carefully documents the cultural practices of the Nacirema, a group he studied and lived with for many years. As you read, make note of any of the cultural practices you find particularly strange, and think about whether this is a group of people that you would ever want to be among.

The anthropologist has become so familiar with the diversity of ways in which different peoples behave in similar situations that he is not apt to be surprised by even the most exotic customs. In fact, if all of the logically possible combinations of behavior have not been found somewhere in the world, he is apt to suspect that they must be present in some yet undescribed tribe. This point has, in fact, been expressed with respect to clan organization by Murdock (1949:71). In this light, the magical beliefs and practices of the Nacirema present such unusual aspects that it seems desirable to describe them as an example of the extremes to which human behavior can go.

Professor Linton first brought the ritual of the Nacirema to the attention of anthropologists twenty years ago (1936:326), but the culture of this people is still very poorly understood. They are a North American group living in the territory between the Canadian Cree, the Yaqui and Tarahumare of Mexico, and the Carib

"Body Ritual Among the Nacirema," by Horace Miner in *American Anthropologist* 58:3, June 1956.

and Arawak of the Antilles. Little is known of their origin, although tradition states that they came from the east. According to Nacirema mythology, their nation was originated by a culture hero, Notgnihsaw, who is otherwise known for two great feats of strength—the throwing of a piece of wampum across the river Pa-To-Mac and the chopping down of a cherry tree in which the Spirit of Truth resided.

Nacirema culture is characterized by a highly developed market economy which has evolved in a rich natural habitat. While much of the people's time is devoted to economic pursuits, a large part of the fruits of these labors and a considerable portion of the day are spent in ritual activity. The focus of this activity is the human body, the appearance and health of which loom as a dominant concern in the ethos of the people. While such a concern is certainly not unusual, its ceremonial aspects and associated philosophy are unique.

The fundamental belief underlying the whole system appears to be that the human body is ugly and that its natural tendency is to debility and disease. Incarcerated in such a body, man's only hope is to avert these characteristics through the use of the powerful influences of ritual and ceremony. Every household has one or more shrines devoted to this purpose. The more powerful individuals in the society have several shrines in their houses and, in fact, the opulence of a house is often referred to in terms of the number of such ritual centers it possesses. Most houses are of wattle and daub construction, but the shrine rooms of the more wealthy are walled with stone. Poorer families imitate the rich by applying pottery plaques to their shrine walls.

While each family has at least one such shrine, the rituals associated with it are not family ceremonies but are private and secret. The rites are normally only discussed with children, and then only during the period when they are being initiated into these mysteries. I was able, however, to establish sufficient rapport with the natives to examine these shrines and to have the rituals described to me.

The focal point of the shrine is a box or chest which is built into the wall. In this chest are kept the many charms and magical potions without which no native believes he could live. These preparations are secured from a variety of specialized practitioners. The most powerful of these are the medicine men, whose assistance must be rewarded with substantial gifts. However, the medicine men do not provide the curative potions for their clients, but decide what the ingredients should be and then write them down in an ancient and secret language. This writing is understood only by the medicine men and by the herbalists who, for another gift, provide the required charm.

The charm is not disposed of after it has served its purpose, but is placed in the charm-box of the household shrine. As these magical materials are specific for certain ills, and the real or imagined maladies of the people are many, the charm-box is usually full to overflowing. The magical packets are so numerous that people forget what their purposes were and fear to use them again. While the natives are very vague on this point, we can only assume that the idea in retaining all the old magical materials is that their presence in the charm-box, before which the body rituals are conducted, will in some way protect the worshipper.

Beneath the charm-box is a small font. Each day every member of the family, in succession, enters the shrine room, bows his head before the charm-box, mingles different sorts of holy water in the font, and proceeds with a brief rite of ablution. The holy waters are secured from the Water Temple of the community, where the priests conduct elaborate ceremonies to make the liquid ritually pure.

In the hierarchy of magical practitioners, and below the medicine men in prestige, are specialists whose designation is best translated "holy-mouth-men." The Nacirema have an almost pathological horror of and fascination with the mouth, the condition of which is believed to have a supernatural influence on all social relationships. Were it not for the rituals of the mouth, they believe that their teeth would fall out, their gums bleed, their jaws shrink, their friends desert them, and their lovers reject them. They also believe that a strong relationship exists between oral and moral characteristics. For example, there is a ritual ablution of the mouth for children which is supposed to improve their moral fiber.

The daily body ritual performed by everyone includes a mouth-rite. Despite the fact that these people are so punctilious about care of the mouth, this rite involves a practice which strikes the uninitiated stranger as revolting. It was reported to me that the ritual consists of inserting a small bundle of hog hairs into the mouth, along with certain magical powders, and then moving the bundle in a highly formalized series of gestures.

In addition to the private mouth-rite, the people seek out a holy-mouth-man once or twice a year. These practitioners have an impressive set of paraphernalia, consisting of a variety of augers, awls, probes, and prods. The use of these objects in the exorcism of the evils of the mouth involves almost unbelievable ritual torture of the client. The holy-mouth-man opens the client's mouth and, using the above mentioned tools, enlarges any holes which decay may have created in the teeth. Magical materials are put into these holes. If there are no naturally occurring holes in the teeth, large sections of one or more teeth are gouged out so that the supernatural substance can be applied. In the client's view, the purpose of these ministrations is to arrest decay and to draw friends. The extremely sacred and traditional character of the rite is evident in the fact that the natives return to the holy-mouth-men year after year, despite the fact that their teeth continue to decay.

It is to be hoped that, when a thorough study of the Nacirema is made, there will be careful inquiry into the personality structure of these people. One has but to watch the gleam in the eye of a holy-mouth-man, as he jabs an awl into an exposed nerve, to suspect that a certain amount of sadism is involved. If this can be established, a very interesting pattern emerges, for most of the population shows definite masochistic tendencies. It was to these that Professor Linton referred in discussing a distinctive part of the daily body ritual which is performed only by men. This part of the rite involves scraping and lacerating the surface of the face with a sharp instrument. Special women's rites are performed only four times during each lunar month, but what they lack in frequency is made up in barbarity. As part of this ceremony, women bake their heads in small ovens for about an hour. The theoretically interesting point is that what seems to be a preponderantly masochistic people have developed sadistic specialists.

The medicine men have an imposing temple, or *latipso*, in every community of any size. The more elaborate ceremonies required to treat very sick patients can only be performed at this temple. These ceremonies involve not only the thaumaturge but a permanent group of vestal maidens who move sedately about the temple chambers in distinctive costume and headdress.

The *latipso* ceremonies are so harsh that it is phenomenal that a fair proportion of the really sick natives who enter the temple ever recover. Small children whose indoctrination is still incomplete have been known to resist attempts to take them to the temple because "that is where you go to die." Despite this fact, sick adults are not only willing but eager to undergo the protracted ritual purification, if they can afford to do so. No matter how ill the supplicant or how grave the emergency, the guardians of many temples will not admit a client if he cannot give a rich gift to the custodian. Even after one has gained admission and survived the ceremonies, the guardians will not permit the neophyte to leave until he makes still another gift.

The supplicant entering the temple is first stripped of all his or her clothes. In every-day life the Nacirema avoids exposure of his body and its natural functions. Bathing and excretory acts are performed only in the secrecy of the household shrine, where they are ritualized as part of the body-rites. Psychological shock results from the fact that body secrecy is suddenly lost upon entry into the *latipso*. A man, whose own wife has never seen him in an excretory act, suddenly finds himself naked and assisted by a vestal maiden while he performs his natural functions into a sacred vessel. This sort of ceremonial treatment is necessitated by the fact that the excreta are used by a diviner to ascertain the course and nature of the client's sickness. Female clients, on the other hand, find their naked bodies are subjected to the scrutiny, manipulation and prodding of the medicine men.

Few supplicants in the temple are well enough to do anything but lie on their hard beds. The daily ceremonies, like the rites of the holy-mouth-men, involve discomfort and torture. With ritual precision, the vestals awaken their miserable charges each dawn and roll them about on their beds of pain while performing ablutions, in the formal movements of which the maidens are highly trained. At other times they insert magic wands in the supplicant's mouth or force him to eat substances which are supposed to be healing. From time to time the medicine men come to their clients and jab magically treated needles into their flesh. The fact that these temple ceremonies may not cure, and may even kill the neophyte, in no way decreases the people's faith in the medicine men.

There remains one other kind of practitioner, known as a "listener." This witch-doctor has the power to exorcise the devils that lodge in the heads of people who have been bewitched. The Nacirema believe that parents bewitch their own children. Mothers are particularly suspected of putting a curse on children while teaching them the secret body rituals. The counter-magic of the witch-doctor is unusual in its lack of ritual. The patient simply tells the "listener" all his troubles and fears, beginning with the earliest difficulties he can remember. The memory displayed by the Nacirema in these exorcism sessions is truly remarkable. It is not uncommon for the patient to bemoan the rejection he felt upon being weaned as a babe, and a few individuals even see their troubles going back to the traumatic effects of their own birth.

In conclusion, mention must be made of certain practices which have their base in native esthetics but which depend upon the pervasive aversion to the natural body and its functions. There are ritual fasts to make fat people thin and ceremonial feasts to make thin people fat. Still other rites are used to make women's breasts larger if they are small, and smaller if they are large. General dissatisfaction with breast shape is symbolized in the fact that the ideal form is virtually outside the range of human variation. A few women afflicted with almost inhuman hypermammary development are so idolized that they make a handsome living by simply going from village to village and permitting the natives to stare at them for a fee.

Reference has already been made to the fact that excretory functions are ritualized, routinized, and relegated to secrecy. Natural reproductive functions are similarly distorted. Intercourse is taboo as a topic and scheduled as an act. Efforts are made to avoid pregnancy by the use of magical materials or by limiting intercourse to certain phases of the moon. Conception is actually very infrequent. When pregnant, women dress so as to hide their condition. Parturition takes place in secret, without friends or relatives to assist, and the majority of women do not nurse their infants.

Our review of the ritual life of the Nacirema has certainly shown them to be a magic-ridden people. It is hard to understand how they have managed to exist so long under the burdens which they have imposed upon themselves. But even such exotic customs as these take on real meaning when they are viewed with the insight provided by Malinowski when he wrote (1948:70):

Looking from far and above, from our high places of safety in the developed civilization, it is easy to see all the crudity and irrelevance of magic. But without its power and guidance early man could not have mastered his practical difficulties as he has done, nor could man have advanced to the higher stages of civilization.

DISCUSSION QUESTIONS

1. Which practices described by Miner did you find to be particularly odd?

2. If you were given the chance to accompany a research team to live with the Nacirema for a semester as an internship, would you be willing to do so?

3. How do our assumptions about what is normal and what is deviant affect how we interpret the beliefs and practices of other cultures?

4. How might our cultural obsession with social media, texting, and the Internet be described by someone not familiar with Americans' cultural practices?

5. Reread the sections of the article that had the practices you thought were most strange in from Question 1 above. Does anything sound familiar about them?

REFERENCES CITED

Linton, Ralph 1936 The Study of Man. New York, D. Appleton-Century Co.

Malinowski, Bronislaw 1948 Magic, Science, and Religion. Glencoe, The Free Press.

Murdock, George P. 1949 Social Structure. New York, The Macmillan Co.

7

Islands of Meaning

Eviatar Zerubavel

If you've ever spent any time around children, you've probably been either amused, grossed out, or both by their lack of appreciation for norms that adults take for granted. Perhaps you've had to explain to a disappointed child why he or she can't order ice cream for dinner, that scissors aren't toys, or why it's OK to jump on the trampoline outside but not on the bed inside. What children have not yet learned are the socially appropriate ways to categorize the world. For example, ice cream belongs in the dessert category, not the dinner category, and trampolines are toys, whereas beds are furniture. In this article, Zerubavel argues that learning the socially appropriate categorization conventions of one's culture is fundamental to creating the reality that we generally take for granted as simply existing objectively out in the physical world. One of the first things that new members of a society must do is learn how to see the islands of meaning (i.e., categories) that are conventionally used in that particular culture.

Zerubavel explains why categorization is so important to the process of socialization, and he describes the different processes used to create these islands of meaning, including lumping, splitting, and creating mental gaps. As you read, pay special attention to the language he uses to describe these processes; the words he uses are very physical in nature. He also uses numerous examples to show how what we tend to perceive as the inherent logic of categorizations are actually simply social conventions that could just as logically be arranged in a different way. If the categorizations were somehow inherent and obvious, children would never ask to have ice cream for dinner.

W̲e transform the natural world into a social one by carving out of it mental chunks we then treat as if they were discrete, totally detached from their surroundings. The way we mark off islands of property is but one example of the general process by which we create meaningful social entities.

In order to endow the things we perceive with meaning, we normally ignore their uniqueness and regard them as typical members of a particular class of objects (a relative, a present), acts (an apology, a crime), or events (a game, a conference). After all, "If each of the many things in the world were taken as distinct, unique, a thing in itself unrelated to any other thing, perception of the world would disintegrate into complete meaninglessness." Indeed, things become meaningful only when placed in some category. A clinical symptom, for instance, is quite meaningless until we find some diagnostic niche (a cold, an allergic reaction) within which to situate and thus make sense of it. Our need to arrange the world around us in categories is so great that, even when we encounter mental odds and ends that do not seem to belong in any conventional category, we nonetheless "bend" them so as to fit them into one anyway, as we usually do with the sexually ambiguous or the truly novel work of art. When such adjustment does not suffice, we even create special categories (avant-garde, others, miscellaneous) for these mental pariahs.

〲 MENTAL GAPS

Creating islands of meaning entails two rather different mental processes—lumping and splitting. On the other hand, it involves grouping "similar" items together in a single mental cluster—sculptors and filmmakers ("artists"), murder and arson ("felonies"), foxes and camels ("animals"). At the same time, it also involves separating in our mind "different" mental clusters from one another—artists from scientists, felonies from misdemeanors, animals from humans. In order to carve out of the flux surrounding us meaningful entities with distinctive identities, we must experience them as separate from one another.

Separating one island of meaning from another entails the introduction of some mental void between them. As we carve discrete mental chunks out of continuous streams of experience, we normally visualize substantial gaps separating them from one another. Such mental versions of the great divides that split continuous stretches of land following geological upheavals underlie our basic experience of mental entities as situated amid blank stretches of emptiness. It is our perception of the void among these islands of meaning that makes them separate in our mind, and its magnitude reflects the degree separateness we perceive among them.

Gaps are critical to our ability to experience insular entities. The experiential separateness of the self, for example, is clearly enhanced by the actual gap of "personal space" that normally envelops it. By literally insulating the self from contact with others, such a gap certainly promotes its experience as an insular entity. A similar experience of an island situated in a vacuum often leads us to confine our horizons to, and never venture beyond, our neighborhood, hometown, or country. The great divides we visualize between women and men, children and adults, and blacks and whites like wise promote our perception of such entities as discrete.

Mental gaps are often represented by token partitions. Like the ancient Assyrians, who used mere doorways to demarcate the borders of their empire, we often use a partial wall or a column to create the illusion of a discrete work space or sitting area in a room. And like the ancient Egyptians, who used cartouches to cut off visually the names of monarchs from the rest of the text in which they were embedded, thus substantiating the social gulf that separated royalty from ordinary folk, we often use lines to portray the mental gap between news and commercial ads in newspapers.

Often, however, we represent mental gaps quite literally by blank spaces. When we wish not only to rank entities but also to portray the relative magnitude of the mental distances among them, a visual representation of the latter is of considerable help. I recall, for example, my eight-year-old daughter ranking her favorite restaurants and finding it necessary to "leave some space" between the first two and the third. The ability to visualize mental gaps is even more critical, of course, when we wish to depict the precise magnitude of such intervals.

Often, however, we need more than a blank space or silence to substantiate mental gaps. Along with the rites of passage that help us articulate transitions from one mental entity to another, we also use various "rites of separation" to highlight the gaps we visualize among them. Holidays, reunions, and parties, for example, inevitably dramatize the mental gap separating members who are invited to participate from nonmembers who are excluded. In so doing, they clearly promote our experience of ethnic groups, families, and fraternities as insular entities.

Rites of separation are often designed to dramatize the mental gap between the old and new selves of people whose social identity is radically transformed as a result of crossing some critical mental partition. Thus, for example, as they go through basic military training (in which they become soldiers), puberty rites (in which they officially become adults), and initiations into monastic orders (in which they are symbolically transformed into brides of Christ), recruits, children, and ordinary girls practically undergo a symbolic death. To dramatize the considerable mental gaps (separating civilians from soldiers, childhood from adulthood, and so on) involved in such transformations, they must ritually destroy their old self before they can assume their new identity. Men about to be married thus attend bachelor parties given by their old friends, newly enlisted soldiers relinquish their civilian clothes and much of their hair, and new nuns renounce their entire former life. A ritual name change helps monks, converts, slaves, brides, and adoptees articulate similar symbolic metamorphoses and dramatize the gap between their old identity and the new one.

Mental reality, in short, is deeply embedded in social reality. The gaps we perceive among the supposedly discrete entities that constitute social reality as well as the quantum leaps necessary for crossing them are admittedly mental. Nonetheless, once they are institutionalized, they become seemingly inevitable facts that we can no longer ignore or wish away. Along with the islands of meaning they help delineate, they are the very stuff that our social life is made of. Given their centrality to the way we organize our everyday life, such gaps are therefore quite real in their felt presence. Thus, if we perceive the world as made up of discrete entities, it is because, in a way, they indeed *are* discrete.

☖ THE SOCIAL LENS

I have thus far drawn a deliberately one-sided picture of reality as an array of insular entities neatly separated from one another by great divides. Such discontinuity, however, is not as inevitable as we normally take it to be. It is a pronouncedly mental scalpel that helps us carve discrete mental slices out of reality: "You get the illusion that [entities] are just there and are being named as they exist. But they can be . . . organized quite differently depending on how the knife moves. . . . It is important to see this knife for what it is and not to be fooled into thinking that [entities] are the way they are just because the knife happened to cut it up that way. It is important to concentrate on the knife itself." The scalpel, of course, is a *social* scalpel. It is society that underlies the way we generate meaningful mental entities.

Reality is not made up of insular chunks unambiguously separated from one another by sharp divides, but, rather, of vague, blurred-edge essences that often "spill over" into one another. It normally presents itself not in black and white, but, rather, in subtle shades of gray, with mental twilight zones as well as intermediate essences connecting entities. Segmenting it into discrete islands of meaning usually rests on some social convention, and most boundaries are, therefore, mere social arti-facts. As such, they often vary from one society to another as well as across historical periods within each society. Moreover, the precise location—not to mention the very existence—of such mental partitions is often disputed even within any given society.

〰 CULTURE AND CLASSIFICATION

There is more than one way to carve discrete chunks out of a given continuum, and different cultures indeed mold out of the same reality quite different archipelagos of meaning. While all cultures, for example, distinguish the edible from the ined-ible or the young from the old, they usually differ from one another in where they draw the lines between them. The distinction between the sexually accessible and inaccessible is likewise universal (all cultures, for example, have an incest taboo), yet the specific delineation of those who are considered off limits often varies from one culture to another. Surrounding oneself with a bubble of "personal space," too, is a universal practice, yet, in marked contrast to other species, humans exhibit substantial subspecific cultural variations in where they draw its boundaries. (Along similar lines, the precise delineation of one's "personal" circle of intimates also varies from one culture to another.) By the same token, not everyone who is considered "black" in America would necessarily be classified as such in the West Indies or Brazil.

    Languages differ from one another in the way they generate distinct lexical particles, and it is not unusual that a single word in one language would cover the semantic range of several separate words in another. Thus, for example, while there is a single word for both rats and mice in Latin, insects and airplanes in Hopi, and brothers-in-law and grandnephews in the Algonquian language of the Fox, there are separate words for blankets that are folded and spread out, for water in buckets and in lakes, and for dogs that stand and sit in Navajo. Such differences have considerable cognitive implications. After all, it is much easier to isolate a distinct mental entity from its surroundings when one has a word to denote it. That explains why the Navajo, who use different verbs to denote the handling of objects with different shapes, indeed tend to classify objects according to shape much more than English speakers. By the same token, lacking the necessary lexical tools for differentiating, it took me, a native speaker of Hebrew, a long time before I could actually notice the mental gaps—so obvious to English-speakers—that separate jelly from jam or preserves.

While such cross-cultural variability often leads us to look down on other cultures' classificatory schemas as primitive or "confused," it ought to help us recognize and accept the relative validity of our own. Only their ethnocentric blinders prevent those who claim that "savages" fail to notice obvious mental discontinuities from appreciating the highly sophisticated classificatory skills of these people, who clearly do make distinctions, though rarely among the things that we do.

Any notion of logic is valid only within a particular cultural milieu, and our own classifications are no more logical than those of "savages." We must therefore resist the ethnocentric tendency to regard our own way of classifying reality as the only reasonable way to do it. That entails giving up the idea that some ways of classifying are more correct and "logical" than others and, therefore, also reconsidering the standard tests through which we usually measure intelligence. Thus, for example, "a person, asked in what way wood and alcohol are alike [should not be] given a zero score if he answers: 'Both knock you out' [just] because the examiner prefers logical categories of scientific classification." By the same token, nor should we penalize someone who maintains (as did my daughter, when she was five) that the difference between a bus and an airplane lies in the fact that we need not pay the pilot on boarding a plane.

Ways of classifying reality vary not only across cultures but also across historical periods within the same culture. The last couple of centuries, for example, saw substantial shifts in the location of the lines we draw between the sexes, the "races," public and private, family and community.

Only two centuries ago, the mental gap between the sexes was so wide that women were perceived as "closer" to animals than to men and granting them political rights seemed as ludicrous as extending such rights to beasts. That this sounds so utterly absurd today only comes to show that absurdity is a function of where we draw lines, and that mental distances may change over time. Before the Civil War, when blacks were regarded in the United States as objects rather than persons, granting then civil rights would have legally been just as ludicrous. (In fact, public signs as Negroes and Dogs Not Allowed suggest that, until quit recently, they were still perceived in the South as "closer" to animals than to whites.) Only a few decades ago, the idea that homosexuals should be regarded as a distinct political minority would have been as absurd as granting such status to music teachers, baseball fans, or vegetarians. Rights have historically been extended to new social categories (prisoners, noncitizens, children, the insane, the preborn) whose legal standing prior to that would have been inconceivable.

Since it is the very basis of society reality, we often forget that language rests on mere convention and regard such mental entities, which are own creation, as if they were real.

It is society that helps us carve discrete islands of meaning out of our experience. Only English speakers, for example, can "hear" the gaps between the separate words in "perhaps they should have tried it earlier," which everyone else hears as a single chain of sound. Along similar lines, while people who hear jazz for the first time can never understand why a seemingly continuous stretch of music is occasionally interrupted by bursts of applause, jazz connoisseurs can actually "hear" the purely mental divides separating piano, bass, or drum "solos" from mere "accompaniment." Being a member of society entails "seeing" the world through special mental lenses. It is these lenses, which we acquire only through socialization, that allow us to perceive "things." The proverbial Martian cannot see the mental partitions separating Catholics from Protestants, classical from popular music, or the funny from the crude. Like the contours of constellations, we "see" such fine lines only when we learn that we should expect them there. As real as they may feel to us, boundaries are mere figments of our minds. Only the socialized can "see" them. To all cultural outsiders they are totally invisible.

Only through such "glasses" can entities be "seen." As soon as we remove them, boundaries practically disappear and the "things" they delineate fade away. What we then experience is as continuous as is Europe or the Middle East when seen from space or in ancient maps, or our own neighborhood when fog or heavy snow covers curbs and property lines, practically transforming familiar milieus into a visually undifferentiated flux. This is the way reality must appear to the unsocialized—boundless, unbroken world with no lines. That is the world we would have inhabited were it not for society.

℣ DISCUSSION QUESTIONS

1. Make a list of all the terms that Zerubavel uses to describe the process of categorization that are more conventionally used to describe physical acts. Why do you think he chose to use these types of terms?

2. How are lumping, splitting, and mental gaps part of the process of creating islands of meaning?

3. Zerubavel notes that mental gaps between categories are often reflected in physical gaps. Think about your classroom or where you work. Where do physical gaps reinforce mental gaps?

4. Think about your last trip to the grocery store. How are food items and other supplies generally organized? Have you ever had difficulty finding an item because it was categorized differently (and therefore in a different place in the store) than you thought it would be?

8

The Presentation of Self in Everyday Life

Erving Goffman

Most of us enter, participate in, and leave countless interactions each day without giving much thought to any of them. In fact, one of the most remarkable things about social interactions is how often they go smoothly. Simply getting to class, buying dinner, or spending time watching TV with friends involves an impressive amount of information gathering, decision making, action, and response. These mundane, often repeated, daily interactions wouldn't seem like they could have anything significant to tell us about the nature of social interaction, but in fact they do.

In this article, Erving Goffman introduces us to dramaturgy, *which illuminates the underlying principles that govern just such mundane interactions. Dramaturgy is a theoretical perspective based on the analogy that face-to-face social interactions are like a theatrical performance. Goffman argues that in any face-to-face encounter, the participants engage in "the presentation of self," performing a role (student, employee, friend, significant other, etc.) just as a performer in a stage production would. Successful social actors look the part (appearance), act in a way that matches their role (manner), and play their role in the appropriate place (setting). These are referred to as* sign vehicles.

For Goffman, we use sign vehicles to answer the question "what's going on here?" in every face to face interaction we have. The agreed upon answer to this question is what he refers to as the definition of the situation, *which must be determined every time we enter into an interaction. We tend to only consciously notice this when things don't go as we expected. You probably didn't think too much about class the last time you arrived at your classroom. But imagine instead that you had arrived at your classroom to find all of the chairs pushed to the edges of the room, a disco ball hanging from the ceiling, your professor moonwalking, and 80s music playing from the computer. You would be very likely to ask or at least think, "What's going on here?" In Goffman's terms, the* definition of the situation *has been called into question. Your teacher's presentation of self does not match what we expect of a teacher in terms of appearance and manner and the setting has changed significantly.*

Importantly, from a dramaturgical perspective, we go through the same process of using sign vehicles to figure out the definition of the situation even when an interaction unfolds exactly as expected and we don't consciously think, "What's going on here." It's a bit like driving on a long stretch of boring road. You may have had the experience of zoning out while driving and suddenly realizing that 20 minutes had passed.[1] It wasn't that you stopped driving; you probably passed a few cars, tapped the brake a few times, and maybe even changed the radio station. But just because you weren't actively attending to the task of driving (as you might when you notice a police officer following behind you) doesn't mean you weren't paying attention and making decisions that are necessary to drive safely. Similarly, just because we don't actively attend to the assumptions and decisions we make about what's going on in most face-to-face interactions doesn't mean we're not still doing the cognitive work to arrive at a definition of the situation based on the sign vehicles we see.

Goffman's dramaturgical ideas are wonderfully easy to apply to your day-to-day life since dramaturgy is a microlevel theory. As you read, think about examples from your own life of the types of behaviors and interactional strategies that he describes.

⚬ PREFACE

The perspective employed in this report is that of the theatrical performances; the principles derived are dramaturgical ones. I shall consider the way in which the individual in ordinary work situations presents himself and his activity to others, the ways in which he guides and controls the impression they form of him, and the kinds of things he may and may not do while sustaining his performance before them.

〽 INTRODUCTION

When an individual enters the presence of others, they commonly seek to acquire information about him or to bring into play information about him already possessed. They will be interested in his general socio-economic status, his conception of self, his attitude toward them, his competence, his trustworthiness, etc. Although some of this information seems to be sought almost as an end in itself, there are usually quite practical reasons for acquiring it. Information about the individual helps to define the situation, enabling others to know in advance what he will expect of them and what they may expect of him. Informed in these ways, the others will know how best to act in order to call forth a desired response from him.

For those present, many sources of information become accessible and many carriers (or "sign-vehicles") become available for conveying this information. If unacquainted with the individual, observers can glean clues from his conduct and appearance which allow them to apply their previous experience with individuals roughly similar to the one before them or, more important, to apply untested stereotypes at him. They can also assume from past experience that only individuals of a particular kind are likely to be found in a given social setting. They can rely on what the individual says about himself or on documentary evidence he provides as to who and what he is. If they know, or know of, the individual by virtue of experience prior to the interaction, they can rely on assumptions as to the persistence and generality of psychological traits as a means of predicting his present and future behavior.

Taking communication in both its narrow and broad sense, one finds that when the individual is in the immediate presence of others, his activity will have a promissory character. The others are likely to find that they must accept the individual on faith, offering him a just return while he is present before them in exchange for something whose true value will not be established until after he has left their presence. (Of course, the others also live by inference in their dealings with the physical world, but it is only in the world of social interaction that the objects about which they make inferences will purposely facilitate and hinder this inferential process.) The security that they justifiably feel in making inferences about the individual will vary, of course, depending on such factors as the amount of information they already possess about him, but no amount of such past evidence can entirely obviate the necessity of acting on the basis of inferences.

I have said that when an individual appears before others his actions will influence the definition of the situation which they come to have. Sometimes the individual will act in a thoroughly calculating manner, expressing himself in a given way solely in order to give the kind of impression to others that is likely to evoke from them a specific response he is concerned to obtain. Sometimes the individual will be calculating in his activity but be relatively unaware that this is the case. Sometimes he will intentionally and consciously express himself in a particular way, but chiefly because the tradition of his group or social status require this kind of expression and not because of any particular response (other than vague acceptance or approval) that is likely to be evoked from those impressed by the expression. Sometimes the traditions of an individual's role will lead him to give a well-designed impression of a particular kind and yet he may be neither consciously nor unconsciously disposed to create such an impression. The others, in their turn, may be suitably impressed by the individual's efforts to convey something, or may misunderstand the situation and come to conclusions that are warranted neither by the individual's intent nor by the facts. In any case, in so far as the others act *as if* the individual had conveyed a particular impression, we may take a functional or pragmatic view and say that the individual has "effectively" projected a given definition of the situation and "effectively" fostered the understanding that a given state of affairs obtains.

When we allow that the individual projects a definition of the situation when he appears before others, we must also see that the others, however passive their role may seem to be, will themselves effectively project a definition of the situation by virtue of their response to the individual and by virtue of any lines of action the initiate to him. Ordinarily the definitions of the situation projected by the several different participants are sufficiently attuned to one another so that open contradiction will not occur. I do not mean that there will be the kind of consensus that arises when each individual present candidly expresses what he really feels and honestly agrees with the expressed feelings of the others present. This kind of harmony is an optimistic ideal and in any case not necessary for the smooth working of society. Rather, each participant is expected to suppress his immediate heartfelt feelings, conveying a view of the situation which he feels the others will be able to find at least temporarily acceptable. The maintenance of this surface of agreement, this veneer of consensus, is facilitated by each participant concealing his own wants behind statements which assert values to which everyone present feels obliged to give lip service. Further, there is usually a kind of division of definitional labor. Each participant is allowed to establish the tentative official ruling regarding matters which are vital to him but not immediately important to others, e.g., the rationalizations and justifications by which he accounts for his past activity. In exchange for this courtesy he remains silent or non-committal on matters important to others but not immediately important to him. We have then a kind of interactional *modus vivendi*. Together the participants contribute to a single overall definition of the situation which involves not so much a real agreement as to what exists but rather a real agreement as to whose claims concerning what issues will be temporarily honored. Real agreement will also exist concerning the desirability of avoiding an open conflict of definitions of the situation.[2] I will refer to this level of agreement as a "working consensus." It is to be understood that the working consensus established in one interaction setting will be quite different in content from the working consensus established in a different type of setting

For the purpose of this report, interaction (that is, face-to-face interaction) may be roughly defined as the reciprocal influence of individuals upon one another's actions when in one another's immediate physical presence. *An* interaction may be defined as all the interaction which occurs throughout any one occasion when a given set of individuals are in one another's continuous presence; the term "an encounter" would do as well. A "performance" may be defined as all the activity of a given participant on a given occasion which serves to influence in any way any of the other participants. Taking a particular participant and his performance as a basic point of reference, we may refer to those who contribute the other performances as the audience, observers, or co-participants. The pre-established pattern of action which is unfolded during a performance and which may be presented or played through on other occasions may be called a "part" "routine."[3] These situational terms can easily be related to conventional structural ones. When an individual or performer plays the same part to the same audience on different occasions, a social relationship is likely to arise. Defining social role as the enactment of rights and duties attached to a given status, we can say that a social role will involve one or more parts and that each of these different parts may be presented by the performer on a series of occasions to the same kinds of audience or to an audience of the same persons.

⟋⟍ FRONT

I have been using the term "performance" to refer to all the activity of an individual which occurs during a period marked by his continuous presence before a particular set of observers and which has some influence on the observers. It will be convenient to label as "front" that part of the individual's performance which regularly functions in a general and fixed fashion to define the situation for those who observe the performance. Front, then, is the expressive equipment of a standard kind intentionally or unwittingly employed by the individual during his performance. For preliminary purposes, it will be convenient to distinguish and label what seem to be the standard parts of front.

First, there is the "setting," involving furniture, décor, physical layout, and other background items which supply the scenery and stage props for the spate of human action played out before, within, or upon it.

If we take the term "setting" to refer to the scenic parts of expressive equipment, one may take the term "personal front" to refer to the other items of expressive equipment, the items that we most intimately identify with the performer himself and that we naturally expect will follow the performer wherever he goes. As part of personal front we may include: insignia of office or rank; clothing; sex, age, and racial characteristics; size and looks; posture; speech patterns; facial expressions; bodily gestures; and the like. Some of these vehicles for conveying signs, such as racial characteristics, are relatively fixed and over a span of time do not vary for the individual from one situation to another. On the other hand, some of these sign vehicles are relatively mobile or transitory, such as facial expression, and can vary during a performance from one moment to the next.

It is sometimes convenient to divide the stimuli which make up personal front into "appearance" and "manner," according to the function performed by the information that these stimuli convey. "Appearance" may be taken to refer to those stimuli which function at the time to tell us of the performer's social statuses. These stimuli also tell us of the individual's temporary ritual state, that is, whether he is engaging in formal social activity, work, or informal recreation, whether or not he is celebrating a new phase in the season cycle or in his life-cycle. "Manner" may be taken to refer to those stimuli which function at the time to warn us of the interaction role the performer will expect to play in the oncoming situation. Thus a haughty, aggressive manner may give the impression that the performer expects to be the one who will initiate the verbal interaction and direct its course. A meek, apologetic manner may give the impression that the performer expects to follow the lead of others, or at least that he can be led to do so.

〵 REGIONS AND REGION BEHAVIOR

It was suggested earlier that when one's activity occurs in the presence of other persons, some aspects of the activity are expressively accentuated and other aspects, which might discredit the fostered impression, are suppressed. It is clear that accentuated facts make their appearance in what I have called a front region; it should be just as clear that there may be another region—a "back region" or "back-stage"—where the suppressed facts make an appearance.

A back region or backstage may be defined as a place, relative to a given performance, where the impression fostered by the performance is knowingly contradicted as a matter of course. There are, of course, many characteristic functions of such places. It is here that the capacity of a performance to express something beyond itself may be painstakingly fabricated; it is here that illusions and impressions are openly constructed. Here stage props and items of personal front can be stored in a kind of compact collapsing of whole repertoires of actions and characters.[4] Here grades of ceremonial equipment, such as different types of liquor or clothes, can be hidden so that the audience will not be able to see the treatment accorded them in comparison with the treatment that could have been accorded them. Here devices such as the telephone are sequestered so that they can be used "privately." Here costumes and other parts of personal front may be adjusted and scrutinized for flaws. Here the team can run through its performance, checking for offending expressions when no audience is present to be affronted by them; here poor members of the team, who are expressively inept, can be schooled or dropped from the performance. Here the performer can relax; he can drop his front, forgo speaking his lines, and step out of character.

THE ROLE OF EXPRESSION IN CONVEYING IMPRESSIONS OF SELF

Perhaps a moral note can be permitted at the end. In this report the expressive component of social life has been treated as a source of impressions given to or taken by others. Impression, in turn, has been treated as a source of information about unapparent facts and as a means by which the recipients can guide their response to the informant without having to wait for the full consequences of the informant's actions to be felt. Expression, then, has been treated in terms of the communicative role it plays during social interaction and not, for example, in terms of consumatory or tension-release function it might have in expresser.[5]

Underlying all social interaction there seems to be a fundamental dialectic. When one individual enters the presence of others, he will want to discover the facts of the situation. Were he to possess this information, he could know, and make allowances for, what will come to happen and he could give the others present as much of their due as is consistent with his enlightened self-interest. To uncover fully the factual nature of the situation, it would be necessary for the individual to know all the relevant social data about the others. It would also be necessary for the individual to know the actual outcome or end product of the activity of the others during the interaction, as well as their innermost feelings concerning him. Full information of this order is rarely available; in its absence, the individual tends to employ substitutes—cues, tests, hints, expressive gestures, status symbols, etc.—as predictive devices. In short, since the reality that the individual is concerned with is unperceivable at the moment, appearances must be relied upon in its stead. And, paradoxically, the more the individual is concerned with the reality that is not available to perception, the more must he concentrate his attention on appearances.

The individual tends to treat the others present on the basis of the impression they give now about the past and the future. It is here that communicative acts are translated into moral ones. The impressions that the others give tend to be treated as claims and promises they have implicitly made, and claims and promises tend to have a moral character. In his mind the individual says: "I am using these impressions of you as a way of checking up on you and your activity, and you ought not to lead me astray." The peculiar thing about this is that the individual tends to take this stand even though he expects the others to be unconscious of many of their expressive behaviors and even though he may expect to exploit the others on the basis of the information he gleans about them. Since the sources of impression used by the observing individual involve a multitude of standards pertaining to politeness and decorum, pertaining both to social intercourse and task-performance, we can appreciate afresh how daily life is enmeshed in moral lines of discrimination.

DISCUSSION QUESTIONS

1. Goffman proposes that in every interaction we are each playing a role and that we must work to present our desired self to our audience. Is he saying that we are all being fake in all of our social interactions?

2. In what kinds of social situations are you most likely to be aware of your impression management efforts?

3. What are some of the examples of the impression management you do each time you are in class?

4. Can you think of an interaction that was either confusing or embarrassing because someone's performance did not go well? Using dramaturgical terms, explain why the interaction was uncomfortable.

5. How might Goffman's ideas be updated or modified to shed light on the ways people use online spaces like Facebook to present a self to the world?

6. Give two examples from your day-to-day life of when you are front stage and when you are backstage.

〰 NOTES

1. Note that this is VERY different from distracted driving, like texting or talking on a cell phone when you really aren't paying attention to the fundamentals of driving. This example is about distraction-free driving when you might be described as lost in your own thoughts or just listening to music or the radio.

2. An interaction can be purposely set up as a time and place for voicing differences in opinion, but in such cases participants must be careful to agree not to disagree on the proper tone of voice, vocabulary, and degree of seriousness in which all arguments are to be phrased, and upon the mutual respect which disagreeing participants must carefully continue to express toward one another. This debaters' or academic definition of the situation may also be invoked suddenly and judiciously as a way of translating a serious conflict of views into one that can be handled within a framework acceptable to all present.

3. For comments on the importance of distinguishing between a routine of interaction and any particular instance when this routine is played through, see John von Neumann and Oskar Morgenstern, *The Theory of Games and Economic Behaviour* (2nd ed.; Princeton: Princeton University Press, 1947), p.49.

4. As Métraux (*op. cit.*, p. 24) suggests, even the practice of voodoo cults will require such facilities:

   > Every case of possession has its theatrical side, as shown in the matter of disguises. The rooms of the sanctuary are not unlike the wings of a theater where the possessed find the necessary accessories. Unlike the hysteric, who reveals his anguish and his desires through symptoms—a personal means of expression—the ritual of possession must conform to the classic image of a mythical personage.

5. A recent treatment of this kind may be found in Talcott Parsons, Robert F. Bales, and Edward A. Shils, Working Papers in the Theory of Action (Glencoe, Ill.: The Free Press, 1953), Chap. II, "The Theory of Symbolism in Relation to Action."

9

Anybody's Son Will Do

Gwynne Dyer

Socialization is the process of learning culture. One aspect of this is learning the expected behaviors and attitudes that go along with the different roles in a particular culture. We must learn what behaviors and attitudes are expected of men and women, college students, employees, friends, spouses, student athletes, or musicians just to name a few. Many roles can simply be added to our cultural repertoires, while others require the unlearning of a previous role. This type of significant resocialization is often done with the help of what Erving Goffman referred to as total *institutions. These are places where groups of people are physically separated from the outside world and have much of their daily activities managed by specialized staff whose goal is to resocialize them in some significant way.*

The military is an example of a total institution, and in this article Gwynne Dyer documents the impressively effective strategies used by the Marines to resocialize civilians into soldiers in just a few short weeks. This is no small task as many aspects of the role of civilian and solider are fundamentally at odds with each other. As Dyer notes, the strategies used by the Marines work equally well on volunteers and conscripted (drafted) individuals, which is quite impressive. As you read, think about what other social institutions you may encounter in your life that might affect a similar level of change on you.

Y*ou think about it and you know you're going to have to kill but you don't understand the implications of that, because in the society in which you've lived murder is the most heinous of crimes . . . and you are in a situation in which it's turned the other way round. . . . When you do actually kill someone the experience, my experience, was one of revulsion and disgust.*

I was utterly terrified—petrified—but I knew there had to be a Japanese sniper in a small fishing shack near the shore. He was firing in the other direction at Marines in another battalion, but I knew as soon as he picked off the people there—there was a window on our side—that he would start picking us off. And there was nobody else to go . . . and so I ran towards the shack and broke in and found myself in an empty room.

There was a door which meant there was another room and the sniper was in that—and I just broke that down. I was just absolutely gripped by the fear that this man would expect me and would shoot me. But as it turned out he was in a sniper harness and he couldn't turn around fast enough. He was entangled in the harness so I shot him with a .45 and I felt remorse and shame. I can remember whispering foolishly, "I'm sorry" and then just throwing up. . . . I threw up all over myself. It was a betrayal of what I'd been taught since a child.

—*William Manchester*

Yet he did kill the Japanese soldier, just as he had been trained to—the revulsion only came afterward. And even after Manchester knew what it was like to kill another human being, a young man like himself, he went on trying to kill his "enemies" until the war was over. Like all the other tens of millions of soldiers who had been taught from infancy that killing was wrong, and had then been sent off to kill for their countries, he was almost helpless to disobey, for he had fallen into the hands of an institution so powerful and so subtle that it could quickly reverse the moral training of a lifetime.

The whole vast edifice of the military institution rests on its ability to obtain obedience from its members even unto death—and the killing of others. It has enormous powers of compulsion at its command, of course, but all authority must be based ultimately on consent. The task of extracting that consent from its members has probably grown harder in recent times, for the gulf between the military and the civilian worlds has undoubtedly widened: civilians no longer perceive the threat of violent death as an everyday hazard of existence, and the categories of people whom it is not morally permissible to kill have broadened to include (in peacetime) the entire human race. Yet the armed forces of every country can still take almost any young male civilian and turn him into a soldier with all the right reflexes and attitudes in only a few weeks. Their recruits usually have no more than twenty years' experience of the world, most of it as children, while the armies have had all of history to practice and perfect their techniques.

All soldiers belong to the same profession, no matter what country they serve, and it makes them different from everybody else. They have to be different, for their job is ultimately about killing and dying, and those things are not a natural vocation for any human being. Yet all soldiers are born civilians. The method for turning young men into soldiers—people who kill other people and expose themselves to death—is basic training. It's essentially the same all over the world, and it always has been, because young men everywhere are pretty much alike.

Human beings are fairly malleable, especially when they are young, and in every young man there are attitudes for any army to work with: the inherited values and postures, more or less dimly recalled, of the tribal warriors who were once the model for every young boy to emulate. Civilization did not involve a sudden clean break in the way people behave, but merely the progressive distortion and redirection of all the ways in which people in the old tribal societies used to behave, and modern definitions of maleness still contain a great deal of the old warrior ethic. The anarchic machismo of the primitive warrior is not what modern armies really need in their soldiers, but it does provide them with promising raw material for the transformation they must work in their recruits.

Just how this transformation is wrought varies from time to time and from country to country. In totally militarized societies—ancient Sparta, the samurai class of medieval Japan, the areas controlled by organizations like the Eritrean People's Liberation Front today—it begins at puberty or before, when the young boy is immersed in a disciplined society in which only the military values are allowed to penetrate. In more sophisticated modern societies, the process is briefer and more concentrated, and the way it works is much more visible. It is, essentially, a conversion process in an almost religious sense—and as in all conversion phenomena, the emotions are far more important than the specific ideas.

Soldiers are not just robots; they are ordinary human beings with national and personal loyalties, and many of them do feel the need for some patriotic or ideological justification for what they do. But which nation, which ideology, does not matter: men will fight as well and die as bravely for the Khmer Rouge as for "God, King, and Country." Soldiers are the instruments of politicians and priests, ideologues and strategists, who may have high national or moral purposes in mind, but the men down in the trenches fight for more basic motives. The closer you get to the front line, the fewer abstract nouns you hear.

Armies know this. It is their business to get men to fight, and they have had a long time to work out the best way of doing it. All of them pay lip service to the symbols and slogans of their political masters, though the amount of time they must devote to this activity varies from country to country. It is less in the United States than in the Soviet Union, and it is still less in a country like Israel, which actually fights frequent wars. Nor should it be thought that the armies are hypocritical—most of their members really do believe in their particular national symbols and slogans. But their secret is that they know these are not the things that sustain men in combat.

What really enables men to fight is the their own self-respect, and a special kind of love that has nothing to do with sex or idealism. Very few men have died in battle, when the moment actually arrived, for the United States of America or for the sacred cause of Communism, or even for their homes and families; if they had any choice in the matter at all, they chose to die for each other and for their own vision of themselves.

Once you get out there and you realize a guy is shooting at you, your first instinct, regardless of all your training, is to live. . . . But you can't turn around and run the other way. Peer pressure, you know? There's people here with you that have probably saved your life or will save your life in the future; you can't back down

—*USMC Vietnam veteran*

This is going to sound really strange, but there's a love relationship that is nurtured in combat because the man next to you—you're depending on him for the most important thing you have, your life, and if he lets you down you're either maimed or killed. If you make a mistake the same thing happens to him, so the bond of trust has to be extremely close, and I'd say this bond is stronger than almost anything, with the exception of parent and child. It's a hell of a lot stronger than man and wife—your life is in his hands, you trust that person with the most valuable thing you have. And you'll find that people who pursue the aphrodisiac of combat or whatever you want to call it are there because they're friends, the same people show up in the same wars time and again.

—*Capt. John Early, ex-U.S. Army, Vietnam, ex-mercenary, Rhodesia*

John Early is an intelligent and sensitive man who became a combat junkie ("I'm a contradiction in terms, and I can't explain it") and as such he is a rarity. For most men, the trust and intimacy of a small unit in combat never compensate for the fear and revulsion. But the selfless identification of the soldier with the other men in his unit is what makes armies work in combat, and the foundations for it must be laid in peacetime. "Fighting is a social art, based upon collective activity, cooperation and mutual support," an Israeli soldier observed. "This utter reliance on others is an integral part of the effort to meet the enemy irrespective of odds, and it largely determines men's willingness to risk their lives in pressing the attack. . . . In short there is rarely brotherhood in facing death when there is none in peace."[1]

The way armies produce this sense of brotherhood in a peacetime environment is basic training: a feat of psychological manipulation on the grand scale which has been so consistently successful and so universal that we fail to notice it as remarkable. In countries where the army must extract its recruits in their late teens, whether voluntarily or by conscription, from a civilian environment that does not share the military values, basic training involves a brief but intense period of indoctrination whose purpose is not really to teach the recruits basic military skills, but rather to change their values and their loyalties. "I guess you could say we brainwash them a little bit," admitted a U.S. Marine drill instructor, "but you know they're good people."

The duration and intensity of basic training, and even its major emphases, depend on what kind of society the recruits are coming from, and on what sort of military organization they are going to. It is obviously quicker to train men from a martial culture than from one in which the dominant values are civilian and commercial, and easier to deal with volunteers than with reluctant conscripts. Conscripts are not always unwilling, however; there are many instances in which the army is popular for economic reasons.

In the United States, where the contrast between the austerity, hierarchy, and discipline of military life and the prevailing civilian values is most extreme, basic training—the conversion of young civilian males into soldiers—is given a greater emphasis than almost anywhere else.

The degree of emphasis, however, depends heavily on what the American volunteer is going to do in military life. The great majority of military personnel in the armed forces of all industrialized countries these days are not combat soldiers, and a man or woman whose time will be spent in manning one of the navy's radar sets or filing air force documents does not need to learn the very special attitudes and loyalties that are necessary in ground combat. Learning to look military, obey orders, and perform their jobs will suffice. But the U.S. Army, which reckons that all its members could, under some circumstances, find themselves in a combat zone, insists on seven weeks' basic training, followed by advanced individual training in a specific trade—and the U.S. Marine Corps gives eleven weeks of basic training to every man and woman who joins the Corps.

It is a very old-fashioned organization (the last of the U.S. armed forces to get its hands on any desirable piece of new weapons technology), which clings to the belief that every Marine must be a qualified combat rifleman first, even if his subsequent specialty will be cooking or supply. It is also an elite assault force, whose battle doctrine accepts the necessity, on occasion, of trading casualties for time. The entire orientation of the Marine Corps is toward the demands of combat: it informs everything the Corps does.

This makes the Marines atypical of contemporary armed forces in the United States or anywhere else, which generally consist of very large numbers of pseudo-military personnel doing technical, administrative, and even public relations jobs, surrounding a much smaller combat core. The Marines is almost all core. But for this very reason it is a virtually ideal case study in how basic training works: it draws its recruits from the most extravagantly individualistic civilian society in the world and turns them into elite combat soldiers in eleven weeks.

It's easier if you catch them young. You can train older men to be soldiers; it's done in every major war. But you can never get them to believe that they like it, which is the major reason armies try to get their recruits before they are twenty. There are other reasons too, of course, like the physical fitness, lack of dependents, and economic dispensability of teenagers, that make armies prefer them, but the most important qualities teenagers bring to basic training are enthusiasm and naivete. Many of them actively want the discipline and the closely structured environment that the armed forces will provide, so there is no need for the recruiters to deceive the kids about what will happen to them after they join.

Young civilians who have volunteered and have been accepted by the Marine Corps arrive at Parris Island, the Corps's East Coast facility for basic training, in a state of considerable excitement and apprehension: most are aware that they are about to undergo an extraordinary and very difficult experience. But they do not make their own way to the base; rather they trickle in to Charleston airport on various flights throughout the day on which their training platoon is due to form, and are held there, in a state of suppressed but mounting nervous tension, until late in the evening. When the buses finally come to carry them the seventy-six miles to Parris Island, it is often after midnight—and this is not an administrative oversight. The shock treatment they are about to receive will work most efficiently if they are worn out and somewhat disoriented when they arrive.

The basic training organization is a machine, processing several thousand young men every month, and every facet and gear of it has been designed with the sole purpose of turning civilians into Marines as efficiently as possible. Provided it can have total control over their bodies and their environment for approximately three months, it can practically guarantee converts. Parris Island provides that controlled environment, and the recruits do not set foot outside it again until they graduate as Marine privates eleven weeks later.

They're allowed to call home, so long as it doesn't get out of hand—every three weeks or so they can call home and make sure everything's all right, if they haven't gotten a letter or there's a particular set of circumstances. If it's a case of an emergency call coming in, then they're allowed to accept that call; if not, one of my staff will take the message. . . .

In some cases I'll get calls from parents who haven't quite gotten adjusted to the idea that their son had cut the strings—and in a lot of cases that's what they're doing. The military provides them with an opportunity to leave home but they're still in a rather secure environment.

—Captain Brasstngton, USMC

For the young recruits, basic training is the closest thing their society can offer to a formal rite of passage, and the institution probably stands in an unbroken line of descent from the lengthy ordeals by which young males in precivilized groups were initiated into the adult community of warriors. But in civilized societies it is a highly functional institution whose product is not anarchic warriors, but trained soldiers.

Basic training is not really about teaching people skills; it's about changing them, so that they can do things they wouldn't have dreamt of otherwise. It works by applying enormous physical and mental pressure to men who have been isolated from their normal civilian environment and placed in one where the only right way to think and behave is the way the Marine Corps wants them to. The key word the men who run the machine use to describe this process is motivation.

I can motivate a recruit and in third phase, if I tell him to jump off the third deck, he'll jump off the third deck. Like I said before, it's a captive audience and I can train that guy; I can get him to do anything I want him to do. . . . They're good kids and they're out to do the right thing. We get some bad kids, but you know, we weed those out. But as far as motivation here, we can motivate them to do anything you want, in recruit training.

—USMC drill instructor, Parris Island

☷ STEP 1 - SURRENDER

Surrender Former Identity

The first three days the raw recruits spend at Parris Island are actually relatively easy, though they are hustled and shouted at continuously. It is during this time that they are documented and inoculated, receive uniforms, and learn the basic orders of drill that enable young Americans (who are not very accustomed to this aspect of life) to do everything simultaneously in large groups. But the most important thing that happens in "forming" is the surrender of the recruits' own clothes, their hair—all the physical evidence of their individual civilian identities.

During a period of only seventy-two hours, in which they are allowed little sleep, the recruits lay aside their former lives in a series of hasty rituals (like being shaven to the scalp) whose symbolic significance is quite clear to them even though they are quite deliberately given absolutely no time for reflection, or any hint that they might have the option of turning back from their commitment. The men in charge of them know how delicate a tightrope they are walking, though, because at this stage the recruits are still newly caught civilians who have not yet made their ultimate inward submission to the discipline of the Corps.

The frantic bustle of forming is designed to give the recruit no time to think about resisting what is happening to him. And so the recruits emerge from their initiation into the system, stripped of their civilian clothes, shorn of their hair, and deprived of whatever confidence in their own identity they may previously have had as eighteen-year-olds, like so many blanks ready to have the Marine identity impressed upon them.

The first stage in any conversion process is the destruction of an individual's former beliefs and confidence, and his reduction to a position of helplessness and need. It isn't really as drastic as all that, of course, for three days cannot cancel out eighteen years; the inner thoughts and the basic character are not erased. But the recruits have already learned that the only acceptable behavior is to repress any unorthodox thoughts and to mimic the character the Marine Corps wants. Nor are they, on the whole, reluctant to do so, for they *want* to be Marines. From the moment they arrive at Parris Island, the vague notion that has been passed down for a thousand generations that masculinity means being a warrior becomes an explicit article of faith, relentlessly preached: to be a man means to be a Marine.

There are very few eighteen-year-old boys who do not have highly romanticized ideas of what it means to be a man, so the Marine Corps has plenty of buttons to push. And it starts pushing them on the first day of real training: the officer in charge of the formation appears before them for the first time, in full dress uniform with medals, and tells them how to become men.

The United States Marine Corps has 205 years of illustrious history to speak for itself. You have made the most important decision in your life . . . by signing your name, your life, your pledge to the Government of the United States, and even more importantly, to the United States Marine Corps—a brotherhood, an elite unit. In 10.3 weeks you are going to become a member of that history, those traditions, this organization—if you have what it takes.

All of you want to do that by virtue of your signing your name as a man. The Marine Corps says that we build men. Well, I'll go a little bit further. We develop the tools that you have—and everybody has those tools to a certain extent right now. We're going to give you the blueprints, and we are going to show you how to build a Marine. You've got to build a Marine—you understand?

—*Captain Pingree, USMC*

The recruits, gazing at him with awe and adoration, shout in unison, "Yes, sir!" just as they have been taught. They do it willingly, because they are volunteers—but even conscripts tend to have the romantic fervor of volunteers if they are only eighteen years old. Basic training, whatever its hardships, is a quick way to become a man among men, with an undeniable status, and beyond the initial consent to undergo it, it doesn't even require any decisions.

☒ STEP 2 - SUBMIT

The training, when it starts, seems impossibly demanding physically for most of the recruits—and then it gets harder week by week. There is a constant barrage of abuse and insults aimed at the recruits, with the deliberate purpose of breaking down their pride and so destroying their ability to resist the transformation of values and attitudes that the Corps intends them to undergo. At the same time the demands for constant alertness and for instant obedience are continuously stepped up, and the standards by which the dress and behavior of the recruits are judged become steadily more unforgiving. But it is all carefully calculated by the men who run the machine, who think and talk in terms of the stress they are placing on the recruits: "We take so many c.c.'s of stress and we administer it to each man—they should be a little bit scared and they should be unsure, but they're adjusting." The aim is to keep the training arduous but just within most of the recruits' capability to withstand. One of the most striking achievements of the drill instructors is to create and maintain the illusion that basic training is an extraordinary challenge, one that will set those who graduate apart from others, when in fact almost everyone can succeed.

Just the sheer physical exercise, administered in massive doses, soon has the recruits feeling stronger and more competent than ever before. Inspections, often several times daily, quickly build up their ability to wear the uniform and carry themselves like real Marines, which is a considerable source of pride. The inspections also help to set up the pattern in the recruits of unquestioning submission to military authority: standing stock-still, staring straight ahead, while somebody else examines you closely for faults is about as extreme a ritual act of submission as you can make with your clothes on.

But they are not submitting themselves merely to the abusive sergeant making unpleasant remarks about the hair in their nostrils. All around them are deliberate reminders—the flags and insignia displayed on parade, the military music, the marching formations and drill instructors' cadenced calls—of the idealized organization, the "brotherhood" to which they will be admitted as full members if they submit and conform. Nowhere in the armed forces are the military courtesies so elaborately observed, the staffs' uniforms so immaculate (some DIs change several times a day), and the ritual aspects of military life so highly visible as on a basic training establishment.

Even the seeming inanity of close-order drill has a practical role in the conversion process. It has been over a century since mass formations of men were of any use on the battlefield, but every army in the world still drills its troops, especially during basic training, because marching in formation, with every man moving his body in the same way at the same moment, is a direct physical way of learning two things a soldier must believe: that orders have to be obeyed automatically and instantly, and that you are no longer an individual, but part of a group.

※ STEP 3 - IDENTITY WITH GROUP

The recruits' total identification with the other members of their unit is the most important lesson of all, and everything possible is done to foster it. They spend almost every waking moment together—a recruit alone is an anomaly to be looked into at once—and during most of that time they are enduring shared hardships. They also undergo collective punishments, often for the misdeed or omission of a single individual (talking in the ranks, a bed not swept under during barracks inspection), which is a highly effective way of suppressing any tendencies toward individualism. And, of course, the DIs place relentless emphasis on competition with other "serials" in training: there may be something infinitely pathetic to outsiders about a marching group of anonymous recruits chanting, "Lift your heads and hold them high, 3313 is a-passin' by," but it doesn't seem like that to the men in the ranks.

※ STEP 4 - BUILD CONFIDENCE

Nothing is quite so effective in building up a group's morale and solidarity, though, as a steady diet of small triumphs. Quite early in basic training, the recruits begin to do things that seem, at first sight, quite dangerous: descend by ropes from fifty-foot towers, cross yawning gaps hand-over-hand on high wires (known as the Slide for Life, of course), and the like. The common denominator is that these activities are daunting but not really dangerous: the ropes will prevent anyone from falling to his death off the rappelling tower, and there is a pond of just the right depth—deep enough to cushion a falling man, but not deep enough that he is likely to drown—under the Slide for Life. The goal is not to kill recruits, but to build up their confidence as individuals and as a group by allowing them to overcome apparently frightening obstacles.

> *You have an enemy here at Parris Island. The enemy that you're going to have at Parris Island is in every one of us. It's in the form of cowardice. The most rewarding experience you're going to have in recruit training is standing on line every evening, and you'll be able to look into each other's eyes, and you'll be able to say to each other with your eyes: "By God, we've made it one more day! We've defeated the coward."*
>
> —Captain Pingree, USMC

If somebody does fail a particular test, he tends to be alone, for the hurdles are deliberately set low enough that most recruits can clear them if they try. In any large group of people there is usually a goat: someone whose intelligence or manner or lack of physical stamina marks him for failure and contempt. The competent drill instructor, without deliberately setting up this unfortunate individual for disgrace, will use his failure to strengthen the solidarity and confidence of the rest. When one hapless young man fell off the Slide for Life into the pond, for example, his drill instructor shouted the usual invective—"Well, get out of the water. Don't contaminate it all day"—and then delivered the payoff line: "Go back and change your clothes. You're useless to your unit now."

"Useless to your unit" is the key phrase, and all the recruits know that what it means is "useless *in battle*." The Marine drill instructors at Parris Island know exactly what they are doing to the recruits, and why. They are not rear-echelon people filling comfortable jobs, but the most dedicated and intelligent NCOs the Marine Corps can find; even now, many of them have combat experience. The Corps has a clear-eyed understanding of precisely what it is training its recruits for—combat—and it ensures that those who do the training keep that objective constantly in sight.

The DIs "stress" the recruits, feed them their daily ration of synthetic triumphs over apparent obstacles, and bear in mind all the time that the goal is to instill the foundations for the instinctive, selfless reactions and the fierce group loyalty that is what the recruits will need if they ever see combat. They are arch-manipulators, fully conscious of it, and utterly unashamed. These kids have signed up as Marines, and they could well see combat; this is the way they have to think if they want to live.

Combat is the ultimate reality that Marines—or any other soldiers, under any flag—have to deal with. Physical fitness, weapons training, battle drills, are all indispensable elements of basic training, and it is absolutely essential that the recruits learn the attitudes of group loyalty and interdependency which will be their sole hope of survival and success in combat. The training inculcates or fosters all of those things, and even by the halfway point in the eleven-week course, the recruits are generally responding with enthusiasm to their tasks.

But there is nothing in all this (except the weapons drill) that would not be found in the training camp of a professional football team. What sets soldiers apart is their willingness to kill. But it is not a willingness that comes easily to most men—even young men who have been provided with uniforms, guns, and official approval to kill those whom their government has designated as enemies. They will, it is true, fall very readily into the stereotypes of the tribal warrior group. Indeed, most of them have had at least a glancing acquaintance in their early teens with gangs (more or less violent, depending on, among other things, the neighborhood), the modern relic of that ancient institution.

And in many ways what basic training produces is the uniformed equivalent of a modern street gang: a bunch of tough, confident kids full of bloodthirsty talk. But gangs don't actually kill each other in large numbers. If they behaved the way armies do, you'd need trucks to clean the bodies off the streets every morning. They're held back by the civilian belief—the normal human belief—that killing another person is an awesome act with huge consequences.

There is aggression in all of us—men, women, children, babies. Armies don't have to create it, and they can't even increase it. But most of us learn to put limits on our aggression, especially physical aggression, as we grow up. It is true even of New York gangs wearing their colors and looking as mean as they possibly can, or of British football fans who appear to be restaging the battle of Agincourt on the terraces. They make a very careful distinction between aggressive display and actual violence, and most of what seems to be violence is mime.

There is such a thing as a "natural soldier": the kind of man who derives his greatest satisfaction from male companionship, from excitement, and from the con- quering of physical and psychological obstacles. He doesn't necessarily want to kill people as such, but he will have no objections if it occurs within a moral framework that gives him a justification—like war—and if it is the price of gaining admission to the kind of environment he craves. Whether such men are born or made, I do not know, but most of them end up in armies (and many move on again to become mercenaries, because regular army life in peacetime is too routine and boring).

But armies are not full of such men. They are so rare that they form only a modest fraction even of small professional armies, mostly congregating in the commando-type special forces. In large conscript armies they virtually disappear beneath the weight of numbers of more ordinary men. And it is these ordinary men, who do not like combat at all, that the armies must persuade to kill. Until only a generation ago, they did not even realize how bad a job they were doing.

Armies had always assumed that, given the proper rifle training, the average man would kill in combat with no further incentive than the knowledge that it was the only way to defend his own life. After all, there are no historical records of Roman legionnaires refusing to use their swords, or Marlborough's infantrymen refusing to fire their muskets against the enemy. But then dispersion hit the battlefield, removing each rifleman from the direct observation of his companions—and when U.S. Army Colonel S. L. A. Marshall finally took the trouble to inquire into what they were doing in 1943–45, he found that on average only 15 percent of trained combat riflemen fired their weapons at all in battle. The rest did not flee, but they would not kill—even when their own position was under attack and their lives were in immediate danger.

Marshall conducted both individual interviews and mass interviews with over four hundred infantry companies, both in Europe and in the Central Pacific, immediately after they had been in close combat with German or Japanese troops, and the results were the same each time. They were, moreover, as astonishing to the company officers and the troops themselves as they were to Marshall; each man who hadn't fired his rifle thought he had been alone in his defection from duty.

Even more indicative of what was going on was the fact that almost all the crew-served weapons had been fired. Every man had been trained to kill and knew it was his duty to kill, and so long as he was in the presence of other soldiers who could see his actions, he went ahead and did it. But the great majority of the riflemen, each unobserved by the others in his individual foxhole, had chosen not to kill, even though it increased the likelihood of his own death.

By World War II, with the increasing dispersion of infantrymen and their escape from direct observation by their comrades, that fundamental disinclination to kill had become the dominating factor even when a unit was directly engaged in heavy combat. And there is no reason to believe that the phenomenon Marshall found in the American army was any different in the German or Soviet or Japanese armies; there were no comparable studies made, but if a higher proportion of Japanese or Germans had been willing to kill, then the volume of fire they actually managed to produce would have been three, four, or five times greater than a similar number of Americans—and it wasn't. Men will kill under compulsion—men will do almost anything if they know it is expected of them and they are under strong social pressure to comply—but the vast majority of men are not born killers.

But the question naturally arises: if the great majority of men are not instinctive killers, and if most military killing these days is in any case done by weapons operating from a distance at which the question of killing scarcely troubles the operators—then why is combat an exclusively male occupation? The great majority of women, everyone would agree, are not instinctive killers either, but so what? If the remote circumstances in which the killing is done or the deliberate conditioning supplied by the military enable most men to kill, why should it be any different for women?

My own guess would be that it probably wouldn't be very different; it just hasn't been tried very extensively. But it is an important question, because it has to do with the causes and possible cure of war. If men fight wars because that is an intrinsic part of the male character, then nothing can abolish the institution of warfare short of abolishing the male half of the human race (or at least, as one feminist suggested, disfranchising it for a hundred years).

If, on the other hand, wars are a means of allocating power between civilized human groups, in which the actual soldiers have always been male simply because men were more suited to it by their greater physical strength and their freedom from the burden of childbearing, then what we are discussing is not Original Sin, but simply a mode of social behavior. The fact that almost every living male for thousands of generations has imbibed some of the warrior mystique is no proof of a genetic predisposition to be warlike. The cultural continuity is quite enough to transmit such attitudes, and men were specialized in the hunting and warrior functions for the same physical reasons long before civilized war was invented.

It was undoubtedly men, the "hunting" specialists, who invented civilized war, just as it was probably women, specializing in the "gathering" part of the primitive economy, who invented agriculture. That has no necessary relevance today: we all eat vegetables, and we can all die in war. It is a more serious allegation against males to say that all existing forms of political power have been shaped predominantly by men, so that even if wars are about power and not about the darker side of the masculine psyche, war is still a male problem. That has unquestionably been true through all of history (although it remains to be proven that women exercising power respond very differently to its temptations and obsessions). But there is no need to settle that argument; if war and masculinity are not inseparable, then we have already moved onto negotiable ground. For the forms of political power, unlike psyches, are always negotiable.

Unfortunately there is little direct support for this optimistic hypothesis in the prevailing current of opinion among soldiers generally, where war and maleness are indeed seen as inseparable. To say that the combat branches of the armed forces are sexist is like remarking that gravity generally pulls downward, and nowhere is the contempt for women greater than at a recruit training base like Parris Island. The DIs are quite ruthless in exploiting every prejudice and pushing every button that will persuade the recruits to accept the value system they are selling, and one of those buttons (quite a large one) is the conviction of young males—or at least the desire to be convinced—that they are superior to young females. (After all, even recruits want to feel superior to somebody, and it certainly isn't going to be anybody in their immediate vicinity at Parris Island.)

When it's all boys together, especially among the younger men, Marine Corps slang for any woman who isn't the wife, mother, or daughter of anyone present is "Suzie." It is short for "Suzie Rottencrotch"—and Suzie crops up a lot in basic training. Even when the topic of instruction is hand and arm signals in combat.

Privates, if you don't have a little Suzie now, maybe you're going to find one when you get home. You bet. You'll find the first cheap slut you can get back home. What do you mean, "No"? You're a Marine, you're going to do it.

If we get home with little Suzie . . . we're in a nice companionship with little Suzie and here you are getting hot and heavy and then you're getting ready to go down there and make that dive, privates, and Suzie says . . . Suzie says it's the wrong time of the month. Privates, if you don't want to get back home and indulge in this little adventure, you can show your girlfriend the hand and arm signal for "close it up."

And you want her to close up those nasty little thighs of hers, do you not, privates? The hand and arm signal: the arms are laterally shoulder height, the fingers are extended, and the palms are facing toward the front. This is the starting position for "close it up" [tighten up the formation]: just like closing it up, bring the arms together just like that.

Privates, in addition, I want you to dedicate all this training to one very special person. Can anyone tell me who that is, privates?

(Voice) The Senior Drill Instructor, sir?

No, not your Senior Drill Instructor. You're going to dedicate all this training, privates, to your enemy . . . to your enemy. To your enemy: the reason being, so he can die for his country. So who are we going to dedicate all this training to, privates?

—*lecture on hand and arm signals, Parris Island, 1982*

And they shouted enthusiastically: "The enemy, sir! The enemy, sir!" It would not be instantly clear to the disinterested observer from Mars, however, why these spotty-faced male eighteen-year-olds are uniquely qualified to kill the enemy, while their equally spotty-faced female counterparts get to admire them from afar (or so the supposition goes), and get called Suzie Rottencrotch for their trouble.

Interestingly, it isn't entirely clear either to the senior military and civilian officials whose responsibility it is to keep the organization filled up with warm bodies capable of doing the job. Women are not employed in combat roles in the regular armed forces of any country (though increasing numbers of women have been admitted to the noncombat military jobs in the course of this century). But in the last decade the final barrier has come under serious consideration.[2] It was, unsurprisingly, in the United States, where the problems of getting enough recruits for the all-volunteer armed forces converged with the changes of attitude flowing from the women's liberation movement, that the first serious proposals to send women into combat were entertained, during the latter years of the Carter administration.

Despite the anguished cries of military conservatives, both male and female, the reaction of younger officers in the combat branches (all male, of course) was cautious but not entirely negative. The more intelligent ones dismissed at once arguments about strength and stamina—the average American woman, one pointed out, is bigger than the average Vietnamese man—and were as little impressed by the alleged special problems arising from the fact that female soldiers may become pregnant. In the noncombat branches, the army loses less time from its women soldiers due to pregnancy than it loses from desertion, drug abuse, and alcoholism in its male soldiers.

More important, few of the male officers involved in the experimental programs giving combat training to women recruits in the late 1970s had any doubt that the women would function effectively in combat. Neither did the women themselves. Despite their lack of the traditional male notions about the warrior stereotype, the training did its job. As one female trainee remarked: "I don't like the idea of killing anything . . . [and] I may not at this moment go into combat. But knowing that I can fire as well as I can fire now, knowing that today, I'd go in. I believe in my country . . . I'd fight to keep it."

The one major reservation the male officers training the "infantrywomen had was about how the presence of the women in combat would affect the men. The basic combat unit, a small group of men bound together by strong male ties of loyalty and trust, was a time-tested system that worked, and they were reluctant to tamper with it by adding an additional, unknown factor to the equation.

DISCUSSION QUESTIONS

1. What are some other examples of total institutions in our society?

2. What are synthetic triumphs and what purpose do they serve? Can you think of any nonmilitary examples of people using synthetic triumphs for the same type of purpose?

3. In what ways is college a total institution? How do new students go through the same stages of resocialization as marine recruits do during boot camp?

NOTES

1. Rolbart, op. cit., p. 58.

2. In January 2013, the military lifted the ban on women in combat roles. During 2014, the military, including the Marine Corps, began evaluating how to determine where the bar should be in terms of physical fitness for women to be placed in combat units. (http://www.npr.org/2014/11/23/366075916/women-sweat-the-test-to-show-marines-theyre-combat-ready)

10

On Being Sane in Insane Places

David L. Rosenhan

Normal behavior rarely gets much notice; it's generally seen as natural, taken for granted, and expected. However, normality cannot exist without deviance to help define it. What makes something normal is that it is not deviant, and what makes something deviant is that it is not normal. Think of the yin-yang symbol.

The shape of the line dividing yin and yang defines each of them. In a similar way, the behaviors that we consider to be normal and those we define as deviant touch at a point where the dividing line is drawn. You can't have one without the other. When we encounter ideas of normality (healthy) and deviance (illness) in a medical context, we tend to assume that the dividing line between them is natural, inherent, and fixed. But this is not the case, and nowhere is this more true than in definitions surrounding mental health.

In fact, the socially constructed nature of mental illness categories received quite a bit of public attention recently with the publication of the fifth edition of the Diagnostic and Statistical Manual of Mental Illness *(the DSM V) published by the American Psychiatric Association. The DSM, which has been published and updated since 1952, lists all possible mental illnesses, their symptoms, and criteria through diagnosis. But in each edition, both the illnesses and their criteria have changed. For example, until 1974, homosexuality was listed as a mental illness. And changes aren't just in the past. The DSM V published in 2013 has a new mental illness called premenstrual dysphoric disorder, which defines women with severe premenstrual symptoms as mentally ill. Yet narcissistic personality disorder no longer exists as of the DSM V. It's important to note that people didn't suddenly stop being narcissists and droves of women didn't suddenly begin to go crazy from terrible PMS. The* definition *of normal changed, not people's behavior or symptoms.*

In this piece, Rosenhan shares the results of a remarkable study that shows how definitions of mental illness are powerfully shaped by context and labels that radically affect interpretations of behaviors. Originally published in 1973, Rosenhan's findings still echo loudly today in any sociological examination of mental illness. As you read, think about how the social nature of definitions of sanity and insanity might also be useful in helping us understand how categorizations of normality and deviance work in social arenas other than medicine.

I f sanity and insanity exist, how shall we know them?

The question is neither capricious nor itself insane. However much we may be personally convinced that we can tell the normal from the abnormal, the evidence is simply not compelling. It is commonplace, for example, to read about murder trials wherein eminent psychiatrists for the defense are contradicted by equally eminent psychiatrists for the prosecution on the matter of the defendant's sanity. More generally, there are a great deal of conflicting data on the reliability, utility, and meaning of such terms as "sanity," "insanity," "mental illness," and "schizophrenia."[1] Finally, as early as 1934, Benedict suggested that normality and abnormality are not universal.[2] What is viewed as normal in one culture may be seen as quite aberrant in another. Thus, notions of normality and abnormality may not be quite as accurate as people believe they are.

To raise questions regarding normality and abnormality is in no way to question the fact that some behaviors are deviant or odd. Murder is deviant. So, too, are hallucinations. Nor does raising such questions deny the existence of the personal anguish that is often associated with "mental illness." Anxiety and depression exist. Psychological suffering exists. But normality and abnormality, sanity and insanity, and the diagnoses that flow from them may be less substantive than many believe them to be.

At its heart, the question of whether the sane can be distinguished from the insane (and whether degrees of insanity can be distinguished from each other) is a simple matter: do the salient characteristics that lead to diagnoses reside in the patients themselves or in the environments and contexts in which observers find them? From Bleuler, through Kretchmer, through the formulators of the recently revised *Diagnostic and Statistical Manual* of the American Psychiatric Association, the belief has been strong that patients present symptoms, that those symptoms can be categorized, and, implicitly, that the sane are distinguishable from the insane. More recently, however, this belief has been questioned. Based in part on theoretical and anthropological considerations, but also on philosophical, legal, and therapeutic ones, the view has grown that psychological categorization of mental illness is useless at best and downright harmful, misleading, and pejorative at worst. Psychiatric diagnoses, in this view, are in the minds of the observers and are not valid summaries of characteristics displayed by the observed.[345]

Gains can be made in deciding which of these is more nearly accurate by getting normal people (that is, people who do not have, and have never suffered, symptoms of serious psychiatric disorders) admitted to psychiatric hospitals and then determining whether they were discovered to be sane and, if so, how. If the sanity of such pseudopatients were always detected, there would be prima facie evidence that a sane individual can be distinguished from the insane context in which he is found. Normality (and presumably abnormality) is distinct enough that it can be recognized wherever it occurs, for it is carried within the person. If, on the other hand, the sanity of the pseudopatients were never discovered, serious difficulties would arise for those who support traditional modes of psychiatric diagnosis. Given that the hospital staff was not incompetent, that the pseudopatient had been behaving as sanely as he had been outside of the hospital, and that it had never been previously suggested that he belonged in a psychiatric hospital, such an unlikely outcome would support the view that psychiatric diagnosis betrays little about the patient but much about the environment in which an observer finds him.

This article describes such an experiment. Eight sane people gained secret admission to 12 different hospitals.[6] Their diagnostic experiences constitute the data of the first part of this article; the remainder is devoted to a description of their experiences in psychiatric institutions.

⑃ PSEUDOPATIENTS AND THEIR SETTINGS

The eight pseudopatients were a varied group. One was a psychology graduate student in his 20's. The remaining seven were older and "established." Among them were three psychologists, a pediatrician, a psychiatrist, a painter, and a housewife. Three pseudopatients were women, five were men. All of them employed pseudonyms, lest their alleged diagnoses embarrass them later. Those who were in mental health professions alleged another occupation in order to avoid the special attentions that might be accorded by staff, as a matter of courtesy or caution, to ailing colleagues.[7] With the exception of myself (I was the first pseudopatient and my presence was known to the hospital administrator and chief psychologist and, so far as I can tell, to them alone), the presence of pseudopatients and the nature of the research program was not known to the hospital staffs.[8]

The settings were similarly varied. In order to generalize the findings, admission into a variety of hospitals was sought. The 12 hospitals in the sample were located in five different states on the East and West coasts. Some were old and shabby, some were quite new. Some were research-oriented, others not. Some had good staff-patient ratios, others were quite understaffed. Only one was a strictly private hospital. All of the others were supported by state or federal funds or, in one instance, by university funds.

After calling the hospital for an appointment, the pseudopatient arrived at the admissions office complaining that he had been hearing voices. Asked what the voices said, he replied that they were often unclear, but as far as he could tell they said "empty," "hollow," and "thud." The voices were unfamiliar and were of the same sex as the pseudopatient. The choice of these symptoms was occasioned by their apparent similarity to existential symptoms. Such symptoms are alleged to arise from painful concerns about the perceived meaninglessness of one's life. It is as if the hallucinating person were saying, "My life is empty and hollow." The choice of these symptoms was also determined by the *absence* of a single report of existential psychoses in the literature.

Beyond alleging the symptoms and falsifying name, vocation, and employment, no further alterations of person, history, or circumstances were made. The significant events of the pseudopatient's life history were presented as they had actually occurred. Relationships with parents and siblings, with spouse and children, with people at work and in school, consistent with the aforementioned exceptions, were described as they were or had been. Frustrations and upsets were described along with joys and satisfactions. These facts are important to remember. If anything, they strongly biased the subsequent results in favor of detecting sanity, since none of their histories or current behaviors were seriously pathological in any way.

Immediately upon admission to the psychiatric ward, the pseudopatient ceased simulating *any* symptoms of abnormality. In some cases, there was a brief period of mild nervousness and anxiety, since none of the pseudopatients really believed that they would be admitted so easily. Indeed, their shared fear was that they would be immediately exposed as frauds and greatly embarrassed. Moreover, many of them had never visited a psychiatric ward; even those who had, nevertheless had some genuine fears about what might happen to them. Their nervousness, then, was quite appropriate to the novelty of the hospital setting, and it abated rapidly.

Apart from that short-lived nervousness, the pseudopatient behaved on the ward as he "normally" behaved. The pseudopatient spoke to patients and staff as he might ordinarily. Because there is uncommonly little to do on a psychiatric ward, he attempted to engage others in conversation. When asked by staff how he was feeling, he indicated that he was fine, that he no longer experienced symptoms. He responded to instructions from attendants, to calls for medication (which was not swallowed), and to dining-hall instructions. Beyond such activities as were available to him on the admissions ward, he spent his time writing down his observations about the ward, its patients, and the staff. Initially these notes were written "secretly," but as it soon became clear that no one much cared, they were subsequently written on standard tablets of paper in such public places as the dayroom. No secret was made of these activities.

The pseudopatient, very much as a true psychiatric patient, entered a hospital with no foreknowledge of when he would be discharged. Each was told that he would have to get out by his own devices, essentially by convincing the staff that he was sane. The psychological stresses associated with hospitalization were considerable, and all but one of the pseudopatients desired to be discharged almost immediately after being admitted. They were, therefore, motivated not only to behave sanely, but to be paragons of cooperation. That their behavior was in no way disruptive is confirmed by nursing reports, which have been obtained on most of the patients. These reports uniformly indicate that the patients were "friendly," "cooperative," and "exhibited no abnormal indications."

〽 THE NORMAL ARE NOT DETECTABLY SANE

Despite their public "show" of sanity, the pseudopatients were never detected. Admitted, except in one case, with a diagnosis of schizophrenia,[9] each was discharged with a diagnosis of schizophrenia "in remission." The label "in remission" should in no way be dismissed as a formality, for at no time during any hospitalization had any question been raised about any pseudopatient's simulation. Nor are there any indications in the hospital records that the pseudopatient's status was suspect. Rather, the evidence is strong that, once labeled schizophrenic, the pseudopatient was stuck with that label. If the pseudopatient was to be discharged, he must naturally be "in remission"; but he was not sane, nor, in the institution's view, had he ever been sane.

The uniform failure to recognize sanity cannot be attributed to the quality of the hospitals, for, although there were considerable variations among them, several are considered excellent. Nor can it be alleged that there was simply not enough time to observe the pseudopatients. Length of hospitalization ranged from 7 to 52 days, with an average of 19 days. The pseudopatients were not, in fact, carefully observed, but this failure clearly speaks more to traditions within psychiatric hospitals than to lack of opportunity.

Finally, it cannot be said that the failure to recognize the pseudopatients' sanity was due to the fact that they were not behaving sanely. While there was clearly some tension present in all of them, their daily visitors could detect no serious behavioral consequences—nor, indeed, could other patients. It was quite common for the patients to "detect" the pseudopatients' sanity. During the first three hospitalizations, when accurate counts were kept, 35 of a total of 118 patients on the admissions ward voiced their suspicions, some vigorously. "You're not crazy. You're a journalist, or a professor [referring to the continual note-taking]. You're checking up on the hospital." While most of the patients were reassured by the pseudopatient's insistence that he had been sick before he came in but was fine now, some continued to believe that the pseudopatient was sane throughout his hospitalization.[10] The fact that the patients often recognized normality when staff did not raises important questions.

Failure to detect sanity during the course of hospitalization may be due to the fact that physicians operate with a strong bias toward what statisticians call the type 2 error (5). This is to say that physicians are more inclined to call a healthy person sick (a false positive, type 2) than a sick person healthy (a false negative, type 1). The reasons for this are not hard to find: it is clearly more dangerous to misdiagnose illness than health. Better to err on the side of caution, to suspect illness even among the healthy.

But what holds for medicine does not hold equally well for psychiatry. Medical illnesses, while unfortunate, are not commonly pejorative. Psychiatric diagnoses, on the contrary, carry with them personal, legal, and social stigmas.[11] It was therefore important to see whether the tendency toward diagnosing the sane insane could be reversed. The following experiment was arranged at a research and teaching hospital whose staff had heard these findings but doubted that such an error could occur in their hospital. The staff was informed that at some time during the following 3 months, one or more pseudopatients would attempt to be admitted into the psychiatric hospital. Each staff member was asked to rate each patient who presented himself at admissions or on the ward according to the likelihood that the patient was a pseudopatient. A 10-point scale was used, with a 1 and 2 reflecting high confidence that the patient was a pseudopatient.

Judgments were obtained on 193 patients who were admitted for psychiatric treatment. All staff who had had sustained contact with or primary responsibility for the patient—attendants, nurses, psychiatrists, physicians, and psychologists—were asked to make judgments. Forty-one patients were alleged, with high confidence, to be pseudopatients by at least one member of the staff. Twenty-three were considered suspect by at least one psychiatrist. Nineteen were suspected by one psychiatrist *and* one other staff member. Actually, no genuine pseudopatient (at least from my group) presented himself during this period.

The experiment is instructive. It indicates that the tendency to designate sane people as insane can be reversed when the stakes (in this case, prestige and diagnostic acumen) are high. But what can be said of the 19 people who were suspected of being "sane" by one psychiatrist and another staff member? Were these people truly "sane," or was it rather the case that in the course of avoiding the type 2 error the staff tended to make more errors of the first sort—calling the crazy "sane"? There is no way of knowing. But one thing is certain: any diagnostic process that lends itself so readily to massive errors of this sort cannot be a very reliable one.

〰 THE STICKINESS OF PSYCHODIAGNOSTIC LABELS

Beyond the tendency to call the healthy sick—a tendency that accounts better for diagnostic behavior on admission than it does for such behavior after a lengthy period of exposure—the data speak to the massive role of labeling in psychiatric assessment. Having once been labeled schizophrenic, there is nothing the pseudopatient can do to overcome the tag. The tag profoundly colors others' perceptions of him and his behavior.

From one viewpoint, these data are hardly surprising, for it has long been known that elements are given meaning by the context in which they occur. Gestalt psychology made this point vigorously, and Asch[12] demonstrated that there are "central" personality traits (such as "warm" versus "cold") which are so powerful that they markedly color the meaning of other information in forming an impression of a given personality[13]. "Insane," "schizophrenic," "manic-depressive," and "crazy" are probably among the most powerful of such central traits. Once a person is designated abnormal, all of his other behaviors and characteristics are colored by that label. Indeed, that label is so powerful that many of the pseudopatients' normal behaviors were overlooked entirely or profoundly misinterpreted. Some examples may clarify this issue.

Earlier I indicated that there were no changes in the pseudopatient's personal history and current status beyond those of name, employment, and, where necessary, vocation. Otherwise, a veridical description of personal history and circumstances was offered. Those circumstances were not psychotic. How were they made consonant with the diagnosis of psychosis? Or were those diagnoses modified in such a way as to bring them into accord with the circumstances of the pseudopatient's life, as described by him?

As far as I can determine, diagnoses were in no way affected by the relative health of the circumstances of a pseudopatient's life. Rather, the reverse occurred: the perception of his circumstances was shaped entirely by the diagnosis. A clear example of such translation is found in the case of a pseudopatient who had had a close relationship with his mother but was rather remote from his father during his early childhood. During adolescence and beyond, however, his father became a close friend, while his relationship with his mother cooled. His present relationship with his wife was characteristically close and warm. Apart from occasional angry exchanges, friction was minimal. The children had rarely been spanked. Surely there is nothing especially pathological about such a history. Indeed, many readers may see a similar pattern in their own experiences, with no markedly deleterious consequences. Observe, however, how such a history was translated in the psychopathological context, this from the case summary prepared after the patient was discharged.

> This white 39-year-old male . . . manifests a long history of considerable ambivalence in close relationships, which begins in early childhood. A warm relationship with his mother cools during his adolescence. A distant relationship to his father is described as becoming very intense. Affective stability is absent. His attempts to control emotionality with his wife and children are punctuated by angry outbursts and, in the case of the children, spankings. And while he says that he has several good friends, one senses considerable ambivalence embedded in those relationships also. . . .

The facts of the case were unintentionally distorted by the staff to achieve consistency with a popular theory of the dynamics of a schizophrenic reaction.[14] Nothing of an ambivalent nature had been described in relations with parents, spouse, or friends. To the extent that ambivalence could be inferred, it was probably not greater than is found in all human relationships. It is true the pseudopatient's relationships with his parents changed over time, but in the ordinary context that would hardly be remarkable—indeed, it might very well be expected. Clearly, the meaning ascribed to his verbalizations (that is, ambivalence, affective instability) was determined by the diagnosis: schizophrenia. An entirely different meaning would have been ascribed if it were known that the man was "normal."

All pseudopatients took extensive notes publicly. Under ordinary circumstances, such behavior would have raised questions in the minds of observers, as, in fact, it did among patients. Indeed, it seemed so certain that the notes would elicit suspicion that elaborate precautions were taken to remove them from the ward each day. But the precautions proved needless. The closest any staff member came to questioning these notes occurred when one pseudopatient asked his physician what kind of medication he was receiving and began to write down the response. "You needn't write it," he was told gently. "If you have trouble remembering, just ask me again."

If no questions were asked of the pseudopatients, how was their writing interpreted? Nursing records for three patients indicate that the writing was seen as an aspect of their pathological behavior. "Patient engages in writing behavior" was the daily nursing comment on one of the pseudopatients who was never questioned about his writing. Given that the patient is in the hospital, he must be psychologically disturbed. And given that he is disturbed, continuous writing must be a behavioral manifestation of that disturbance, perhaps a subset of the compulsive behaviors that are sometimes correlated with schizophrenia.

One tacit characteristic of psychiatric diagnosis is that it locates the sources of aberration within the individual and only rarely within the complex of stimuli that surrounds him. Consequently, behaviors that are stimulated by the environment are commonly misattributed to the patient's disorder. For example, one kindly nurse found a pseudopatient pacing the long hospital corridors. "Nervous, Mr. X?" she asked. "No, bored," he said.

The notes kept by pseudopatients are full of patient behaviors that were misinterpreted by well-intentioned staff. Often enough, a patient would go "berserk" because he had, wittingly or unwittingly, been mistreated by, say, an attendant. A nurse coming upon the scene would rarely inquire even cursorily into the environmental stimuli of the patient's behavior. Rather, she assumed that his upset derived from his pathology, not from his present interactions with other staff members. Occasionally, the staff might assume that the patient's family (especially when they had recently visited) or other patients had stimulated the outburst. But never were the staff found to assume that one of themselves or the structure of the hospital had anything to do with a patient's behavior. One psychiatrist pointed to a group of patients who were sitting outside the cafeteria entrance half an hour before lunchtime. To a group of young residents he indicated that such behavior was characteristic of the oral-acquisitive nature of the syndrome. It seemed not to occur to him that there were very few things to anticipate in a psychiatric hospital besides eating.

A psychiatric label has a life and an influence of its own. Once the impression has been formed that the patient is schizophrenic, the expectation is that he will continue to be schizophrenic. When a sufficient amount of time has passed, during which the patient has done nothing bizarre, he is considered to be in remission and available for discharge. But the label endures beyond discharge, with the unconfirmed expectation that he will behave as a schizophrenic again. Such labels, conferred by mental health professionals, are as influential on the patient as they are on his relatives and friends, and it should not surprise anyone that the diagnosis acts on all of them as a self-fulfilling prophecy. Eventually, the patient himself accepts the diagnosis, with all of its surplus meanings and expectations, and behaves accordingly.

The inferences to be made from these matters are quite simple. Much as Zigler and Phillips have demonstrated that there is enormous overlap in the symptoms presented by patients who have been variously diagnosed,[15] so there is enormous overlap in the behaviors of the sane and the insane. The sane are not "sane" all of the time. We lose our tempers "for no good reason." We are occasionally depressed or anxious, again for no good reason. And we may find it difficult to get along with one or another person—again for no reason that we can specify. Similarly, the insane are not always insane. Indeed, it was the impression of the pseudopatients while living with them that they were sane for long periods of time—that the bizarre behaviors upon which their diagnoses were allegedly predicated constituted only a small fraction of their total behavior. If it makes no sense to label ourselves permanently depressed on the basis of an occasional depression, then it takes better evidence than is presently available to label all patients insane or schizophrenic on the basis of bizarre behaviors or cognitions. It seems more useful, as Mischel[16] has pointed out, to limit our discussions to *behaviors,* the stimuli that provoke them, and their correlates.

It is not known why powerful impressions of personality traits, such as "crazy" or "insane," arise. Conceivably, when the origins of and stimuli that give rise to a behavior are remote or unknown, or when the behavior strikes us as immutable, trait labels regarding the *behaver* arise. When, on the other hand, the origins and stimuli are known and available, discourse is limited to the behavior itself. Thus, I may hallucinate because I am sleeping, or I may hallucinate because I have ingested a peculiar drug. These are termed sleep-induced hallucinations, or dreams, and drug-induced hallucinations, respectively. But when the stimuli to my hallucinations are unknown, that is called craziness, or schizophrenia—as if that inference were somehow as illuminating as the others.

\\\\ SUMMARY AND CONCLUSIONS

It is clear that we cannot distinguish the sane from the insane in psychiatric hospitals. The hospital itself imposes a special environment in which the meanings of behavior can easily be misunderstood. The consequences to patients hospitalized in such an environment—the powerlessness, depersonalization, segregation, mortification, and self-labeling—seem undoubtedly counter-therapeutic.

I do not, even now, understand this problem well enough to perceive solutions. But two matters seem to have some promise. The first concerns the proliferation of community mental health facilities, of crisis intervention centers, of the human potential movement, and of behavior therapies that, for all of their own problems, tend to avoid psychiatric labels, to focus on specific problems and behaviors, and to retain the individual in a relatively non-pejorative environment. Clearly, to the extent that we refrain from sending the distressed to insane places, our impressions of them are less likely to be distorted. (The risk of distorted perceptions, it seems to me, is always present, since we are much more sensitive to an individual's behaviors and verbalizations than we are to the subtle contextual stimuli that often promote them. At issue here is a matter of magnitude. And, as I have shown, the magnitude of distortion is exceedingly high in the extreme context that is a psychiatric hospital.)

The second matter that might prove promising speaks to the need to increase the sensitivity of mental health workers and researchers to the *Catch 22* position of psychiatric patients. Simply reading materials in this area will be of help to some such workers and researchers. For others, directly experiencing the impact of psychiatric hospitalization will be of enormous use. Clearly, further research into the social psychology of such total institutions will both facilitate treatment and deepen understanding.

I and the other pseudopatients in the psychiatric setting had distinctly negative reactions. We do not pretend to describe the subjective experiences of true patients. Theirs may be different from ours, particularly with the passage of time and the necessary process of adaptation to one's environment. But we can and do speak to the relatively more objective indices of treatment within the hospital. It could be a mistake, and a very unfortunate one, to consider that what happened to us derived from malice or stupidity on the part of the staff. Quite the contrary, our overwhelming impression of them was of people who really cared, who were committed and who were uncommonly intelligent. Where they failed, as they sometimes did painfully, it would be more accurate to attribute those failures to the environment in which they, too, found themselves than to personal callousness. Their perceptions and behavior were controlled by the situation, rather than being motivated by a malicious disposition. In a more benign environment, one that was less attached to global diagnosis, their behaviors and judgments might have been more benign and effective.

☒ DISCUSSION QUESTIONS

1. Not everyone thought that the pseudopatients were insane. Who was most likely to pick up the normality of the pseudopatients and why do you think this was the case?

2. Rosenhan notes that mental illness labels are "sticky." What does he mean by this and what are some of the consequences? Can you think of other labels, unrelated to health, that once applied, are very hard for people to get rid of?

3. News coverage and commentary of mass shootings focus heavily on determining whether or not the shooters were mentally ill. Is there any way to see these unfortunate events as normal (if negative and undesirable) rather than a sign of mental illness or personality?

NOTES

1. P. Ash, *J. Abnorm. Soc. Psychol.* **44**, 272 (1949); A. T. Beck, *Amer. J. Psychiat.* **119**, 210 (1962); A. T. Boisen, *Psychiatry* **2**, 233 (1938); N. Kreitman, *J. Ment. Sci.* **107**, 876 (1961); N. Kreitman, P. Sainsbury, J. Morrisey, J. Towers, J. Scrivener, *ibid.*, p. 887; H. O. Schmitt and C. P. Fonda, *J. Abnorm. Soc. Psychol.* **52**, 262 (1956); W. Seeman, *J .Nerv. Ment. Dis.* **118**, 541 (1953). For an analysis of these artifacts and summaries of the disputes, see J. Zubin, *Annu. Rev. Psychol.* **18**, 373 (1967); L. Phillips and J. G. Draguns, *ibid.* **22**, 447 (1971).

2. R. Benedict, *J.Gen. Psychol.* **10**, 59 (1934).

3. See in this regard H. Becker *Outsiders: Studies in the Sociology of Deviance* (Free Press, New York, 1963); B. M. Braginsky. D. D. Braginsky, K. Ring, *Methods of Madness: The Mental Hospital as a Last Resort* (Holt, Rinehart & Winston, New York, 1969); G. M. Crocetti and P. V. Lemkau, *Amer. Sociol. Rev.* **30**, 577 (1965); E. Goffman, *Behavior in Public Places* (Free Press, New York, 1964); R. D. Laing, *The Divided Self: A Study of Sanity and Madness* (Quadrangle, Chicago, 1960); D. L. Phillips, *Amer. Sociol. Rev.* **28**, 963 (1963); T. R. Sarbin, *Psychol. Today* **6**, 18 (1972); E. Schur, *Amer. J. Sociol.* **75**, 309 (1969); T. Szasz, *Law, Liberty and Psychiatry* (Macmillan, New York, 1963); *The Myth of Mental Illness: Foundations of a Theory of Mental Illness* (Hoeber Harper, New York. 1963). For a critique of some of these views, see W. R. Gove, *Amer. Sociol. Rev.* **35**, 873 (1970).

4. E. Goffman, *Asylums* (Doubleday, Garden City. N.Y., 1961).

5. T. J. Scheff, *Being Mentally Ill: A Sociological Theory* (Aldine, Chicago, 1966).

6. Data from a ninth pseudopatient are not incorporated in this report because, although his sanity went undetected, he falsified aspects of his personal history, including his marital status and parental relationships. His experimental behaviors therefore were not identical to those of the other pseudopatients.

7. Beyond the personal difficulties that the pseudopatient is likely to experience in the hospital, there are legal and social ones that, combined, require considerable

attention before entry. For example, once admitted to a psychiatric institution, it is difficult, if not impossible, to be discharged on short notice, state law to the contrary notwithstanding. I was not sensitive to these difficulties at the outset of the project, nor to the personal and situational emergencies that can arise, but later a writ of habeas corpus was prepared for each of the entering pseudopatients and an attorney was kept "on call" during every hospitalization. I am grateful to John Kaplan and Robert Bartels for legal advice and assistance in these matters.

8. However distasteful such concealment is, it was a necessary first step to examining these questions. Without concealment, there would have been no way to know how valid these experiences were; nor was there any way of knowing whether whatever detections occurred were a tribute to the diagnostic acumen of the staff or to the hospital's rumor network. Obviously, since my concerns are general ones that cut across individual hospitals and staffs, I have respected their anonymity and have eliminated clues that might lead to their identification.

9. Interestingly, of the 12 admissions, 11 were diagnosed as schizophrenic and one, with the identical symptomatology, as manic-depressive psychosis. This diagnosis has a more favorable prognosis, and it was given by the only private hospital in our sample. On the relations between social class and psychiatric diagnosis, see A. B. Hollingshead and F. C. Redlich, *Social Class and Mental Illness: A Community Study* (Wiley, New York, 1958).

10. It is possible, of course, that patients have quite broad latitudes in diagnosis and therefore are inclined to call many people sane, even those whose behavior is patently aberrant. However, although we have no hard data on this matter, it was our distinct impression that this was not the case. In many instances, patients not only singled us out for attention, but came to imitate our behaviors and styles.

11. J. Cumming and E. Cumming, *Community Ment. Health* **1**, 135 (1965); A. Farina and K. Ring, *J. Abnorm. Psychol.* **70**, 47 (1965); H. E. Freeman and O. G. Simmons, *The Mental Patient Comes Home* (Wiley, New York, 1963); W. J. Johannsen, *Ment. Hygiene* **53**, 218 (1969); A. S. Linsky, *Soc. Psychiat.* **5**, 166 (1970).

12. S. E. Asch, *J. Abnorm. Soc. Psychol.* **41**, 258 (1946); *Social Psychology* (Prentice-Hall, New York, 1952).

13. See also I. N. Mensh and J. Wishner, *J. Personality* **16**, 188 (1947); J. Wishner, *Psychol. Rev.* **67**, 96 (1960); J. S. Bruner and R. Tagluri, in *Handbook of Social Psychology*, G. Lindzey, Ed. (Addison-Wesley, Cambridge, Mass., 1954), vol. 2, pp. 634–654; J. S. Bruner, D. Shapiro, R. Tagiuri, in *Person Perception and Interpersonal Behavior*, R. Tagiuri and L. Petrullo, Eds. (Stanford Univ. Press, Stanford, Calif., 1958), pp. 277–288.

14. For an example of a similar self-fulfilling prophecy, in this instance dealing with the "central" trait of intelligence, see R. Rosenthal and L. Jacobson, *Pygmalion in the Classroom* (Holt, Rinehart & Winston, New York, 1968).

15. E. Zigler and L. Phillips, *J. Abnorm. Soc. Psychol,* **63,** 69 (1961). See also R. K. Freudenberg and J. P. Robertson, AMA. *Arch. Neurol. Psychiatr.* **76,** 14 (1956).

16. W. Mischel, *Personality and Assessment* (Wiley, New York, 1968).

AUTHORS' NOTE: The author is professor of psychology and law at Stanford University, Stanford, California 94305. Portions of these data were presented to colloquiums of the psychology departments at the University of California at Berkeley and at Santa Barbara; University of Arizona, Tucson; and Harvard University, Cambridge, Massachusetts.

11

The Rise of Viagra

Meika Loe

In the previous article, Rosenhan focuses on the socially constructed nature of mental illness. Here, sociologist Meika Loe applies similar thinking and maps changing definitions of normal sexual function in men, brought on by the discovery of Viagra. Viagra was a happy accident, discovered by researchers at the pharmaceutical company Pfizer who were trying to find a cure for angina (a condition in which the heart does not get enough blood.) But Pfizer had a marketing problem it had to solve before it could turn Viagra into the best selling drug in the world. The inability to get and maintain an erection was almost always either considered a natural part of aging, the result of stress, or caused by relationships or emotional issues. Only in very rare cases did men have an actual physical condition that led to problems, and many of those were related to lifestyle (smoking, lack of physical exercise, etc.) This condition was referred to as impotence, *a term that was highly stigmatized and had significant negative connotations (even today it is grammatically correct to refer to someone who is ineffective in their job as impotent). While this had started to change between 1970 and 1990, it was Pfizer and Viagra that ushered in the widespread* medicalization *of impotence. Medicalization is the process of redefining a nonmedical condition as a medical one. This started with a name change, impotence became* erectile dysfunction *(ED); it was followed by an emphasis on physical mechanics of erections (or lack thereof) that intentionally ignored the emotional and social dimensions of the issue. At the same time, Pfizer's marketing of Viagra redefined normal male sexual performance. A healthy man of 60 who occasionally had trouble either getting or maintaining an erection now could be diagnosed with mild ED and prescribed the infamous little blue pill.*

As you read, think about the social and cultural context that Viagra and related drugs came from. What ideas and insecurities about masculinity does Viagra play into? Who benefits and who loses from this new definition of men's sexuality?

A s a Pfizer Pharmaceuticals sales representative, one of the first things you learn is that erectile dysfunction is a disease. Training manuals counsel that one of the greatest ED myths is that the problem "is all in your mind." A training chart that Pfizer representatives must memorize reveals that "up until the 1970s, erectile dysfunction was deemed 90% psychogenic," or mental, "and 10% organic," or physical. Conversely, the "current medical consensus on erectile dysfunction is 10–30% psychogenic, and 70–90% organic." Today, none of this information sounds strange to us; Pfizer's PR teams and sales representatives have succeeded in converting these "medical facts" into cultural common sense. In fact, most sexual dysfunction reporting takes this organic, or biological, causality "consensus" for granted. But do these sales representatives understand what changed after the 1970s and how these changes created fertile ground for Viagra's debut?

Today, with Viagra offered as a solution, assertions about impotence as an "organic" problem are almost everywhere, with medical practitioners, many of whom were paid researchers or consultants for Pfizer Pharmaceuticals, monopolizing mainstream discussions about impotence. But this wasn't always the case. For most of the twentieth century, sexual problems were attributed to psychological, emotional, relational, and social factors.

Today, most sexual problems are seen as "correctable" physiological problems. How, why, and when this shift towards an "organic model" took place is rarely questioned. What explains the shift in terminology from "impotence" to "erectile dysfunction"? And how do we understand the move from psychologists to urologists as the sex experts of a new era?

The answers to these questions reveal the history of how Viagra came to be. To understand the cultural paradigm shift that occurred between the 1970s and 1990s, one must take into account a changing medical landscape and the rise of social groups that together made this shift possible. As journalist Malcolm Gladwell suggests in his best-selling book, *The Tipping Point,* "Epidemics are a function of the people who transmit infectious agents, the infectious agent itself, and the environment in which the infectious agent is operating." As we will see, in the 1990s, erectile dysfunction took on "epidemic" proportions due to the coordinated efforts of scientific experts and corporations. Specifically, the story of the rise of erectile dysfunction and the emergence of Viagra is a fascinating tale colored by shifting blame, medical accidents, public demonstrations, Puritan intentions, profit motives, vested interests, and medical, scientific, and technological discovery.

⑊ THE NEW EMPHASIS ON "HYDRAULICS"

According to medical historian Robert Aronowitz, the medical profession's large-scale rejection of psychosomatic models for illness can be traced back to a 1933 *JAMA* article, in which medical critic Franz Alexander claimed that medicine's aversion to psycho-social factors harkened back to "the remote days of medicine as sorcery, expelling demons from the body." Alexander claimed that twentieth-century medicine was "dedicated to forgetting its dark, magical past" in favor of "emphasizing exactness and keeping out of field anything that endangers the appearance of science."

In the 1950s, social theorist Talcott Parsons wanted to understand the social function and allure of medicalization. Parsons argued that medical explanations can remove responsibility and blame from the patient. This "sick-role" theory can be applied to the man with sexual failure who is relieved to place blame on his physiology rather than his mind. More recently, sociologists Conrad and Schneider add that medicalization offers optimistic outcomes, such as treatments and cures associated with the prestige of the medical profession.

Clinical psychologist Leonore Tiefer, author of the book *Sex Is Not a Natural Act*, suggests that physiological explanations for impotence fit with the "natural" penile functioning model that men are taught to believe—that the penis is immune when it comes to psychological problems, anxieties, and fears. Biotechnological solutions also allow men to avoid psychological treatments such as marital or sex therapy, which they may find threatening or embarrassing. The trade-off is a potentially embarrassing doctor's visit, which can also be avoided through internet consultations and pharmaceutical purchasing options.

In the 1980s, professional and popular discussions of male sexuality had begun to emphasize physical causes and treatments for sexual problems over and above the earlier respected psychogenic model. Referring to her own experiences working with the Department of Urology at a New York medical center, Tiefer wrote that of the eight hundred men who had been seen since 1981 for erection problems, 90 percent believed their problem to be physical. After examination, only 45 percent of those patients were diagnosed with predominantly medically caused erectile problems. Tiefer was one of the first scholars to question biomedical assumptions, suggesting that they are based on problematic medical models as well as on expectations that normal men must always be interested in sex and that that interest leads easily and directly to erection. Tiefer links these expectations to Masters and Johnson's famous statement that "sex is a natural act," which implies that there is no "natural" reason for decline, so erectile problems must reveal (unnatural) bodily dysfunction, which can be corrected (and bodies restored to normal) with suitable treatment.

Others working in the field of sexual medicine have different explanations for how this paradigm shift came about. Some point to social trends in constant flux, recent influential sex research, or the economic of health care. For example, John Bancroft, former director of the Kinsey Institute for Research on Sex, Gender, and Reproduction, cites a number of factors as crucial to the shift in thinking and practice regarding sexual "function" from psychology to biology: cycles of interest in medicine, changing priorities with increasing technological developments, the need for clinicians to make money, and the high level of involvement of pharmaceutical companies in medical-scientific research and development. Others, like University of Washington psychologist Julia Heiman, explain the change by pointing out the role of researchers Masters and Johnson and the restructuring of health care and coverage in leading the way for a paradigm shift:

> [Medicalization] preceded the Viagra phenomenon. If you think of Masters and Johnson, she was a nurse and he was a medical doctor. They did not do a lot of medicalization for a medical team. They used a much more nonmedical approach. But it favored physiology. Fifteen or twenty years afterwards there's a reaction against this which moves towards the biological. For example, the story of male erection treatment is dominated by medicine. So this is back to the 1970s, when things shifted to the biological. Also, this was part of a larger movement when treatment became considered a medical act. Diagnosis is only available in the DSM, so if you diagnose, this is what you use. Psycho-social diagnoses can be done but they aren't usually because they don't communicate anything to one's colleagues, and there is no reimbursement for that. It's really a guild issue. Anyone doing treatment that is diagnosis related is usually associated with medicine.

Journalistic examples from Viagra media coverage exemplify the seductiveness of medical reasoning in relation to sexual problems. In 1997, two very different publications (to say the least), *JAMA* and *Playboy*, posited similar arguments that: impotence is "mechanical," ignoring psychological dimensions entirely and relying exclusively on biomedical explanations. It is perhaps fair to say that *JAMA* may be invested in promoting the idea that impotence is primarily biological for many reasons, including the fact that this construction is in line with *JAMA*'s regular promotion of medical-science models, as well as the medical community's interest in further developing medical subfields, such as urology. *Playboy,* on the other hand, may have other reasons. Promoting the idea that impotence is a mechanical dysfunction, easily fixed, relieves *Playboy*'s male readership of personal responsibility, blame, or guilt by portraying the condition as one in which the sufferer has no control (but happily, does have access to optimistic outcomes).

In the Viagra era, impotence is no longer blamed on the mind or the wife but, more likely, on human physiology. Locating the problem in the body enables many to benefit, including the patient himself. Lynne Luciano sums up the benefits of medicalizing impotence as follows:

> Transforming impotence into a medical ailment was beneficial not only to physicians but also pharma companies, penile implant manufacturers, and hospitals. Medicalized articles and advertising made information about impotence more acceptable to the mass media by treating it as a scientific issue. Most significantly, medicalization of impotence made men more accepting of it, both because of the centrality of the erections to their self esteem and because modern urology seemed to offer a near-magical technofix—pill, a shot, and not a long session of psychoanalysis. Medical approaches seemed action-oriented. Doctors were doing something about impotence, not just talking about it. In addition, in the 1980s, as health care cutbacks and the proliferation of HMOs eliminated coverage for therapeutic counseling, genuine medical problems were more likely to be covered by insurance. And treating the condition as a medical problem made it more palatable to men by absolving them of blame and failure.

In the 1980s, ideas were changing about who and what to blame for sexual problems. But practitioners and journalists still needed convincing that physiology prevailed over psychology. In 1983, the urologists got their proof.

〰 THE "HAPPY ACCIDENT"

The story of Viagra's discovery is a powerful one—a story that Pfizer has carefully crafted for the public. In 1989 the chemical composition of sildenafil existed in Pfizer Pharmaceuticals labs and test tubes as UK-92,480, a cure for angina. In development and then in clinical tests from 1989 to 1994 in Sandwich, England, at Pfizer Pharmaceutical's research headquarters, sildenafil's success in sending blood to the hearts of trial subjects was not realized. Instead, trial subjects and clinicians discovered that sildenafil increased blood flow to the genital region, causing and sustaining erections, and noted this as a common "side-effect." After a preliminary ten-day safety trial for the angina treatment in 1992, one clinician who was running the trials reported common side effects to his supervisor, Allen, at Pfizer.

> He mentioned that at 50 mg taken every 8 hours for 10 days, there were episodes of indigestion [and of] aches in patients' backs and legs. And he said, "Oh, there are some reports of penile erections." It was not a Eureka moment, as portrayed in some popular accounts, said Allen. It was "just an observation." Obviously, a crucial one.

Overall, the most common Viagra origin story in the mainstream media prior to Viagra's public debut in 1998 recounts the "accidental" discovery of a drug that created and sustained erections and produced intense demand among dumbfounded yet delighted trial subjects. The story generally goes on to suggest that such demand and subsequent public curiosity fueled Pfizer Pharmaceutical's effort to develop and market an impotence drug they later named Viagra.

Such "unanticipated consequence" stories carry public cachet, but only in certain circles. Social scientists Latour and Woolgar argue that scientific accounts are fundamentally about the "creation of order" out of disorder. In this vein, when an article in *JAMA* declared that "better understanding of the mechanisms of erection led to the development of the new oral agent sildenafil," the scientist authors of this article (many of whom worked for Pfizer) predictably tell a more staid version of this story that avoids mention of medical "accidents" and instead favors an ordered, scientific-method approach.

The substitution of science over mischance is repeated by a senior vice president at Pfizer, Dr. David McGibney, in a talk delivered to the Royal Society for the Encouragement of Arts, Manufactures & Commerce in February 1999, one year after Viagra's public debut:

> A Nobel prizewinner has said: "Research is the art of seeing what others see, but thinking what others don't think." That was certainly true of one of our recent discoveries, Viagra, with our own preclinical and clinical studies, together with emerging science from academic laboratories, refocusing our therapeutic target from angina to erectile dysfunction.

In Dr. McGibney's narrative, Viagra's discovery is not accidental but the result of creative thinking, research, and "refocusing." Happy clinical trial subjects are nowhere to be found. Dr. McGibney's pride in Viagra one year after its debut also hides Pfizer's initial corporate ambivalence about developing and marketing this drug. By 2001, the "happy accident" story had become popularized enough that Pfizer published and distributed a version of it to Pfizer-affiliated sexual-dysfunction specialists. But it seems that in order to maintain its reputation in the public sphere as a serious company dedicated to drug development and disease treatment, Pfizer continued to develop a corporate strategy and promotional campaign that associated Viagra with debilitating medical dysfunction or disease. And this is exactly what they did, with astounding success.

⩗ "BRANDING" ERECTILE DYSFUNCTION

By the 1990s, several people and events had set the stage for Viagra. A paradigm shift had taken place in scientific understandings of sexuality, which now located the source of sexual problems in the body, not the mind, the society, or the relationship. Brindley paved the way for the chemical treatment of erections. Urologists were now recognized as the new sex experts, with some poised to become paid consultants to the pharmaceutical industry. A drug for treating impotence was accidentally discovered. Now Pfizer needed a marketing plan that would sanitize and sell sildenafil.

Before starting clinical trials, Pfizer had to solve the problem of how to construct a market for their product and build up public anticipation and practitioner interest. According to philosopher Carl Elliott, author of *Better Than Well*, the industry has learned that the key to selling psychiatric drugs is to sell the illnesses they treat. Doctors treat "patients" and must be convinced that the problem being addressed is a medical disorder. In other words, from a doctor's perspective, Paxil must treat social phobia rather than relieve shyness, and Ritalin must treat attention-deficit disorder rather than improve concentration. The technology in question must treat the proper illness, or else there is no reason why doctors should be obliged to provide it.

One writer in the trade journal *Pharmaceutical Executive* compliments Pfizer on successfully claiming and "branding" ED. To do so, Pfizer had to make sure that from the beginning Viagra and its corresponding medical disorder, ED, were clearly understood and inseparable in the public imagination.

How many people knew ten years ago that there would be such a term as "erectile dysfunction"? That's brilliant branding. And it's not just about branding the drug; it's branding the condition, and by inference, a branding of the patient. . . .What kind of patient does a blockbuster create? We're creating patient populations just as we're creating medicines, to make sure that products become blockbusters.

Although the diagnostic category "erectile dysfunction" existed prior to Viagra's debut, Pfizer borrowed the term and introduced it and Viagra together in 1998, thus constructing a public association between problem and treatment. According to journalists Stipp and Whitaker writing for Fortune, over ten years before Bob Dole made "ED" a house-hold term in television ads as a Viagra spokesperson, erectile dysfunction was a medical category redefined by Irwin Goldstein and his team of researchers in the first federally funded study on impotence, Aging Study (MMAS), which took place from 1987 to 1989. In this important study for the field of urology, impotence was assigned a new name and redefined more broadly. A new subjective and elastic category, "erectile dysfunction" replaced the older stigmatized term "impotence," thereby blurring disease and discontent. Impotence, which is the inability to get an erection, was replaced by ED, which is "the inability to get and maintain an erection adequate for satisfactory sexual performance."

Thus, the MMAS questionnaire characterized erectile potency not as an either/or but as if potency existed on a continuum. Subjects were asked to rate their potency on a scale of one to four: (1) not impotent, (2) minimally impotent, (3) moderately impotent, or (4) completely impotent. These responses were then assigned gradations of erectile dysfunction, ranging from "no ED" to "mild ED (usually able)" to "moderate ED (sometimes able)" to "severe ED (never able)." In other words, men who reported "unsatisfactory sexual performance" or who were "usually able to penetrate partner" were included in the "mild ED" category. Given these flexible definitions, of 1,290 men surveyed, aged forty to seventy, 52 percent fell somewhere in the "mild, moderate, or complete erectile dysfunction" categories. This statistic—that half of men over forty experience ED—is now cited regularly by Pfizer Pharmaceuticals. Thus, by measuring erectile dysfunction both physiologically and subjectively, Pfizer created a "wider range of troubles" to address.

But "diagnostic expansion," or the expansion of medical boundaries and medical categories, may be what is sending record numbers of men to their doctors and spurring record-breaking profits for Pfizer. The big picture of diagnostic augmentation, embedded within a corporate context of market expansion, is that more people are prescribing, selling, taking, and profiting from prescription drugs than ever before. Philosopher and bioethicist Carl Elliot explains,

Drug companies are not simply making up diseases out of thin air, and psychiatrists are not being gulled into diagnosing well people as sick. No one doubts that some people genuinely suffer from, say, depression. . .or that the right medications make these disorders better. But surrounding the core of many of these disorders is a wide zone of ambiguity that can be chiseled out and expanded. The bigger the diagnostic category, the more patients who fit within its boundaries, the more psychoactive drugs will be prescribed.

With the change in definition and nomenclature, initial impotence numbers tripled. Pfizer promotional materials for 2000 confusingly pronounce erectile dysfunction a "common condition that's commonly undertreated." In 2001, Pfizer's official website, www.Viagra.com, used the MMAS statistics to claim, "Erectile dysfunction (ED) affects over 30 million men *to some degree* in the United States" (emphasis added). Apparently, erectile dysfunction, while appearing to be a precise, objective measure, is flexible and subjective enough to include almost any male with sexual insecurities, dissatisfaction, concerns, or intermittent erectile "failures."

⫸ DISEASE MONGERING AND DOCTOR SALESMEN

Pfizer's shifting of medical definitions in what looks like an attempt to create and expand markets is common in contemporary medical marketing. Medical journalist Lynn Payer shares these concerns in her book *The Disease-Mongers.*

> Disease mongering—trying to convince essentially well people that they are sick, or slightly sick, or slightly sick people that they are very ill, is big business. To market drugs to the widest possible audience, pharmaceutical companies must convince people—or their physicians—that they are sick. . . .To tell us about a disease and then to imply that there is a high likelihood that we have it. . .by citing the fact that huge numbers of Americans do. . .is to gnaw away at our self-confidence. And that may really make us sick.

> Disease mongering can include turning ordinary ailments into medical problems, seeing mild symptoms as serious, treating personal problems as medical, seeing risks as diseases, and framing prevalence estimates to maximise potential markets.

With the publicity machine in gear and public anticipation high, thanks to the work of Goldstein and other Pfizer consultants, the final phase of preparing

America for Viagra required quickly concluding clinical trials, earning fast FDA approval, and associating sildenafil with a name that people would remember. Viagra symbolism and imagery were particularly useful when it came to naming, one of the final stages in the making of the drug.

According to sociologist Joel Best, "naming" is crucial because it "shapes the problem" and the solution. Various journalists have suggested that "Viagra" is a mixture of the words "vigor" and "Niagara"—thus constructing the little blue pill as a powerful, vital, potent, thundering entity, and thereby implying that "the problem" is vulnerability, powerlessness, and helplessness and the solution is the opposite of these states. Such symbolism appears regularly in popular media, as in the *Harper's Bazaar* suggestion, "[Viagra's] name seems meant to evoke the pounding power of Niagara Falls. . . .It's expected to thunder onto the market sometime this year." And this symbolic name is no coincidence. According to Greider, it is common for pharmaceutical companies to hire outside consultants to conduct market research and screen names, because the name is central to "branding" the product.

The product name and inflated statistics infused investors' hopes for the Viagra bull market. Pfizer stocks rose 75 percent in anticipation of the pill that could work on anyone. "Among the ideas that excited some analysts was the possibility that millions of men and women with no medical need for the new drugs would take them to enhance sex, vastly amplifying sales." Pfizer would never officially admit that Viagra was for anyone but those with medical need, but it did profit from the widespread concern with sexual dissatisfaction it helped to create.

◊◊◊ MANUFACTURING NEED

As this chapter has shown, the story of Viagra is not just about the manufacture of a little blue pill. It is also about manufacturing "needs," so that every man in America could see himself as a potential Viagra consumer. If nothing else, Pfizer advertisements and expert claims might cause a man to question whether he is young enough, sexual enough, or man enough. While this may seem exaggerated, it is the case that currently most, if not all, American insurance providers pay for Viagra prescriptions, granting legitimacy and value to Viagra and erectile dysfunction, as well as to efforts to normalize male potency and confidence levels, *and* making it possible for all insured men to simply "ask their doctor." It is not accidental that most insurance companies cover Viagra. Kaiser Permanente, the nation's largest HMO, aroused a furor by initially declaring that it would not pay for Viagra, but then backed off. Oxford Health Plans, a Connecticut-based HMO, refused to cover Viagra and became the first insurer to be sued by an irate client. Even the Pentagon agreed to cover the drug once it was estimated that Viagra could eat up one-fifth of the entire pharmaceutical budget of the Veterans Affairs Department, roughly the cost of forty-five Tomahawk Cruise missiles. It is important to note that while insurers tend to cover Viagra, most limit the prescription to six pills a month, with "doctor-diagnosed" erectile dysfunction. Many commentators have pointed out that when the most powerful members of our society or those who control our economy make demands, they are answered. Meanwhile, women's prescriptions such as birth control are still not covered by most insurance plans.[1] Insurance coverage of Viagra and not birth control has spurred a "contraceptive equity movement" nationwide, in which fifteen states have passed contraceptive equity laws that require insurers to cover birth control.

Erectile difficulties are real. But so are the fears that men have about such difficulties, as well as cultural ideals conflating potency, manhood, and individualism. Taken together, those men suffering from erectile problems, those fearful of developing impotence, and those interested in ensuring potency provide Pfizer with a sizeable market for its product. Herein lies the problem for anyone concerned about the construction of normal masculinity and the sexual body. Pfizer and its networks are uniquely positioned to send an important message to men about illness, sexuality, and masculinity—and many will listen. But, the message they have chosen to send is disappointing, for it is the most profitable message they can send: illness in epidemic proportions. The target audience is individual men with aging bodies. And the goal is to get men to their doctors. While this marketing move makes sense, it is oversimplified and highly problematic. Male insecurity may reach epidemic proportions, but the number of men with severe ED is much smaller. By targeting individual men and their dysfunctional bodies, Pfizer obscures the impact that "dysfunctional" social norms or relationships can have on men's insecurities and bodies. Sending men to doctors may be a good thing, but shouldn't they talk with others—such as partners and friends? Pfizer's overemphasis on individuals obscures the sociocultural, medical, relationship-based, and age-related factors that contribute to the concerns and difficulties of men, and it therefore results in mass reinforcement of silence and social insecurity.

⑅ DISCUSSION QUESTIONS

1. Viagra is just one example of medicalization. What other nonmedical conditions can you think of that have been redefined over time as medical issues?

2. Viagra is marketed heavily toward middle-aged and older heterosexual men. Why do you think that Viagra isn't marketed to homosexual men?

3. Why might visiting the doctor for a prescription be more appealing to men than going to talk to a counselor or discussing the issue with their partner?

⁀ NOTE

1. This changed with the passage of the Affordable Care Act in 2010 which requires health insurance plans on the federal health insurance exchanges to cover women's contraception, although not all options are covered. There have been challenges to this portion of the law by religious organizations.

12

Situational Ethics and College Student Cheating

Emily E. LaBeff, Robert E. Clark, Valerie J. Haines,
and George M. Diekhoff

Have you ever cheated on an exam or some other type of schoolwork? If so, you're not alone. The Internet is rife with websites where students can buy term papers, and new digital technologies make it easier than ever to share tests or other work. Some schools even outsource their anticheating efforts by using websites such as Turnitin.com to check student work against that submitted by others. Even an old-fashioned glance at a classmate's test or copying homework before class still happens with impressive frequency. Adults aren't exempt from this either. A recent spate of news stories has revealed that academics, politicians, journalists, and all sorts of other authors plagiarized writing and presented it as their own. Yet as widespread as cheating in various forms may be, it's something that is viewed by the wider society as deviant. If you've ever cheated, you probably didn't drop into your teacher's office or call your parents to brag about how proud you were of how you cheated. People know that cheating is wrong. While people may claim that they didn't realize a behavior counted as cheating, few would argue that they had no idea that cheating itself is wrong.

So how can we explain why cheating is so widespread when it is a form of behavior that is almost universally acknowledged as wrong (i.e., deviant?) In this article, LaBeff et al. provide us with one set of answers. They argue that students who cheat use what they call techniques of neutralization *to justify their actions. These rationalizations allow students to reconcile the wider cultural value that cheating is wrong, while simultaneously redefining their actions in such a way that does not feel that they have committed a deviant act.*

As you read, think about whether you or those you know have ever used these techniques of neutralization and how they might be applied to behaviors considered deviant other than cheating.

This report examines instances of self-reported cheating engaged in by college students, fifty-four percent of whom reported at least one incidence of cheating. Descriptive responses are analyzed in the context of techniques of neutralization. The neutralizing attitude held by these student cheaters suggests that situational ethics are involved. Although the respondents indicate disapproval of cheating, many students feel justified in cheating under certain circumstances.

⧖ INTRODUCTION

Studies have shown that cheating in college is epidemic, and some analysts of this problem estimate that fifty percent of college students may engage in such behavior (e.g., Pavela 1976; Baird 1980; Wellborn 1980; Haines, Diekhoff, LaBeff, and Clark 1986). Such studies have examined demographic and social characteristics of students such as age, sex, academic standing, major, classification, extracurricular activity, level of test anxiety, degree of sanctioned threat, and internal social control. Each of these factors has been found to be related, to some extent, to cheating although the relationship of these factors varies considerably from study to study (Bonjean and McGee 1965; Harp and Taietz 1966; Stannord and Bowers 1970; Fakouri 1972; Johnson and Gormly 1972; Bronzaft, Stuart, and Blum 1973; Tittle and Rowe 1973; Liska 1978; Baird 1980; Leming 1980; Barnett and Dalton 1981, Eve and Bromley 1981; Newhouse 1982; Singhal 1982; Haines et al. 1986).

In our freshmen classes, we often informally ask students to discuss whether they have cheated in college and, if so, how. Some students have almost bragged about which of their methods have proven most effective including writing notes on shoes and caps and on the backs of calculators. Rolling up a tiny cheat sheet into a pen cap was mentioned. And one student said he had "incredibly gifted eyes" which allowed him to see the answers of a smart student four rows in front of him. One female student talked about rummaging through the dumpsters at night close to final examination time looking for test dittos. She did find at least one examination. A sorority member informed us that two of her term papers in her freshman year were sent from a sister chapter of the sorority at another university, retyped and submitted to the course professor. Further, many of these students saw nothing wrong with what they were doing, although they verbally agreed with the statement that cheating was unethical.

It appears that students hold qualified guidelines for behavior which are situationally determined. As such, the concept of situational ethics might well describe this college cheating in that rules for behavior may not be considered rigid but depend on the circumstances involved (Norris and Dodder 1979, p. 545). Joseph Fletcher, in his well known philosophical treatise, *Situation Ethics: The New Morality* (1966), argues that this position is based on the notion that any action may be considered good or bad depending on the social circumstances. In other words, what is wrong in most situations might be considered right or acceptable if the end is defined as appropriate. This concept focuses on contextual appropriateness, not necessarily what is good or right, but what is viewed as fitting, given the circumstances. Central to this process is the idea that situations alter cases, thus altering the rules and principles guiding behavior (Edwards 1967).

Of particular relevance to the present study is the work of Gresham Sykes and David Matza (1957) who first developed the concept of neutralization to explain delinquent behavior. Neutralization theory in the study of delinquency expresses the process of situationally defining deviant behavior. In this view, deviance is based upon ". . . an unrecognized extension of defenses to crimes, in the form of justifications . . . seen as valid by the delinquent but not by . . . society at large" (Sykes and Matza 1957, p. 666). Through neutralization individuals justify violation of accepted behavior. This provides protection ". . . from self blame and the blame of others . . ." (Sykes and Matza 1957, p. 666). They do this before, during, and after the act. Such techniques of neutralization are separated into five categories: denial of responsibility, condemnation of condemners, appeal to higher loyalties, denial of victim, and denial of injury. In each case, individuals profess a conviction about a particular law but argue that special circumstances exist which cause them to violate the rules in a particular instance. However, in recent research, only Liska (1978) and Haines et al. (1986) found neutralization to be an important factor in college student cheating.

※ METHODOLOGY

The present analysis is based on a larger project conducted during the 1983–1984 academic year when a 49-item questionnaire about cheating was administered to students at a small southwestern university. The student body (N = 4950) was evenly distributed throughout the university's programs with a disproportionate number (twenty-seven percent) majoring in business administration. In order to achieve a representative sample from a cross-section of the university student body, the questionnaire was administered to students enrolled in courses classified as a part of the university's core curriculum. Freshmen and sophomores were overrepresented (eighty-four percent of the sample versus sixty percent of the university population). Females were also overrepresented (sixty-two percent of the sample versus fifty-five percent of the university population).

There are obvious disadvantages associated with the use of self-administered questionnaires for data-gathering purposes. One such problem is the acceptance of student responses without benefit of contest. To maximize the return rate, questionnaires were administered during regularly scheduled class periods. Participation was on a voluntary basis. In order to establish the validity of responses, students were guaranteed anonymity. Students were also instructed to limit their reponses regarding whether they had cheated to the current academic year.

Previous analysis (e.g., Haines et al. 1986) focused on the quantitative aspects of the questionnaire. The present analysis is intended to assess the narrative responses to the incidence of cheating in three forms, namely on major examinations, quizzes, and class assignments, as well as the perceptions of and attitudes held by students toward cheating and the effectiveness of deterrents to cheating. Students recorded their experiences in their own words. Most students (eighty-seven percent) responded to the open-ended portion of the questionnaire.

※ RESULTS

Of the 380 undergraduate students who participated in the spring survey, fifty-four percent indicated they had cheated during the previous six month period. Students were requested to indicate whether cheating involved examination, weekly quizzes, and/or homework assignments. Much cheating took the form of looking on someone else's paper, copying homework, and either buying term papers or getting friends to write papers for them. Only five of the 205 students who admitted cheating reported being caught by the professor. However, seven percent (n = 27) of the students reported cheating more than five times during the preceding six month period. Twenty percent (n = 76) indicated that most students openly approved of cheating. Only seventeen students reported they would inform the instructor if they saw another student cheating. Many students, especially older students, indicated they felt resentment toward cheaters, but most also noted that they would not do anything about it (i.e., inform the instructor).

To more fully explore the ways in which students neutralize their behavior, narrative data from admitted student cheaters were examined (n = 149). The narrative responses were easily classified into three of the five techniques described by Sykes and Matza (1957).

〰 DENIAL OF RESPONSIBILITY

Denial of responsibility was the most often identified response. This technique involves a declaration by the offenders that, in light of circumstances beyond their control, they cannot be held accountable for their actions. Rather than identifying the behavior as "accidental," they attribute wrongdoing to the influence of outside forces. In some instances, students expressed an inability to withstand peer pressure to cheat. Responses show a recognition of cheating as an unacceptable behavior, implying that under different circumstances cheating would not have occurred. One student commented:

> I was working forty plus hours a week and we had a lot to read for that day. I just couldn't get it all in. . . . I'm not saying cheating is okay, sometimes you just have to.

Another student explained her behavior in the following statement:

> . . . I had the flu the week before . . . had to miss several classes so I had no way of knowing what was going to be on the exam (sic). My grades were good up to that point and I hadn't cheated. . . . I just couldn't risk it.

It is noteworthy that these statements indicate the recognition that cheating is wrong under normal circumstances.

Other responses demonstrate the attempt by students to succeed through legitimate means (e.g., taking notes and studying) only to experience failure. Accordingly, they were left with no alternative but to cheat. One student commented:

. . . even though I've studied in the past, I've failed the exam (sic) so I cheated on my last test hoping to bring a better grade.

Another student explained his behavior in the following manner:

I studied for the exam (sic) and I studied hard but the material on the test was different from what I expected. . . . I had to make a good grade.

In some accounts, students present a unique approach to the denial of responsibility. Upon entering the examination setting, these students had no intention of cheating, but the opportunity presented itself. The following statement by one student provides a clear illustration of this point:

. . . I was taking the test and someone in another part of the room was telling someone else an answer. I heard it and just couldn't not (sic) write it down.

Although viewing such behavior as dishonest, the blame for any wrongdoing is quickly transferred to those who provide the answers. Another student justified her action in the following manner:

. . . I didn't mean to cheat but once you get the right answer it's hard, no impossible, not to. How could you ignore an answer that you knew was right?

In addition, some students reported accidentally seeing other students' test papers. In such instances, the cheaters chastised classmates for not covering up their answer sheets. As one student wrote, such temptation simply cannot be overcome:

I studied hard for the exam (sic) and needed an A. I just happened to look up and there was my neighbor's paper uncovered. I found myself checking my answers against his through the whole test.

⑈ APPEAL TO HIGHER LOYALTIES

Conflict also arises between peer group expectations and the normative expectations of the larger society. When this occurs, the individual may choose to sacrifice responsibility, thereby maintaining the interest of peers. Such allegiance allows these individuals to supercede moral obligations when special circumstances arise.

Students who invoke this technique of neutralization frequently described their behavior as an attempt to help another. One student stated:

I only cheated because my friend had been sick and she needed help. . . . it (cheating) wouldn't have happened any other time.

Another student denied any wrongdoing on her part as the following statement illustrates:

I personally have never cheated. I've had friends who asked for help so I let them see my test. Maybe some would consider that to be cheating.

These students recognize the act of cheating is wrong. However, their statements also suggest that in some situations cheating can be overlooked. Loyalty to a friend in need takes precedence over honesty in the classroom. Another student described his situation in the following manner:

I was tutoring this girl but she just couldn't understand the material. . . . I felt I had to help her on the test.

〰 CONDEMNATION OF CONDEMNERS

Cheaters using this technique of neutralization attempt to shift attention from their own actions to the actions of others, most often authority figures. By criticizing those in authority as being unfair or unethical, the behavior of the offender seems less consequential by comparison. Therefore, dishonest behavior occurs in reaction to the perceived dishonesty of the authority figure. Students who utilize this technique wrote about uncaring, unprofessional instructors with negative attitudes who were negligent in their behavior. These incidents were said to be a precursor to their cheating behavior. The following response illustrates this view:

The teachers here are boring and I dislike this school. The majority of teachers here don't care about the students and are rude when you ask them for help.

In other instances, students cite unfair teaching practices which they perceive to be the reason for their behavior. One student stated:

Major exams (sic) are very important to your grade and it seems that the majority of instructors make up the exams (sic) to try and trick you instead of testing your knowledge.

In this case, the instructor is thought to engage in a deliberate attempt to fail the students by making the examinations difficult. Also within this category were student accounts which frequently express a complaint of being overworked. As one student wrote:

> One instructor assigns more work than anyone could possibly handle . . . at least I know I can't, so sometimes cheating is the answer.

Another student described his situation as follows:

> Sometimes it seems like these instructors get together and plan to make it difficult. . . . I had three major tests in one day and very little time to study . . .

Although less frequently mentioned, perceived parental pressure also serves as a neutralizing factor for dishonesty. One student stated:

> During my early years at school my parents constantly pressured me for good grades. . . . they would have withheld money if grades were bad.

Another student blamed the larger society for his cheating:

> In America, we're taught that results aren't achieved through beneficial means, but through the easiest means.

Another stated:

> Ted Kennedy has been a modeling (sic) example for many of us. . . . This society teaches us to survive, to rationalize. . . . (it) is built on injustice and expediency.

This student went on to say that he cheated throughout a difficult science course so he could spend more time studying for major courses which he enjoyed.

\\\ DENIAL OF INJURY AND DENIAL OF THE VICTIM

Denial of injury and denial of the victim do not appear in the student accounts of their cheating. In denial of injury, the wrongdoer states that no one was harmed or implies that accusations of injury are grossly exaggerated. In the second case, denial of the victim, those who violate norms often portray their targets as legitimate. Due to certain factors such as the societal role, personal characteristics, or lifestyle of the victim, the wrongdoer felt the victim "had it coming."

It is unlikely that students will either deny injury or deny the victim since there are no real targets in cheating. However, attempts to deny injury are possible when the one who is cheating argues that cheating is a personal matter rather than a public one. It is also possible that some students are cognizant of the effect their cheating activities have upon the educational system as a whole and, therefore, choose to neutralize their behavior in ways which allow them to focus on the act rather than the consequences of cheating. By observing their actions from a myopic viewpoint, such students avoid the larger issues of morality.

⚜ CONCLUSION

The purpose of this report was to analyze student responses to cheating in their college coursework. Using Sykes and Matza's model of techniques neutralization, we found that students rationalized their cheating behavior and do so without challenging the norm of honesty. Student responses fit three of the five techniques of neutralization. The most common technique is a denial of responsibility. Second, students tend to "condemn the condemners," blaming faculty and testing procedures. Finally, students "appeal to higher loyalties" by arguing that it is more important to help a friend than to avoid cheating. The use of these techniques of neutralization conveys the message that students recognize and accept cheating as an undesirable behavior which, nonetheless, can be excused under certain circumstances. Such findings reflect the prevalence of situational ethics.

The situation appears to be one in which students are not caught and disciplined by instructors. Additionally, students who cheat do not concern themselves with overt negative sanctions from other students. In some groups, cheating is planned, expected, and often rewarded in that students may receive better grades That leaves a student's ethical, internalized control as a barrier to cheating. However, the neutralizing attitude allows students to sidestep issues of ethics and guilt by placing the blame for their behavior elsewhere. Neutralization allows them to state their belief that in general cheating is wrong, but in some circumstances cheating is acceptable, even necessary.

Given such widespread acceptance of cheating in the university setting, it may be useful to further test the salience of neutralization and other such factors in more diverse university environments. This study is limited to a small state university. It is important also to extend the research to a wider range of institutions including prestigious private colleges, large state universities, and church-related schools.

Cross-cultural studies of cheating may also prove useful for identifying broader social and cultural forces which underlie situational ethics and cheating behavior. In this regard, the process involved in learning neutralizing attitudes could be integrated with work in the field of deviance in order to expand our understanding of rule breakers along a continuum of minor to major forms of deviance.

⚟ DISCUSSION QUESTIONS

1. How does the context in which deviance takes place affect whether a behavior is defined as deviant? Are there people you would openly discuss cheating with but others you would not? What is different about these groups?

2. How might these techniques of neutralization be used by someone who steals office supplies, time, or other things of value from his or her place of work?

3. Do you think that there might be cross-cultural variations in techniques of neutralization? Or might there be more techniques of neutralization from your culture that you could add to this list? How else do we justify deviant acts in ourselves or others?

4. Is sharing work and coordinating intellectual effort with other students always deviant? Under what circumstances is this not only accepted but encouraged by your teacher?

⚟ REFERENCES

Baird, John S. 1980. "Current Trends in College Cheating." *Psychology in the Schools* 17:512–522.

Barnett, David C., and J. C. Dalton. 1981. "Why College Students Cheat." *Journal of College Student Personnel* 22:545–551.

Bonjean, Charles M., and Reece McGee. 1965. "Undergraduate Scholastic Dishonesty: A Comparative Analysis of Deviance and Control Systems." *Social Science Quarterly* 65:289–296.

Bronzaft, Arline L., Irving R. Stuart, and Barbara Blum. 1973. "Test Anxiety and Cheating on College Examinations." *Psychological Reports* 32:149–150.

Edwards, Paul 1967. *The Encyclopedia of Philosophy, #3,* edited by Paul Edwards. New York: Macmillan Company and Free Press.

Eve, Raymond, and David G. Bromley. 1981. "Scholastic Dishonesty Among College Undergraduates: A Parallel Test of Two Sociological Explanations." *Youth and Society* 13:629–640.

Fakouri, M. E. 1972. "Achieving Motivation and Cheating." *Psychological Reports* 31:629–640.

Fletcher, Joseph. 1966 *Situation Ethics: The New Morality.* Philadelphia: The Westminster Press.

Haines, Valerie J., George Diekhoff, Emily LaBeff, and Robert Clark. 1986. "College Cheating: Immaturity, Lack of Commitment, and the Neutralizing Attitude." *Research in Higher Education* 25:342–354.

Harp, John, and Philip Taietz. 1966. "Academic Integrity and Social Structure: A Study of Cheating Among College Students." *Social Problems* 13:365–373.

Johnson, Charles D., and John Gormly, 1972. "Academic Cheating: The Contribution of Sex, Personality, and Situational Variables." *Developmental Psychology* 6:320–325.

Leming, James S. 1980. "Cheating Behavior, Subject Variables, and Components of the Internal-External Scale Under High and Low Risk Conditions." *Journal of Education Research* 74:83–87

Liska, Allen. 1987 "Deviant Involvement, Associations, and Attitudes: Specifying the Underlying Causal Structures." *Sociology and Social Research* 63:73–88.

Newhouse, Robert C. 1982. "Alienation and Cheating Behavior in the School Environment." *Psychology in the Schools* 19:234–237.

Norris, Terry D., and Richard A. Dodder. 1979. "A Behavioral Continuum Synthesizing Neutralization Theory, Situational Ethics and Juvenile Delinquency." *Adolescence* 55:545–555.

Pavela, Gary. 1976, "Cheating on the Campus: Who's Really to Blame?" *Time* 107 (June 7):24.

Singhal, Avinash C. 1982. "Factors in Student Dishonesty." *Psychological Reports* 51:775–780.

Stannord, Charles I., and William J. Bowers. 1970. "College Fraternity as an Opportunity Structure for Meeting Academic Demands." *Social Problems* 17:371–390.

Sykes, Gresham, and David Matza. 1957. "Techniques of Neutralization: A Theory of Delinquency." *American Sociological Review* 22:664–670.

Tittle, Charles and Alan Rowe. 1973. "Moral Appeal, Sanction Threat, and Deviance: An Experimental Test." *Social Problems* 20:448–498.

Wellborn, Stanley N. 1980. "Cheating in College Becomes Epidemic" *U.S News and World Report* 89 (October 20):39–42.

13

The Way We Weren't: The Myth and Reality of the "Traditional" Family

Stephanie Coontz

Sociologists sometimes refer to the family as a cornerstone social institution. That's because what happens in the family intersects with so many other important institutions. The family is the first place where new members of society are socialized, and what happens in other institutions often reverberates in families and vice versa. For example, in the years following the economic crisis in 2008, the divorce rate went down significantly. That's not because people suddenly had happier marriages; it's because they couldn't afford to get divorced because the economy was so bad. Similarly, schools and families are strongly tied to each other, with changes in one affecting what happens in the other. Indeed, a huge proportion of social problems debated in the public sphere can somehow be linked to experiences or changes in the family. Gun violence is blamed on bad childhoods. Poor school performance is blamed on lack of parental involvement. Health problems are blamed on the eating and exercise habits kids learned (or didn't learn) at home. Crime is blamed on lack of discipline or broken families.

"The way we weren't: the myth and reality of the "traditional" family," by Stephanie Coontz in *National Forum*, Vol. 76, No. 4 (Fall 1996). Reprinted by permission of Stephanie Coontz, Council on Contemporary Families.

It's not inappropriate to look to the family and changes within in it to try to see what the consequences of those changes in family experiences are. But it's just as important to realize that other social institutions affect the family just as much as the family affects them. Many people give in to the temptation to assume that in the past families were safe, stable, wholesomely positive places where adults were more committed to relationships and children benefited almost universally by being raised by two loving and committed parents. The image of the traditional nuclear family, where dad was the breadwinner and mom stayed home and raised children, is often held up as the common and ideal form of family from the past. The fact that few children today spend their childhood in such a home is often seen as the culprit for a host of social ills. But as historian Stephanie Coontz explains in this article, our rather nostalgic image of families in the past does not match the reality. Historically, there's only been one brief point in American history, immediately after World War II, where a majority of children grew up in a traditional nuclear family, and even then it was only slightly over half of children. Constructing the traditional nuclear family as historically typical and normal is not only inaccurate; it ignores the significant variations by race and class that have existed in family structures and experiences throughout history. Coontz recommends that we look carefully at the influence of other social institutions and how they shape family life rather than blaming individuals for changes in family structures. As you read, pay attention to how the different family types she describes were shaped by larger social forces; this is a great example of sociological imagination in action!

Families face serious problems today, but proposals to solve them by reviving "traditional" family forms and values miss two points. First, no single traditional family existed to which we could return, and none of the many varieties of families in our past has had any magic formula for protecting its members from the vicissitudes of socioeconomic change, the inequities of class, race, and gender, or the consequences of interpersonal conflict. Violence, child abuse, poverty, and the unequal distribution of resources to women and children have occurred in every period and every type of family.

Second, the strengths that we also find in many families of the past were rooted in different social, cultural, and economic circumstances from those that prevail today. Attempts to reproduce any type of family outside of its original socioeconomic context are doomed to fail.

▧ COLONIAL FAMILIES

American families always have been diverse, and the male breadwinner-female homemaker, nuclear ideal that most people associate with "the" traditional family has predominated for only a small portion of our history. In colonial America, several types of families coexisted or competed. Native American kinship systems subordinated the nuclear family to a much larger network of marital alliances and kin obligations, ensuring that no single family was forced to go it alone. Wealthy settler families from Europe, by contrast, formed independent households that pulled in labor from poorer neighbors and relatives, building their extended family solidarities on the backs of truncated families among indentured servants, slaves, and the poor. Even wealthy families, though, often were disrupted by death; a majority of colonial Americans probably spent some time in a stepfamily. Meanwhile, African Americans, denied the legal protection of marriage and parenthood, built extensive kinship networks and obligations through fictive kin ties, ritual co-parenting or godparenting, adoption of orphans, and complex naming patterns designed to preserve family links across space and time.

The dominant family values of colonial days left no room for sentimentalizing childhood. Colonial mothers, for example, spent far less time doing child care than do modern working women, typically delegating this task to servants or older siblings. Among white families, patriarchal authority was so absolute that disobedience by a wife or child was seen as a small form of treason, theoretically punishable by death, and family relations were based on power, not love.

▧ THE NINETEENTH-CENTURY FAMILY

With the emergence of a wage-labor system and a national market in the first third of the nineteenth century, white middle-class families became less patriarchal and more child-centered. The ideal of the male breadwinner and the nurturing mother now appeared. But the emergence of domesticity for middle-class women and children depended on its absence among the immigrant, working class, and African American women or children who worked as servants, grew the cotton, or toiled in the textile mills to free middle-class wives from the chores that had occupied their time previously.

Even in the minority of nineteenth-century families who could afford domesticity, though, emotional arrangements were quite different from nostalgic images of "traditional" families. Rigid insistence on separate spheres for men and women made male-female relations extremely stilted, so that women commonly turned to other women, not their husbands, for their most intimate relations. The idea that all of one's passionate feelings should go toward a member of the opposite sex was a twentieth-century invention—closely associated with the emergence of a mass consumer society and promulgated by the very film industry that "traditionalists" now blame for undermining such values.

◊◊ EARLY TWENTIETH-CENTURY FAMILIES

Throughout the nineteenth century, at least as much divergence and disruption in the experience of family life existed as does today, even though divorce and unwed motherhood were less common. Indeed, couples who marry today have a better chance of celebrating a fortieth wedding anniversary than at any previous time in history. The life cycles of nineteenth-century youth (in job entry, completion of schooling, age at marriage, and establishment of separate residence) were far more diverse than they became in the early twentieth-century. At the turn of the century a higher proportion of people remained single for their entire lives than at any period since. Not until the 1920s did a bare majority of children come to live in a male breadwinner-female homemaker family, and even at the height of this family form in the 1950s, only 60 percent of American children spent their entire childhoods in such a family.

From about 1900 to the 1920s, the growth of mass production and emergence of a public policy aimed at establishing a family wage led to new ideas about family self-sufficiency, especially in the white middle class and a privileged sector of the working class. The resulting families lost their organic connection to intermediary units in society such as local shops, neighborhood work cultures and churches, ethnic associations, and mutual-aid organizations.

As families related more directly to the state, the market, and the mass media, they also developed a new cult of privacy, along with heightened expectations about the family's role in fostering individual fulfillment. New family values stressed the early independence of children and the romantic coupling of husband and wife, repudiating the intense same-sex ties and mother-infant bonding of earlier years as unhealthy. From this family we get the idea that women are sexual, that youth is attractive, and that marriage should be the center of our emotional fulfillment.

Even aside from its lack of relevance to the lives of most immigrants, Mexican Americans, African Americans, rural families, and the urban poor, big contradictions existed between image and reality in the middle-class family ideal of the early twentieth century. This is the period when many Americans first accepted the idea that the family should be sacred from outside intervention; yet the development of the private, self-sufficient family depended on state intervention in the economy, government regulation of parent-child relations, and state-directed destruction of class and community institutions that hindered the development of family privacy. Acceptance of a youth and leisure culture sanctioned early marriage and raised expectations about the quality of married life, but also introduced new tensions between the generations and new conflicts between husband and wife over what were adequate levels of financial and emotional support.

The nineteenth-century middle-class ideal of the family as a refuge from the world of work was surprisingly modest compared with emerging twentieth-century demands that the family provide a whole alternative world of satisfaction and intimacy to that of work and neighborhood. Where a family succeeded in doing so, people might find pleasures in the home never before imagined. But the new ideals also increased the possibilities for failure: America has had the highest divorce rate in the world since the turn of the century.

In the 1920s, these contradictions created a sense of foreboding about "the future of the family" that was every bit as widespread and intense as today's. Social scientists and popular commentators of the time hearkened back to the "good old days," bemoaning the sexual revolution, the fragility of nuclear family ties, the cult of youthful romance, the decline of respect for grandparents, and the threat of the "New Woman." But such criticism was sidetracked by the stock-market crash, the Great Depression of the 1930s, and the advent of World War II.

Domestic violence escalated during the Depression, while murder rates were as high in the 1930s as in the 1980s. Divorce rates fell, but desertion increased and fertility plummeted. The war stimulated a marriage boom, but by the late 1940s one in every three marriages was ending in divorce.

⚞ THE 1950s FAMILY

At the end of the 1940s, after the hardships of the Depression and war, many Americans revived the nuclear family ideals that had so disturbed commentators during the 1920s. The unprecedented postwar prosperity allowed young families to achieve consumer satisfactions and socioeconomic mobility that would have been inconceivable in earlier days. The 1950s family that resulted from these economic and cultural trends, however, was hardly "traditional." Indeed, it is best seen as a historical aberration. For the first time in 100 years, divorce rates dropped, fertility soared, the gap between men's and women's job and educational prospects widened (making middle-class women more dependent on marriage), and the age of marriage fell—to the point that teenage birth rates were almost double what they are today.

Admirers of these very nontraditional 1950s family forms and values point out that household arrangements and gender roles were less diverse in the 1950s than today, and marriages more stable. But this was partly because diversity was ruthlessly suppressed and partly because economic and political support systems for socially-sanctioned families were far more generous than they are today. Real wages rose more in any single year of the 1950s than they did in the entire decade of the 1980s; the average thirty-year-old man could buy a median-priced home on 15 to 18 percent of his income. The government funded public investment, home ownership, and job creation at a rate more than triple that of the past two decades, while 40 percent of young men were eligible for veteran's benefits. Forming and maintaining families was far easier than it is today.

Yet the stability of these 1950s families did not guarantee good outcomes for their members. Even though most births occurred within wedlock, almost a third of American children lived in poverty during the 1950s, a higher figure than today. More than 50 percent of black married-couple families were poor. Women were often refused the right to serve on juries, sign contracts, take out credit cards in their own names, or establish legal residence. Wife-battering rates were low, but that was because wife-beating was seldom counted as a crime. Most victims of incest, such as Miss America of 1958, kept the secret of their fathers' abuse until the 1970s or 1980s, when the women's movement became powerful enough to offer them the support denied them in the 1950s.

THE POST-1950s FAMILY

In the 1960s, the civil rights, antiwar, and women's liberation movements exposed the racial, economic, and sexual injustices that had been papered over by the Ozzie and Harriet images on television. Their activism made older kinds of public and private oppression unacceptable and helped create the incomplete, flawed, but much-needed reforms of the Great Society. Contrary to the big lie of the past decade that such programs caused our current family dilemmas, those antipoverty and social justice reforms helped overcome many of the family problems that prevailed in the 1950s.

In 1964, after fourteen years of unrivaled family stability and economic prosperity, the poverty rate was still 19 percent; in 1969, after five years of civil rights activism, the rebirth of feminism, and the institution of nontraditional if relatively modest government welfare programs, it was down to 12 percent, a low that has not been seen again since the social welfare cutbacks began in the late 1970s. In 1965, 20 percent of American children still lived in poverty; within five years, that had fallen to 15 percent. Infant mortality was cut in half between 1965 and 1980. The gap in nutrition between low-income Americans and other Americans narrowed significantly, as a direct result of food stamp and school lunch programs. In 1963, 20 percent of Americans living below the poverty line had never been examined by a physician; by 1970 this was true of only 8 percent of the poor.

Since 1973, however, real wages have been falling for most Americans. Attempts to counter this through tax revolts and spending freezes have led to drastic cutbacks in government investment programs. Corporations also spend far less on research and job creation than they did in the 1950s and 1960s, though the average compensation to executives has soared. The gap between rich and poor, according to the April 17, 1995, New York Times, is higher in the United States than in any other industrial nation.

⧳ FAMILY STRESS

These inequities are not driven by changes in family forms, contrary to ideologues who persist in confusing correlations with causes; but they certainly exacerbate such changes, and they tend to bring out the worst in all families. The result has been an accumulation of stresses on families, alongside some important expansions of personal options. Working couples with children try to balance three full-time jobs, as employers and schools cling to policies that assume every employee has a "wife" at home to take care of family matters. Divorce and remarriage have allowed many adults and children to escape from toxic family environments, yet our lack of social support networks and failure to forge new values for sustaining intergenerational obligations have let many children fall through the cracks in the process.

Meanwhile, young people find it harder and harder to form or sustain families. According to an Associated Press report of April 25, 1995, the median income of men aged twenty-five to thirty-four fell by 26 percent between 1972 and 1994, while the proportion of such men with earnings below the poverty level for a family of four more than doubled to 32 percent. The figures are even worse for African American and Latino men. Poor individuals are twice as likely to divorce as more affluent ones, three to four times less likely to marry in the first place, and five to seven times more likely to have a child out of wedlock.

As conservatives insist, there is a moral crisis as well as an economic one in modem America: a pervasive sense of social alienation, new levels of violence, and a decreasing willingness to make sacrifices for others. But romanticizing "traditional" families and gender roles will not produce the changes in job structures, work policies, child care, medical practice, educational preparation, political discourse, and gender inequities that would permit families to develop moral and ethical systems relevant to 1990s realities.

America needs more than a revival of the narrow family obligations of the 1950s, whose (greatly exaggerated) protection for white, middle-class children was achieved only at tremendous cost to the women in those families and to all those who could not or would not aspire to the Ozzie and Harriet ideal. We need a concern for children that goes beyond the question of whether a mother is waiting with cookies when her kids come home from school. We need a moral language that allows us to address something besides people's sexual habits. We need to build values and social institutions that can reconcile people's needs for independence with their equally important rights to dependence, and surely we must reject older solutions that involved balancing these needs on the backs of women. We will not find our answers in nostalgia for a mythical "traditional family."

DISCUSSION QUESTIONS

1. What is a family? Is a cohabiting couple without children a family? What about former in-laws after a divorce? How does where you are and when you are affect what we define as family?

2. How has the family structure of the poor and those who are not White been historically different than the family structure of middle- and upper-class Whites?

3. What kind of family did you grow up in? What about your friends? Do you know anyone who spent all 18 years of childhood in a traditional nuclear family?

4. Visit the section of the census website that collects data on families at http://www.census.gov/hhes/families/ and look through the latest table, America's Family and Living Arrangements. What types of families are most common?

⫸ SOURCE CITATION

Coontz, Stephanie. "The way we weren't: the myth and reality of the 'traditional' family." *National Forum* 76.4 (1996): 45+. *Academic OneFile*. Web. 17 July 2014.

14

Doing Gender

Candace West and Don H. Zimmerman

Gender is one of the central organizing features of social life. While we have many different roles we play in different contexts (employee, student, friend, significant other), and we each have personality traits that we may turn up in some situations and down in others (shyness, sense of humor, talkativeness), we are always gendered beings. There is not a social option to be genderless, and those that try, such as parents who for 1 year kept their babies gender to themselves, are met with immediate and harsh social sanctions.[1]

Most people think of gender as a trait that someone simply has, much like eye color. On the other hand, many sociologists see gender as a role that people learn rather than something they have, in this article West and Zimmerman argue that gender should be thought of not as a role that we learn but as an accomplishment, something that we actively do and that is a product of our interactions. This outcome of gender is usually seen as justification of institutional arrangements that separate the genders, but West and Zimmerman argue that in fact by doing gender, we create through social interaction the very differences that we think of as being natural and normal. For example, public restrooms, even those with single stalls, are gender segregated and this is seen as a necessity because of the natural biological differences between men and women. Yet bathrooms in homes are not segregated, and men and women quite happily hare the same bathrooms with the same setup in their private lives. We don't have separate stalls for women because they need them, we think we need them because there are separate stalls. As you read, think about your own gender performance each day and how it reinforces existing institutional arrangements between men and women.

West, C., & Zimmerman, D. H. (1987). Doing gender. Gender and Society, 1(2), 125-151. doi: 10.1177/0891243287001002002.

Our purpose in this article is to propose an ethnomethodologically informed, and therefore distinctively sociological, understanding of gender as a routine, methodical, and recurring accomplishment. We contend that the "doing" of gender is undertaken by women and men whose competence as members of society is hostage to its production. Doing gender involves a complex of socially guided perceptual, interactional, and micropolitical activities that cast particular pursuits as expressions of masculine and feminine "natures."

When we view gender as an accomplishment, an achieved property of situated conduct, our attention shifts from matters internal to the individual and focuses on interactional and, ultimately, institutional arenas. In one sense, of course, it is individuals who "do" gender. But it is a situated doing, carried out in the virtual or real presence of others who are presumed to be oriented to its production. Rather than as a property of individuals, we conceive of gender as an emergent feature of social situations: both as an outcome of and a rationale for various social arrangements and as a means of legitimating one of the most fundamental divisions of society.

To advance our argument, we undertake a critical examination of what sociologists have meant by *gender,* including its treatment as a role enactment in the conventional sense and as a "display" in Goffman's (1976) terminology. Both *gender role* and *gender display* focus on behavioral aspects of being a woman or a man (as opposed, for example, to biological differences between the two). However, we contend that the notion of gender as a role obscures the work that is involved in producing gender in everyday activities, while the notion of gender as a display relegates it to the periphery of interaction. We argue instead that participants in interaction organize their various and manifold activities to reflect or express gender, and they are disposed to perceive the behavior of others in a similar light.

To elaborate our proposal, we suggest at the outset that important but often overlooked distinctions be observed among *sex, sex category,* and *gender.* Sex is a determination made through the application of socially agreed upon biological criteria for classifying persons as females or males.[2] The criteria for classification can be genitalia at birth or chromosomal typing before birth, and they do not necessarily agree with one another. Placement in a *sex category* is achieved through application of the sex criteria, but in everyday life, categorization is established and sustained by the socially required identificatory displays that proclaim one's membership in one or the other category. In this sense, one's sex category presumes one's sex and stands as proxy for it in many situations, but sex and sex category can vary independently; that is, it is possible to claim membership in a sex category even when the sex criteria are lacking. *Gender,* in contrast, is the activity of managing situated conduct in light of normative conceptions of attitudes and activities appropriate for one's sex category. Gender activities emerge from and bolster claims to membership in a sex category.

We argue that gender is not a set of traits, nor a variable, nor a role, but the product of social doings of some sort. What then is the social doing of gender? It is more than the continuous creation of the meaning of gender through human actions (Gerson and Peiss 1985). We claim that gender itself is constituted through interaction.[3]

⟍⟍ SEX, SEX CATEGORY, AND GENDER

Garfinkel's (1967, pp. 118–40) case study of Agnes, a transsexual raised as a boy who adopted a female identity at age 17 and underwent a sex reassignment operation several years later, demonstrates how gender is created through interaction and at the same time structures interaction. Agnes, whom Garfinkel characterized as a "practical methodologist," developed a number of procedures for passing as a "normal, natural female" both prior to and after her surgery. She had the practical task of managing the fact that she possessed male genitalia and that she lacked the social resources a girl's biography would presumably provide in everyday interaction. In short, she needed to display herself as a woman, simultaneously learning what it was to be a woman. Of necessity, this full-time pursuit took place at a time when most people's gender would be well-accredited and routinized. Agnes had to consciously contrive what the vast majority of women do without thinking. She was not "faking" what "real" women do naturally. She was obliged to analyze and figure out how to act within socially structured circumstances and conceptions of femininity that women born with appropriate biological credentials come to take for granted early on. As in the case of others who must "pass," such as transvestites, Kabuki actors, or Dustin Hoffman's "Tootsie," Agnes's case makes visible what culture has, made invisible—the accomplishment of gender.

Garfinkel's (1967) discussion of Agnes does not explicitly separate three analytically distinct, although empirically overlapping, concepts—sex, sex category, and gender.

Sex

Agnes did not possess the socially agreed upon biological criteria for classification as a member of the female *sex*. Still, Agnes regarded herself as a female, albeit a female with a penis, which a woman ought not to possess. The penis, she insisted, was a "mistake" in need of remedy (Garfinkel 1967, pp. 126–27, 131–32).

Like other competent members of our culture, Agnes honored the notion that there *are* "essential" biological criteria that unequivocally distinguish females from males. However, if we move away from the commonsense viewpoint, we discover that the reliability of these criteria is not beyond question (Money and Brennan 1968; Money and Ehrhardt 1972; Money and Ogunro 1974; Money and Tucker 1975). Moreover, other cultures have acknowledged the existence of "cross-genders" (Blackwood 1984; Williams 1986) and the possibility of more than two sexes (Hill 1935; Martin and Voorheis 1975, pp. 84–107; but see also Cucchiari 1981, pp. 32–35).

More central to our argument is Kessler and McKenna's (1978, pp. 1–6) point that genitalia are conventionally hidden from public inspection in everyday life; yet we continue through our social rounds to "observe" a world of two naturally, normally sexed persons. It is the *presumption* that essential criteria exist and would or should be there if looked for that provides the basis for sex categorization. Drawing on Garfinkel, Kessler and McKenna argue that "female" and "male" are cultural events—products of what they term the "gender attribution process"— rather than some collection of traits, behaviors, or even physical attributes. Illustratively they cite the child who, viewing a picture of someone clad in a suit and a tie, contends, "It's a man, because he has a pee-pee" (Kessler and McKenna 1978, p. 154). Translation: "He must have a pee-pee [an essential characteristic] because I see the *insignia* of a suit and tie." Neither initial sex assignment (pronouncement at birth as a female or male) nor the actual existence of essential criteria for that assignment (possession of a clitoris and vagina or penis and testicles) has much—if anything—to do with the identification of sex category in everyday life. There, Kessler and McKenna note, we operate with a moral certainty of a world of two sexes. We do not think, "Most persons with penises are men, but some may not be" or "Most persons who dress as men have penises." Rather, we take it for granted that sex and sex category are congruent—that knowing the latter, we can deduce the rest.

Sex Categorization

Agnes's claim to the categorical status of female, which she sustained by appropriate identificatory displays and other characteristics, could be *discredited* before her transsexual operation if her possession of a penis became known and after by her surgically constructed genitalia (see Raymond 1979, pp. 37, 138). In this regard, Agnes had to be continually alert to actual or potential threats to the security of her sex category. Her problem was not so much living up to some prototype of essential femininity but preserving her categorization as female.

This task was made easy for her by a very powerful resource, namely, the process of commonsense categorization in everyday life.

The categorization of members of society into indigenous categories such as "girl" or "boy," or "woman" or "man," operates in a distinctively social way. The act of categorization does not involve a positive test, in the sense of a well-defined set of criteria that must be explicitly satisfied prior to making an identification. Rather, the application of membership categories relies on an "if-can" test in everyday interaction (Sacks 1972, pp. 332–35). This test stipulates that if people *can be seen* as members of relevant categories, *then categorize them that way.* That is, use the category that seems appropriate, except in the presence of discrepant information or obvious features that would rule out its use. This procedure is quite in keeping with the attitude of everyday life, which has us take appearances at face value unless we have special reason to doubt (Schutz 1943; Garfinkel 1967, pp. 272–77; Bernstein 1986).[4] It should be added that it is precisely when we have special reason to doubt that the issue of applying rigorous criteria arises, but it is rare, outside legal or bureaucratic contexts, to encounter insistence on positive tests[5] (Garfinkel 1967, pp. 262–83; Wilson 1970).

Agnes's initial resource was the predisposition of those she encountered to take her appearance (her figure, clothing, hair style, and so on), as the undoubted appearance of a normal female. Her further resource was our cultural perspective on the properties of "natural, normally sexed persons." Garfinkel (1967, pp. 122–28) notes that in everyday life, we live in a world of two—and only two—sexes. This arrangement has a moral status, in that we include ourselves and others in it as "essentially, originally, in the first place, always have been, always will be, once and for all, in the final analysis, either 'male' or 'female'" (Garfinkel 1967, p. 122).

Consider the following case:

> This issue reminds me of a visit I made to a computer store a couple of years ago. The person who answered my questions was truly a *salesperson.* I could not categorize him/her as a woman or a man. What did I look for? (1) Facial hair: She/he was smooth skinned, but some men have little or no facial hair. (This varies by race, Native Americans and Blacks often have none.) (2) Breasts: She/he was wearing a loose shirt that hung from his/her shoulders. And, as many women who suffered through a 1950s' adolescence know to their shame, women are often flat-chested. (3) Shoulders: His/hers were small and round for a man, broad for a woman. (4) Hands: Long and slender fingers, knuckles a bit large for a woman, small for a man. (5) Voice: Middle range, unexpressive for a woman, not at all the exaggerated tones some gay males affect. (6) His/her treatment of me: Gave off no signs that would let

me know if I were of the same or different sex as this person. There were not even any signs that he/she knew his/her sex would be difficult to categorize and I wondered about that even as I did my best to hide these questions so I would not embarrass him/her while we talked of computer paper. I left still not knowing the sex of my salesperson, and was disturbed by that unanswered question (child of my culture that I am). (Diane Margolis, personal communication)

What can this case tell us about situations such as Agnes's (cf. Morris 1974; Richards 1983) or the process of sex categorization in general? First, we infer from this description that the computer salesclerk's identificatory display was ambiguous, since she or he was not dressed or adorned in an unequivocally female or male fashion. It is when such a display *fails* to provide grounds for categorization that factors such as facial hair or tone of voice are assessed to determine membership in a sex category. Second, beyond the fact that this incident could be recalled after "a couple of years," the customer was not only "disturbed" by the ambiguity of the salesclerk's category but also assumed that to acknowledge this ambiguity would be embarrassing to the salesclerk. Not only do we want to know the sex category of those around us (to see it at a glance, perhaps), but we presume that others are displaying it for us, in as decisive a fashion as they can.

Gender

Agnes attempted to be "120 percent female" (Garfinkel 1967, p. 129), that is, unquestionably in all ways and at all times feminine. She thought she could protect herself from disclosure before and after surgical intervention by comporting herself in a feminine manner, but she also could have given herself away by overdoing her performance. Sex categorization and the accomplishment of gender are not the same. Agnes's categorization could be secure or suspect, but did not depend on whether or not she lived up to some ideal conception of femininity. Women can be seen as unfeminine, but that does not make them "unfemale." Agnes faced an ongoing task of *being* a woman—something beyond style of dress (an identificatory display) or allowing men to light her cigarette (a gender display). Her problem was to produce configurations of behavior that would be seen by others as normative gender behavior.

Agnes's strategy of "secret apprenticeship," through which she learned expected feminine decorum by carefully attending to her fiancè's criticisms of other women, was one means of masking incompetencies and simultaneously acquiring the needed skills (Garfinkel 1967, pp. 146–147). It was through her fiancè that Agnes learned that sunbathing on the lawn in front of her apartment was "offensive" (because it put her on display to other men). She also learned from his critiques of other women that she should not insist on having things her way and that she should not offer her opinions or claim equality with men (Garfinkel 1967, pp. 147–148). (Like other women in our society, Agnes learned something about power in the course of her "education.")

Popular culture abounds with books and magazines that compile idealized depictions of relations between women and men. Those focused on the etiquette of dating or prevailing standards of feminine comportment are meant to be of practical help in these matters. However, the use of any such source *as a manual of procedure* requires the assumption that doing gender merely involves making use of discrete, well-defined bundles of behavior that can simply be plugged into interactional situations to produce recognizable enactments of masculinity and femininity. The man "does" being masculine by, for example, taking the woman's arm to guide her across a street, and she "does" being feminine by consenting to be guided and not initiating such behavior with a man.

Agnes could perhaps have used such sources as manuals, but, we contend, doing gender is not so easily regimented (Mithers 1982; Morris 1974). Such sources may list and describe the sorts of behaviors that mark or display gender, but they are necessarily incomplete (Garfinkel 1967, pp. 66–75; Wieder 1974, pp. 183–214; Zimmerman and Wieder 1970, pp. 285–98). And to be successful, marking or displaying gender must be finely fitted to situations and modified or transformed as the occasion demands. Doing gender consists of managing such occasions so that, whatever the particulars, the outcome is seen and seeable in context as gender-appropriate or, as the case may be, gender-*in*appropriate, that is, *accountable*.

〽 RESOURCES FOR DOING GENDER

Doing gender means creating differences between girls and boys and women and men, differences that are not natural, essential, or biological. Once the differences have been constructed, they are used to reinforce the "essentialness" of gender. In a delightful account of the "arrangement between the sexes," Goffman (1977) observes the creation of a variety of institutionalized frameworks through which our "natural, normal sexedness" can be enacted. The physical features of social setting provide one obvious resource for the expression of our "essential" differences. For example, the sex segregation of North American public bathrooms distinguishes "ladies" from "gentlemen" in matters held to be fundamentally biological, even though both "are somewhat similar in the question of waste products and their elimination" (Goffman 1977, p. 315). These settings are furnished with dimorphic equipment (such as urinals for men or elaborate grooming facilities for women), even though both sexes may achieve the same ends through the same means (and apparently do so in the privacy of their own homes). To be stressed here is the fact that:

> The *functioning* of sex-differentiated organs is involved, but there is nothing in this functioning that biologically recommends segregation; *that* arrangement is a totally cultural matter . . . toilet segregation is presented as a natural consequence of the difference between the sex-classes when in fact it is a means of honoring, if not producing, this difference. (Goffman 1977, p. 316)

Standardized social occasions also provide stages for evocations of the "essential female and male natures." Goffman cites organized sports as one such institutionalized framework for the expression of manliness. There, those qualities that ought "properly" to be associated with masculinity, such as endurance, strength, and competitive spirit, are celebrated by all parties concerned—participants, who may be seen to demonstrate such traits, and spectators, who applaud their demonstrations from the safety of the sidelines (1977, p. 322).

Assortative mating practices among heterosexual couples afford still further means to create and maintain differences between women and men. For example, even though size, strength, and age tend to be normally distributed among females and males (with considerable overlap between them), selective pairing ensures couples in which boys and men are visibly bigger, stronger, and older (if not "wiser") than the girls and women with whom they are paired. So, should situations emerge in which greater size, strength, or experience is called for, boys and men will be ever ready to display it and girls and women, to appreciate its display (Goffman 1977, p. 321; West and Iritani 1985).

Gender may be routinely fashioned in a variety of situations that seem conventionally expressive to begin with, such as those that present "helpless" women next to heavy objects or flat tires. But, as Goffman notes, heavy, messy, and precarious concerns can be constructed from *any* social situation, "even though by standards set in other settings, this may involve something that is light, clean, and safe" (Goffman 1977, p. 324). Given these resources, it is clear that *any* interactional situation sets the stage for depictions of "essential" sexual natures. In sum, these situations "do not so much allow for the expression of natural differences as for the production of that difference itself" (Goffman 1977, p. 324).

Many situations are not clearly sex categorized to begin with, nor is what transpires within them obviously gender relevant. Yet any social encounter can be pressed into service in the interests of doing gender. Thus, Fishman's (1978) research on casual conversations found an asymmetrical "division of labor" in talk between heterosexual intimates. Women had to ask more questions, fill more silences, and use more attention-getting beginnings in order to be heard. Her conclusions are particularly pertinent here:

> Since interactional work is related to what constitutes being a woman, with what a woman *is,* the idea that it *is* work is obscured. The work is not seen as what women do, but as part of what they are. (Fishman 1978, p. 405)

We would argue that it is precisely such labor that helps to constitute the essential nature of women *as* women in interactional contexts (West and Zimmerman 1983, pp. 109–11; but see also Kollock, Blumstein, and Schwartz 1985).

Individuals have many social identities that may be donned or shed, muted or made more salient, depending on the situation. One may be a friend, spouse, professional, citizen, and many other things to many different people—or, to the same person at different times. But we are always women or men—unless we shift into another sex category. What this means is that our identificatory displays will provide an ever-available resource for doing gender under an infinitely diverse set of circumstances.

Some occasions are organized to routinely display and celebrate behaviors that are conventionally linked to one or the other sex category. On such occasions, everyone knows his or her place in the interactional scheme of things. If an individual identified as a member of one sex category engages in behavior usually associated with the other category, this routinization is challenged. Hughes (1945, p. 356) provides an illustration of such a dilemma:

> [A] young woman . . . became part of that virile profession, engineering. The designer of an airplane is expected to go up on the maiden flight of the first plane built according to the design. He [sic] then gives a dinner to the engineers and workmen who worked on the new plane. The dinner is naturally a stag party. The young woman in question designed a plane. Her co-workers urged her not to take the risk—for which, presumably, men only are fit—of the maiden voyage. They were, in effect, asking her to be a lady instead of an engineer. She chose to be an engineer. She then gave the party and paid for it like a man. After food and the first round of toasts, she left like a lady.

On this occasion, parties reached an accommodation that allowed a woman to engage in presumptively masculine behaviors. However, we note that in the end, this compromise permitted demonstration of her "essential" femininity, through accountably "ladylike" behavior.

Hughes (1945, p. 357) suggests that such contradictions may be countered by managing interactions on a very narrow basis, for example, "keeping the relationship formal and specific." But the heart of the matter is that even—perhaps, especially— if the relationship is a formal one, gender is still something one is accountable for. Thus a woman physician (notice the special qualifier in her case) may be accorded respect for her skill and even addressed by an appropriate title. Nonetheless, she is subject to evaluation in terms of normative conceptions of appropriate attitudes and activities for her sex category and under pressure to prove that she is an "essentially" feminine being, despite appearances to the contrary (West 1984, pp. 97–101). Her sex category is used to discredit her participation in important clinical activities (Lorber 1984, pp. 52–54), while her involvement in medicine is used to discredit her commitment to her responsibilities as a wife and mother (Bourne and Wikler 1978, pp. 435–37). Simultaneously, her exclusion from the physician colleague community is maintained and her accountability *as a woman* is ensured.

In this context, "role conflict" can be viewed as a dynamic aspect of our current "arrangement between the sexes" (Goffman 1977), an arrangement that provides for occasions on which persons of a particular sex category can "see" quite clearly that they are out of place and that if they were not there, their current troubles would not exist. What is at stake is, from the standpoint of interaction, the management of our "essential" natures, and from the standpoint of the individual, the continuing accomplishment of gender. If, as we have argued, sex category is omnirelevant, then any occasion, conflicted or not, offers the resources for doing gender.

We have sought to show that sex category and gender are managed properties of conduct that are contrived with respect to the fact that others will judge and respond to us in particular ways. We have claimed that a person's gender is not simply an aspect of what one is, but, more fundamentally, it is something that one *does*, and does recurrently, in interaction with others.

〽 GENDER, POWER, AND SOCIAL CHANGE

Let us return to the question: Can we avoid doing gender? Earlier, we proposed that insofar as sex category is used as a fundamental criterion for differentiation, doing gender is unavoidable. It is unavoidable because of the social consequences of sex-category membership: the allocation of power and resources not only in the domestic, economic, and political domains but also in the broad arena of interpersonal relations. In virtually any situation, one's sex category can be relevant, and one's performance as an incumbent of that category (i.e., gender) can be subjected to evaluation. Maintaining such pervasive and faithful assignment of lifetime status requires legitimation.

But doing gender also renders the social arrangements based on sex category accountable as normal and natural, that is, legitimate ways of organizing social life. Differences between women and men that are created by this process can then be portrayed as fundamental and enduring dispositions. In this light, the institutional arrangements of a society can be seen as responsive to the differences—the social order being merely an accommodation to the natural order. Thus if, in doing gender, men are also doing dominance and women are doing deference (cf. Goffman 1967, pp. 47–95), the resultant social order, which supposedly reflects "natural differences," is a powerful reinforcer and legitimator of hierarchical arrangements. Frye observes:

> For efficient subordination, what's wanted is that the structure not appear to be a cultural artifact kept in place by human decision or custom, but that it appear *natural*—that it appear to be quite a direct consequence of facts about the beast which are beyond the scope of human manipulation. . . . That we are trained to behave so differently as women and men, and to behave so differently toward women and men, itself contributes mightily to the appearance of extreme dimorphism, but also, the *ways* we act as women and men, and the *ways* we act toward women and men, mold our bodies and our minds to the shape of subordination and dominance. We do become what we practice being. (Frye 1983, p. 34)

If we do gender appropriately, we simultaneously sustain, reproduce, and render legitimate the institutional arrangements that are based on sex category. If we fail to do gender appropriately, we as individuals—not the institutional arrangements—may be called to account (for our character, motives, and predispositions).

Social movements such as feminism can provide the ideology and impetus to question existing arrangements, and the social support for individuals to explore alternatives to them. Legislative changes, such as that proposed by the Equal Rights Amendment, can also weaken the accountability of conduct to sex category, thereby affording the possibility of more widespread loosening of accountability in general. To be sure, equality under the law does not guarantee equality in other arenas. As Lorber (1986, p. 577) points out, assurance of "scrupulous equality of categories of people considered essentially different needs constant monitoring."

What such proposed changes *can* do is provide the warrant for asking why, if we wish to treat women and men as equals, there needs to be two sex categories at all (see Lorber 1986, p. 577).

The sex category/gender relationship links the institutional and interactional levels, a coupling that legitimates social arrangements based on sex category and reproduces their asymmetry in face-to-face interaction. Doing gender furnishes the interactional scaffolding of social structure, along with a built-in mechanism of social control. In appreciating the institutional forces that maintain distinctions between women and men, we must not lose sight of the interactional validation of those distinctions that confers upon them their sense of "naturalness" and "rightness."

Social change, then, must be pursued both at the institutional and cultural level of sex category and at the interactional level of gender. Such a conclusion is hardly novel. Nevertheless, we suggest that it is important to recognize that the analytical distinction between institutional and interactional spheres does not pose an either/or choice when it comes to the question of effecting social change.

⟨⟨ DISCUSSION QUESTIONS

1. What do the authors mean when they say that gender is something that we "do"?

2. How do the ideas in this article relate to those in Goffman's *Presentation of Self* article from the last section?

3. How does the act of "doing" gender in face-to-face interactions support and legitimize institutionalized gender differences?

4. Are the authors arguing that gendered differences in interactions are reflections of natural differences between men and women or that gendered differences in interactions have the effect of making what are really social differences appear natural?

5. What is the difference between sex, sex category, and gender? Why do the authors argue these distinctions are important?

6. Can you think of an example of an "institutionalized framework" (p. 149) that facilitates or demands that people "do" gender?

7. How do the institutional arrangements that support a dichotomous gender system (men and women) affect the social interactions of those who do not clearly identify with either gender?

⚞ REFERENCES

Bernstein, Richard. 1986. "France Jails 2 in Odd Case of Espionage." *New York Times* (May 11).

Blackwood, Evelyn. 1984. "Sexuality and Gender in Certain Native American Tribes: The Case of Cross-Gender Females." *Signs: Journal of Women in Culture and Society* 10:27–42.

Bourne, Patricia G., and Norma J. Wikler. 1978. "Commitment and the Cultural Mandate: Women in Medicine." *Social Problems* 25:430–40.

Cucchiari, Salvatore. 1981. "The Gender Revolution and the Transition from Bisexual Horde to Patrilocal Band: The Origins of Gender Hierarchy." Pp. 31–79 in *Sexual Meanings: The Cultural Construction of Gender and Sexuality*, edited by S. B. Ortner and H. Whitehead. New York: Cambridge.

Fishman, Pamela. 1978. "Interaction: The Work Women Do." *Social Problems* 25:397–406.

Frye, Marilyn. 1983. *The Politics of Reality: Essays in Feminist Theory*. Trumansburg, NY: The Crossing Press.

Garfinkel, Harold. 1967. *Studies in Ethnomethodology*. Englewood Cliffs, NJ: Prentice Hall.

Gerson, Judith M., and Kathy Peiss. 1985. "Boundaries, Negotiation, Consciousness: Reconceptualizing Gender Relations." *Social Problems* 32:317–31.

Goffman, Erving. 1967 (1956). "The Nature of Deference and Demeanor." Pp. 47–95 in *Interaction Ritual*. New York: Anchor/Doubleday.

—1976. "Gender Display." *Studies in the Anthropology of Visual Communication* 3:69–77.

—1977. "The Arrangement Between the Sexes." *Theory and Society* 4:301–31.

Henley, Nancy M. 1985. "Psychology and Gender." *Signs: Journal of Women in Culture and Society* 11:101–119.

Hill, W. W. 1935. "The Status of the Hermaphrodite and Transvestite in Navaho Culture." *American Anthropologist* 37:273–79.

Hughes, Everett C. 1945. "Dilemmas and Contradictions of Status." *American Journal of Sociology* 50:353–59.

Kessler, Suzanne J., and Wendy McKenna. 1978. *Gender: An Ethnomethodological Approach*. New York: Wiley.

Kollock, Peter, Philip Blumstein, and Pepper Schwartz. 1985. "Sex and Power in Interaction." *American Sociological Review* 50:34–46.

Lorber, Judith. 1984. *Women Physicians: Careers, Status and Power*. New York: Tavistock.

—1986. "Dismantling Noah's Ark." *Sex Roles* 14:567–80.

Martin, M. Kay, and Barbara Voorheis. 1975. *Female of the Species*. New York: Columbia University Press.

Mithers, Carol L. 1982. "My Life as a Man." *The Village Voice* 27 (October 5):1ff.

Money, John. 1974. "Prenatal Hormones and Postnatal Sexualization in Gender Identity Differentiation." Pp. 221–95 in *Nebraska Symposium on Motivation*, Vol. 21, edited by J. K. Cole and R. Dienstbier. Lincoln: University of Nebraska Press.

—and John G. Brennan. 1968. "Sexual Dimorphism in the Psychology of Female Transsexuals." *Journal of Nervous and Mental Disease* 147:487–99.

—and Anke, A. Ehrhardt. 1972. *Man and Woman/Boy and Girl.* Baltimore: John Hopkins.

—and Charles Ogunro. 1974. "Behavioral Sexology: Ten Cases of Genetic Male Intersexuality with Impaired Prenatal and Pubertal Androgenization," *Archives of Sexual Behavior* 3:181–206.

—and Patricia Tucker. 1975. *Sexual Signatures.* Boston: Little, Brown.

Morris, Jan. 1974. *Conundrum.* New York: Harcourt Brace Jovanovich.

Raymond, Janice G. 1979. *The Transsexual Empire.* Boston: Beacon.

Richards, Renee (with John Ames). 1983. *Second Serve: The Renee Richards Story.* New York: Stein and Day.

Sacks, Harvey. 1972. "On the Analyzability of Stories by Children." Pp. 325–45 in *Directions in Sociolinguistics,* edited by J. J. Gumperz and D. Hymes. New York: Holt, Rinehart & Winston.

Schutz, Alfred. 1943. "The Problem of Rationality in the Social World." *Economics* 10:130–49.

West, Candace. 1984. "When the Doctor is a 'Lady': Power, Status and Gender in Physician-Patient Encounters." *Symbolic Interaction* 7:87–106.

—and Bonita Iritani. 1985. "Gender Politics in Mate Selection: The Male-Older Norm." Paper presented at the Annual Meeting of the American Sociological Association, August, Washington, DC.

—and Don H. Zimmerman. 1983. "Small Insults: A Study of Interruptions in Conversations Between Unacquainted Persons." Pp. 102–17 in *Language, Gender and Society,* edited by B. Thorne, C. Kramarae, and N. Henley. Rowley, MA: Newbury House.

Wieder, D. Lawrence. 1974. *Language and Social Reality: The Case of Telling the Convict Code.* The Hague: Mouton.

Williams, Walter L. 1986. *The Spirit and the Flesh: Sexual Diversity in American Indian Culture.* Boston: Beacon.

Wilson, Thomas P. 1970. "Conceptions of Interaction and Forms of Sociological Explanation." *American Sociological Review* 35:697–710.

Zimmerman, Don H., and D. Lawrence Wieder. 1970. "Ethnomethodology and the Problem of Order: Comment on Denzin." Pp. 287–95 in *Understanding Everyday Life,* edited by J. Denzin. Chicago: Aldine.

NOTES

1. http://www.dailymail.co.uk/news/article-1389593/Kathy-Witterick-David-Stocker-raising-genderless-baby.html

2. This definition understates many complexities involved in the relationship between biology and culture (Jaggar 1983, pp. 106–13). However, our point is that the determination of an individual's sex classification is a *social* process through and through.

3. This is not to say that gender is a singular "thing," omnipresent in the same form historically or in every situation. Because normative conceptions of appropriate attitudes and activities for sex categories can vary across cultures and historical moments, the management of situated conduct in light of those expectations can take many different forms.

4. Bernstein (1986) reports an unusual case of espionage in which a man passing as a woman convinced a lover that he/she had given birth to "their" child, who, the lover, thought, "looked like" him.

5. For example, in 2009 South African track star Caster Semenya was required to undergo what was dubbed a "gender test" after her appearance and performance in the 800 meter world championships raised doubts about her sex.

AUTHORS' NOTE: *This article is based in part on a paper presented at the Annual Meeting of the American Sociological Association, Chicago, September 1977. For their helpful suggestions and encouragement, we thank Lynda Ames, Bettina Aptheker, Steven Clayman, Judith Gerson, the late Erving Goffman, Marilyn Lester, Judith Lorber, Robin Lloyd, Wayne Mellinger, Beth E. Schneider, Barrie Thorne, Thomas P. Wilson, and most especially, Sarah Fenstermaker Berk.*

15

Marked: Women in the Workplace

Deborah Tannen

In the previous article, West and Zimmerman note that we are always gendered beings. While other roles such as student, employee, or friend are performed only in certain interactions, there are no social circumstances where we are genderless. Certainly we may not consciously perceive that gender is relevant in an interaction, but that doesn't mean it isn't. The well-known phenomenon of women being judged first on what they look like and second on what they do or say is just one example of this. Yet the social requirement to enact and reproduce gender plays out differently for men and women.

One of the things that shapes our thinking and assumptions about gender is the tendency to leave unmarked *things that are masculine or male and to* mark *that which is feminine or female. This is the phenomenon that linguist Tannen is interested in exploring in this article. As she puts it, "The unmarked form of a word carries the meaning that goes without saying, what you think of when you're not thinking of anything special" (p. 161). Marked words then designate a special category. Sports leagues are a good example of this. The NBA is the National Basketball Association. The WNBA is the Women's National Basketball Association. NBA is unmarked, WMBA is marked.*

Excerpt from Chapter Four: "Marked: Women in the Workplace" pp. 107-117 from *Talking from 9 to 5: Women and Men at Work* by Deborah Tannen. Copyright © 1994 by Deborah Tannen. Reprinted by permission of HarperCollins Publishers and International Creative Management.

This is a concept that can also be applied to things like appearance and behavior. As Tannen notes in this piece, women's appearance in public is almost always marked. It means something to be a woman who wears makeup and heels, just as it means something to be a woman who does not. (In fact for a long time the phrase "a woman in comfortable shoes" was a euphemism for a lesbian!) The same, however, is not true for men and their appearance. Men have the option of having their appearance be unmarked.

Being unmarked is a reflection of what's considered normal, and what is normal tends to be both valued more and also reflective of power. The assumptions that markedness brings with it, to the workplace in particular, can not only be individually frustrating for women, but can also reinforce stereotypical assumptions about gender. For women in any type of work or professional setting, "Whatever she wears, whatever she calls herself, however she talks, will be fodder for interpretation about her character and competence" (p. 164). Just look at the attention given to the appearance of female politicians—in 2008 Sarah Palin and Hillary Clinton were both ridiculed for their appearance, one being deemed too attractive and one not attractive enough.[1] But no one used the relative attractiveness of Barack Obama and John McCain or Mitt Romney as a means of critiquing their fitness for political office.

As you read, think about what aspects of your presentation of self are marked or unmarked in your day-to-day activities.

Some years ago I was at a small working conference of four women and eight men. Instead of concentrating on the discussion, I found myself looking at the three other women at the table, thinking how each had a different style and how each style was coherent.

One woman had dark brown hair in a classic style that was a cross between Cleopatra and Plain Jane. The severity of her straight hair was softened by wavy bangs and ends that turned under. Because she was beautiful, the effect was more Cleopatra than plain.

The second woman was older, full of dignity and composure. Her hair was cut in a fashionable style that left her with only one eye, thanks to a side part that let a curtain of hair fall across half her face. As she looked down to read her prepared paper, the hair robbed her of binocular vision and created a barrier between her and the listeners.

The third woman's hair was wild, a frosted blond avalanche falling over and beyond her shoulders. When she spoke, she frequently tossed her head, thus calling attention to her hair and away from her lecture.

Then there was makeup. The first woman wore facial cover that made her skin smooth and pale, a black line under each eye, and mascara that darkened her already dark lashes. The second wore only a light gloss on her lips and a hint of shadow on her eyes. The third had blue bands under her eyes, dark blue shadow, mascara, bright red lipstick, and rouge; her fingernails also flashed red.

I considered the clothes each woman had worn on the three days of the conference: In the first case, man-tailored suits in primary colors with solid-color blouses. In the second, casual but stylish black T-shirt, a floppy collarless jacket and baggy slacks or skirt in neutral colors. The third wore a sexy jumpsuit; tight sleeveless jersey and tight yellow slacks; a dress with gaping armholes and an indulged tendency to fall off one shoulder.

Shoes? The first woman wore string sandals with medium heels; the second, sensible, comfortable walking shoes; the third, pumps with spike heels. You can fill in the jewelry, scarves, shawls, sweaters—or lack of them.

As I amused myself finding patterns and coherence in these styles and choices, I suddenly wondered why I was scrutinizing only the women. I scanned the table to get a fix on the styles of the eight men. And then I knew why I wasn't studying them. The men's styles were unmarked.

The term "marked" is a staple of linguistic theory. It refers to the way language alters the base meaning of a word by adding something—a little linguistic addition that has no meaning on its own. The unmarked form of a word carries the meaning that goes without saying, what you think of when you're not thinking anything special.

The unmarked tense of verbs in English denotes the present—for example, *visit*. To indicate past, you have to mark the verb for "past" by adding ed to yield *visited*. For future, you add a word: will *visit*. Nouns are presumed to be singular until marked for plural. To convey the idea of more than one, we typically add something, usually s or es. More than one visit becomes visits, and one *dish* becomes two *dishes*, thanks to the plural marking.

The unmarked forms of most English words also convey "male." Being male is the unmarked case. We have endings, such as *ess* and *ette*, to mark words as female. Unfortunately, marking words for female also, by association, tends to mark them for frivolousness. Would you feel safe entrusting your life to a doctorette? This is why many poets and actors who happen to be female object to the marked forms "poetess" and "actress." Alfre Woodard, an Oscar nominee for Best Supporting Actress, says she identifies herself as an actor because actresses worry about eyelashes and cellulite, and women who are actors worry about the characters we are playing. Any marked form can pick up extra meaning beyond what the marking is intended to denote. The extra meanings carried by gender markers reflect the traditional associations with the female gender: not quite serious, often sexual.

I was able to identify the styles and types of the women at the conference because each of us had to make decisions about hair, clothing, makeup and accessories, and each of those decisions carried meaning. Every style available to us was marked. Of course, the men in our group had to make decisions too, but their choices carried far less meaning. The men could have chosen styles that were marked, but they didn't have to, and in this group, none did. Unlike the women, they had the option of being unmarked.

I took account of the men's clothes. There could have been a cowboy shirt with string tie or a three-piece suit or a necklaced hippie in jeans. But there wasn't. All eight men wore brown or blue slacks and standard-style shirts of light colors.

No man wore sandals or boots; their shoes were dark, closed, comfortable, and flat. In short, unmarked.

Although no man wore makeup, you couldn't say the men didn't wear makeup in the sense that you could say a woman didn't wear makeup. For men, no makeup is unmarked. I asked myself what style we women could have adopted that would have been unmarked, like the men's. The answer was: none. There is no unmarked woman.

There is no woman's hairstyle that could be called "standard," that says nothing about her. The range of women's hairstyles is staggering, but if a woman's hair has no particular style, this in itself is taken as a statement that she doesn't care how she looks—an eloquent message that can disqualify a woman for many positions.

Women have to choose between shoes that are comfortable and shoes that are deemed attractive. When our group had to make an unexpected trek, the woman who wore flat laced shoes arrived first. The last to arrive was the woman with spike heels, her shoes in her hand and a handful of men around her.

If a woman's clothes are tight or revealing (in other words, sexy), it sends a message—an intended one of wanting to be attractive but also a possibly unintended one of availability. But if her clothes are not sexy, that too sends a message, lent meaning by the knowledge that they could have been. In her book *Women Lawyers,* Mona Harrington quotes a woman who, despite being a partner in her firm, found herself slipping into this fault line when she got an unexpected call to go to court right away. As she headed out the door, a young (male) associate said to her, "Hadn't you better button your blouse?" She was caught completely off guard. "My blouse wasn't buttoned unusually low," the woman told Harrington. "And this was not a conservative guy. But he thought one more button was necessary for court." And here's the rub: "I started wondering if my authority was being undermined by one button."

A woman wearing bright colors calls attention to herself, but if she avoids bright colors, she has (as my choice of verb in this sentence suggests) avoided something. Heavy makeup calls attention to the wearer as someone who wants to be attractive.

Light makeup tries to be attractive without being alluring. There are thousands of products from which makeup must be chosen and myriad ways of applying them. Yet no makeup at all is anything but unmarked. Some men even see it as a hostile refusal to please them. Women who ordinarily do not wear makeup can be surprised by the transforming effect of putting it on. In a book titled *Face Value*, my colleague Robin Lakoff noted the increased attention she got from men when she went forth from a television station srill professionally made-up.

Women can't even fill out a form without telling stories about themselves. Most application forms now give four choices for titles. Men have one to choose—"Mr."—so their choice carries no meaning other than to say they are male. But women must choose among three, each of them marked. A woman who checks the box for "Mrs." or "Miss" communicates not only whether she has been married but also that she has conservative tastes in forms of address, and probably other conservative values as well. Checking "Ms." declines to let on about marriage (whereas "Mr." declines nothing since nothing was asked), but it also marks the woman who checks it on her form as either liberated or rebellious, depending on the attitudes and assumptions of the one making the judgment.

I sometimes try to duck these variously marked choices by giving my title as "Dr."—and thereby risk marking myself as either uppity (hence sarcastic responses like "Excuse me!") or an over achiever (hence reactions of congratulatory surprise, like "Good for you!").

All married women's surnames are marked. If a woman takes her husband's name, she announces to the world that she is married and also that she is traditional in her values, according to some observers. To others it will indicate that she is less herself, more identified by her husband's identity. If she does not take her husband's name, this too is marked, seen as worthy of comment: She has done something; she has "kept her own name." Though a man can do exactly the same thing—and usually does—he is never said to have "kept his own name," because it never occurs to anyone that he might have given it up. For him, but not for her, using his own name is unmarked.

A married woman who wants to have her cake and eat it too may use her surname plus his. But this too announces that she is or has been married and often results in a tongue-tying string that makes life miserable for anyone who needs to alphabetize it. In a list (Harvey O'Donovan, Jonathon Feldman, Stephanie Woodbury McGillicutty), the woman's multiple name stands out. It is marked.

Pronouns conspire in this pattern as well. Grammar books tell us that "he" means "he or she" and that "she" is used only if a referent is specifically female. But this touting of "he" as the sex-indefinite pronoun is an innovation introduced into English by grammarians in the eighteenth and nineteenth centuries, according to Peter Miihlhausler and Rom Harre in their book *Pronouns and People*.

From at least about the year 1500, the correct sex-indefinite pronoun was "they," as it still is in casual spoken English. In other words, the female was declared by grammarians to be the marked case.

Looking at the men and women sitting around the conference table, I was amazed at how different our worlds were. Though men have to make choices too, and men's clothing styles may be less neutral now than they once were, nonetheless the parameters within which men must choose when dressing for work—the cut, fabric, or shade of jackets, shirts, and pants, and even the one area in which they are able to go a little wild, ties—are much narrower than the riotous range of colors and styles from which women must choose. For women, decisions about whether to wear a skirt, slacks, or a dress is only the start; the length of skirts can range from just above the floor to just below the hips, and the array of colors to choose from would make a rainbow look drab. But even this contrast in the range from which men and women must choose is irrelevant to the crucial point: A man can choose a style that will not attract attention or subject him to any particular interpretation, but a woman can't. Whatever she wears, whatever she calls herself, however she talks, will be fodder for interpretation about her character and competence. In a setting where most of the players are men, there is no unmarked woman.

This does not mean that men have complete freedom when it comes to dress. Quite the contrary—they have much less freedom than women have to express their personalities in their choice of fabrics, colors, styles, and jewelry. But the one freedom they have that women don't is the point of this discussion—the freedom to be unmarked.

That clothing is a metaphor for women's being marked was noticed by David Finkel, a journalist who wrote an article about women in Congress for *The Washington Post Magazine*. He used the contrast between women's and men's dress to open his article by describing the members coming through the doors to the floor of the U.S. House of Representatives:

> So many men, so many suits. Dark suits. Solid suits. Blue suits that look gray, gray suits that look blue. There's Tom Foley—he's in one, and Bob Michel, and Steny Hoyer, and Fred Grandy, and Dick Durbin, and dozens, make that hundreds, more.

So many suits, so many white shirts. And dark ties. And five o'clock shadows. And short haircuts. And loosening jowls. And big, visible ears.
So many, many men.
. . .

And still the members continue to pour through the doors—gray, grayer, grayest—until the moment when, emerging into this humidor, comes a surprise:

The color red.

It is Susan Molinari, a first-termer from New York . . .

Now, turquoise. It is Barbara Boxer . . .

Now, paisley. It is Jill Long . . .

Embroidering his color-of-clothing metaphor, Finkel, whose article appeared in May 1992, concluded, "Of the 435 members of the House of Representatives, 29 are women, which means that if Congress is a gray flannel suit, the women of Congress are no more than a handful of spots on the lapel."

〰 WHEN IS SEXISM REALISM?

If women are marked in our culture, their very presence in professional roles is, more often than not, marked. Many work settings, just like families, come with ready-made roles prescribed by gender, and the ones women are expected to fill are typically support roles. It was not long ago when medical offices and hospitals were peopled by men who were doctors and orderlies and women who were nurses and clerical workers, just as most offices were composed of men who ran the business and women who served them as receptionists, clerks, and secretaries. All members of Congress were men, and women found in the Capitol Building were aides and staff members. When a woman or man enters a setting in an atypical role, that expectation is always a backdrop to the scene.

All the freshmen women in Congress have had to contend with being mistaken for staff, even though they wear pins on their lapels identifying them as members. For her book A *Woman's Place,* Congresswoman Marjorie Margolies-Mezvinsky interviewed her female colleagues about their experiences. One congresswoman approached a security checkpoint with two congressmen when a guard stopped only her and told her to go through the metal detector. When Congresswoman Maria Cantwell needed to get into her office after hours, the guard wanted to know which member she worked for. But her press secretary, Larry West, has gone through the gate unthinkingly without being stopped. When Congresswoman Lynn Schenk attended a reception with a male aide, the host graciously held out his hand to the aide and said, "Oh, Congressman Schenk."

You don't have to be in Congress to have experiences like that. A woman who owned her own business found that if she took any man along on business trips, regardless of whether he was her vice president or her assistant, people she met tended to address themselves to him, certain that he must be the one with power and she his helper. A double-bass player had a similar experience when she arrived for an audition with a male accompanist. The people who greeted them assumed she was the accompanist. A woman who heads a research firm and holds a doctorate finds she is frequently addressed as "Mrs.," while her assistant, who holds only a Master's degree, is addressed as "Dr."

One evening after hours, I was working in my office at Georgetown University. Faculty offices in my building are lined up on both sides of a corridor, with cubicles in the corridor for secretaries and graduate-student assistants. Outside each office is a nameplate with the professor's title and last name. The quiet of the after-hours corridor was interrupted when a woman came to my door and asked if she could use my phone. I was surprised but glad to oblige, and explained that she had to dial "9." She made the call, thanked me, and left. A few minutes later, she reappeared and asked if I had any correction fluid. Again surprised, but still happy to be of help, I looked in my desk drawer but had to disappoint her: Since my typewriter was self-correcting, I had none. My patience began to waver, but my puzzlement was banished when the woman bounded into my office for the third and final time to ask if I was Dr. Murphy's secretary, in which case she would like to leave with me the paper she was turning in to him.

I doubt this woman would have imposed on my time and space to use my telephone and borrow correction fluid if she had known I was a professor, even though I would not have minded had she done so. At least she would probably have been more deferential in intruding. And the experience certainly gave me a taste of how hard it must be for receptionists to get any work done, as everyone regards them as perpetually interruptible. But what amused and amazed me was that my being female had overridden so many clues to my position: My office was along the wall, it was fully enclosed like all faculty offices, my name and title were on the door, and I was working after five, the hour when offices close and secretaries go home. But all these clues were nothing next to the master clue of gender: In the university environment, she expected that professors were men and women were secretaries. Statistics were on her side: Of the eighteen members of my department at the time, sixteen were men; of the five members of Dr. Murphy's department, four were men. So she was simply trusting the world to be as she knew it was. It is not particularly ironic or surprising that the student who mistook me for a secretary was female. Women are no less prone to assume that people will adhere to the norm than are men. And this includes women who themselves are exceptions. A woman physician who works in a specialty in which few of her colleagues are female told me of her annoyance when she telephones a colleague, identifies herself as "Dr. Jones calling for Dr. Smith," and is told by Dr. Smith's receptionist, "I'll go get Dr. Smith while you put Dr. Jones on the line." But this same woman catches herself referring to her patients' general practitioners as "he," even though she ought to know better than anyone that a physician could be a woman.

Children seem to pick up norms as surely as adults do. A woman who was not only a doctor but a professor at a medical school was surprised when her five-year-old said to her, "You're not a doctor, Mommy. You're a nurse." Intent on impressing her daughter, she said, "Yes, I am a doctor. In fact, I teach other doctors how to be doctors." The little girl thought about this as she incorporated the knowledge into her worldview. "Oh," she said. "But you only teach women doctors." (Conversely, male nurses must deal with being mistaken for doctors, and men who work as assistants must deal with being mistaken for their boss.)

Another of my favorite stories in this mode is about my colleague who made a plane reservation for herself and replied to the question "Is that Mrs. or Miss?" by giving her title: "It's Dr." So the agent asked, "Will the doctor be needing a rental car when he arrives?" Her attempt to reframe her answer to avoid revealing her marital status resulted in the agent refraining her as a secretary.

I relate these stories not to argue that sexism is rampant and that we should all try to bear in mind that roles are changing, although I believe these statements to be true. I am inclined to be indulgent of such errors, even though I am made uncomfortable when they happen to me, because I myself have been guilty of them. I recall an occasion when I gave a talk to a gathering of women physicians, and then signed books. The woman who organized the signing told me to save one book because she had met a doctor in the elevator who couldn't make it to the talk but asked to have a book signed nonetheless. I was pleased to oblige and asked, pen poised, to whom I should sign the book—and was surprised when I heard a woman's name. Even though I had just spent the evening with a room full of doctors who were all women, in my mind "a doctor" had called up the image of a man.

So long as women are a minority of professional ranks, we cannot be surprised if people assume the world is as it is. I mention these stories to give a sense of what the world is like for people who are exceptions to expectations—every moment they live in the unexpected role, they must struggle against others' assumptions that do not apply to them, much like gay men and lesbians with regard to their sexual orientation, and, as Ellis Cose documents in his book *The Rage of a Privileged Class*, much like middle-class black professionals in most American settings.

One particular burden of this pattern for a woman in a position of authority is that she must deal with incursions on her time, as others make automatic assumptions that her time is more expendable, although she also may benefit from hearing more information because people find her "approachable." There is a sense in which every woman is seen as a receptionist—available to give information and help, perennially interruptible. A woman surgeon complained that although she has very good relations with the nurses in her hospital, they simply do not wait on her the way they wait on her male colleagues. (The very fact that I must say "woman surgeon" and "male nurse" reflects this dilemma: All surgeons are presumed male, all nurses presumed female, unless proven otherwise. In other words, the unmarked surgeon is male, the unmarked nurse female.

ⲷ A BRAID IS A STRONGER ROPE

Although I describe patterns of women's and men's typical (not universal) styles, and show that styles expected of women can work against them in work settings, I would not advise women to adopt men's style to succeed—although in some cases and in some ways, this might work. In general, that advice is no more practical than advising women to go to work dressed in men's clothes. Instead, I would argue for flexibility and mutual understanding. The frustration of both genders will be reduced, and companies as well as individuals will benefit, if women and men (like Easterners and Southerners, old and young, and people of different classes and ethnic backgrounds) understand each other's styles. Once you understand what is happening to you, you can experiment on your own, trying new ways of behaving to solve your problems. Of course, all problems will not summarily disappear, but the sense of puzzlement and lack of control will at least subside.

Another reason it would be a mistake for women to try to behave like men is that businesses need to communicate with clients of different sorts, including more and more women. For instance, newspapers need to appeal to women as readers in order to sell newspapers, so it would do them no good to hire a slew of women who are just like men. I sometimes give the example of a woman who worked at an appraisal firm. One of her colleagues told her he had just gotten a very strange call from a client. After identifying herself, the client simply told him that she would be going on vacation that week and hung up, without giving him any comprehensible reason for her call. The woman who told me this said she was pretty sure she understood what this was about and called the client back to apologize for the slight delay in the appraisal she had ordered and reassure her that it would be ready when she returned from her vacation.

The appraiser also told me that she had been nonplussed by a client who called her up and began angrily berating her because his appraisal was late. Taken aback by the verbal assault, which seemed to her unacceptable in the context of a business relationship, she had become tongue-tied and unable to give him the assurances she had just given the other client, so she had her colleague call the man back and deal with him. This example shows how pointless it would be to ask which appraiser's style was "best." Each one was best at dealing with certain clients. Rather than trying to determine which style is best and hire a staff with uniform styles, the company clearly is benefiting from having a range of styles among its sales staff.

⚜ WILL TALK ABOUT GENDER DIFFERENCES POLARIZE?

Some people fear that putting people into two categories by talking about "women" and "men" can drive a wedge between us, polarizing us even more. This is a serious concern. I know of at least one instance in which that is exactly what happened. A female executive at a large accounting firm was so well thought of by her firm that they sent her to a weeklong executive-training seminar at the company's expense. Not surprisingly, considering the small number of women at her level, she was the only woman at the seminar, which was composed of high-ranking executives from a variety of the corporation's wide-ranging divisions. This did not surprise or faze her, since she was used to being the only woman among men.

All went well for the first three days of the seminar. But on the fourth, the leaders turned their attention to issues of gender. Suddenly, everyone who had been looking at her as "one of us" began to look at her differently—as a woman, "one of them." She was repeatedly singled out and asked to relate her experiences and impressions, something she did not feel she could do honestly, since she had no reason to believe they would understand or accept what she was talking about. When they said confidently that they were sure there was no discrimination against women in their company, that if women did not get promoted it was simply because they didn't merit promotion, she did not feel she could object. Worst of all, she had to listen to one after another of her colleagues express what she found to be offensive opinions about women's abilities. By the end of the day, she was so demoralized that she was questioning whether she wanted to continue to work for this company at all. Whereas she had started out feeling completely comfortable, not thinking of herself as different from the men, the discussion of gender issues made her acutely aware of how different she was and convinced her she could never again fit comfortably into this group.

The group in which this occurred was made up of people from far-flung offices, not many of whom were from her own home office. As a result, she was able eventually to get past the experience, and it did not poison her day-to-day relationships at work. If a similar workshop had been held among her daily co-workers, it could have been much more destructive. And the saddest part is that the unfortunate outcome resulted from a program designed to help. As anthropologist Gregory Bateson explained in his work on cybernetics, any time people interfere with a system to change it, they risk making things worse, because they don't understand all the elements in the system and how they interrelate.

But the alternative, doing nothing, is not a viable one, because the situation as it is will have to change. In the case of women in the workplace, the situation is changing, whether we talk about it or not. And the hope that all we had to do was open the doors and let women in has simply not been borne out. Twenty years after women began receiving MBAs and entering businesses where they had not been before, they still make up only a small percentage of higher-level executives. The "pipeline" argument has simply not panned out. Years after women entered the pipeline, they just aren't coming through the other end in proportion to their numbers going in. Instead, more and more women are leaving the corporate world, in greater numbers than men, either to start their own businesses, to be independent contractors, or to do other things entirely. (For example, a 1993 survey of those who received MBAs from Stanford University over rhe preceding ten-year period found that 22% of the women, as compared to 8% of the men, had left large corporations to start their own businesses.) Some of this may be a privilege that men too would take advantage of if they had the chance. But a lot of women are seeking alternatives simply because they tire of feeling like strangers in a strange land when they go to work each day, in a word each day. In a word they tire of being marked.

Simply opening the doors and letting in women, or any individuals whose styles do not conform to those already in place, is not enough. As the experience of the executive at the training seminar showed, neither are localized efforts at diversity training, though surely these can help if they are done well. Finally, we can't just tell individuals that they should simply talk one way or another, as if ways of talking were hats you can put on when you enter an office and take off when you leave. For one thing, if you try to adopt a style that does not come naturally to you, you leave behind your intuitions and may well behave in ways inappropriate in any style or betray the discomfort you actually feel. Most important, we do not regard the way we talk—how we say what we mean, how we show consideration or frustration to others—as superficial, masks to be donned and doffed at will. Comprehensive training and awareness are needed, until everyone is working to make the workplace a world where differing styles are understood and appreciated.

DISCUSSION QUESTIONS

1. Whatever your school mascot, how does your school refer to men and women's sports teams on campus? Are the female teams marked or unmarked? Why does this matter?

2. Tannen's article is largely about perceptions of men and women in the workplace. Do you think that her observations hold true in a college setting? Are women marked in class by their appearance? What about in dorms or at parties? When, if at all, might men be marked at school?

3. At the end of the article, Tannen says she doesn't think advising women to act more like men is advisable. Do you agree or disagree with her? How might women behaving more assertively and aggressively backfire? How might it be beneficial?

NOTE

1. For an excellent commentary on this phenomenon using humor see http://www.nbc.com/saturday-night-live/video/sarah-palin-and-hillary-clinton-address-the-nation/n12287

16

The Boy Code

William Pollack

Discussions of gender often focus on women. This is due partly to the importance of noting the sexism that exists in both institutional arrangements and daily life for women. But associating women with the term gender *has additional significance. If you signed up for a class on gender studies, you'd probably assume that you'd be talking mostly about women (race is similarly associated with minorities rather than Whites.) This tendency to think of gender as female implies that men are somehow genderless beings, and nothing could be further from the truth. While many times maleness and masculinity are considered unmarked and normal, gender is still an important social characteristic for men and one that has significant implications. In many ways, men's adherence to what society considers appropriate gender performance is much more strictly enforced, usually by other men, than women's gender performance. Clothing choices are a good example of this. While the previous article noted that women's clothing choices are always marked, women do have many more options than men. A woman can choose to wear a pantsuit or a suit with a skirt. Men cannot make the same choice without significant and severe social ramifications. So while men have the option to be unmarked, they also have fewer options. This is true of behavior as well as appearance. This asymmetry in enforcement of gender roles is referred to as the* gender straightjacket.

Originally titled as Inside the world of boys by William Pollack 1998.

Excerpts from *Real Boys: Rescuing Our Sons from the Myths of Boyhood* by William Pollack. Copyright © 1998 by William Pollack. Used by permission of Random House, an imprint and division of Random House LLC and Zachary Shuster Harmsworth LLC as agents for the author. All rights reserved.

In this article, William Pollack sketches out the dimensions of what he calls the boy code. This set of "assumptions, models, and rules about boys" (p. 176) work as norms for masculinity in contemporary American society. Boys as young as four and five quickly learn that being stoic, being tough and aggressive if necessary, achieving status and power, and avoiding attributes associated with girls are imperative to learning to be a society's definition of a man. As boys grow to adulthood, the boy code is repeatedly reinforced by peer groups, schools, workplaces, and popular culture. As Pollack argues, this has significant negative consequences for boys and men.

As you read, think about where in your culture elements of the boy code are visible. Can you think of any examples from popular culture or your own experiences where elements of the boy code are being challenged?

A dam is a fourteen-year-old boy whose mother sought me out after a workshop I was leading on the subject of boys and families. Adam, she told me, had been performing very well in school, but now she felt something was wrong.

Adam had shown such promise that he had been selected to join a special program for talented students, and the program was available only at a different—and more academically prestigious—school than the one Adam had attended. The new school was located in a well-to-do section of town, more affluent than Adam's own neighborhood. Adam's mother had been pleased when her son had qualified for the program and even more delighted that he would be given a scholarship to pay for it. And so Adam had set off on this new life.

At the time we talked, Mrs. Harrison's delight had turned to worry. Adam was not doing well at the new school. His grades were mediocre, and at midterm he had been given a warning that he might fail algebra. Yet Adam continued to insist, "I'm fine. Everything's just fine." He said this both at home and at school. Adam's mother was perplexed, as was the guidance counselor at his new school. "Adam seems cheerful and has no complaints," the counselor told her. "But something must be wrong." His mother tried to talk to Adam, hoping to find out what was troubling him and causing him to do so poorly in school. "But the more I questioned him about what was going on," she said, "the more he continued to deny any problems."

Adam was a quiet and rather shy boy, small for his age. In his bright blue eyes I detected an inner pain, a malaise whose cause I could not easily fathom. I had seen a similar look on the faces of a number of boys of different ages, including many boys in the "Listening to Boys' Voices" study. Adam looked wary, hurt, closed-in, self-protective. Most of all, he looked alone.

One day, his mother continued, Adam came home with a black eye. She asked him what had happened. "Just an accident," Adam had mumbled. He'd kept his eyes cast down, she remembered, as if he felt guilty or ashamed. His mother probed more deeply. She told him that she knew something was wrong, something upsetting was going on, and that—whatever it was—they could deal with it, they could face it together. Suddenly, Adam erupted in tears, and the story he had been holding inside came pouring out.

Adam was being picked on at school, heckled on the bus, goaded into fights in the schoolyard. "Hey, White Trash!" the other boys shouted at him. "You don't belong here with *us*" taunted a twelfth-grade bully. "Why don't you go back to your own side of town!" The taunts often led to physical attacks, and Adam found himself having to fight back in order to defend himself. "But I never throw the first punch," Adam explained to his mother. "I don't show them they can hurt me. I don't want to embarrass myself in front of everybody."

I turned to Adam. "How do you feel about all this?" I asked. "How do you handle your feelings of anger and frustration?" His answer was, I'm sad to say, a refrain I hear often when I am able to connect to the inner lives of boys.

"I get a little down," Adam confessed, "but I'm very good at hiding it. It's like I wear a mask. Even when the kids call me names or taunt me, I never show them how much it crushes me inside. I keep it all in."

"What do you do with the sadness?" I asked.

"I tend to let it boil inside until I can't hold it any longer, and then it explodes. It's like I have a breakdown, screaming and yelling. But I only do it inside my own room at home, where nobody can hear. Where nobody will know about it." He paused a moment. "I think I got this from my dad, unfortunately."

Adam was doing what I find so many boys do: he was hiding behind a mask, and using it to hide his deepest thoughts and feelings—his real self—from everyone, even the people closest to him. This mask of masculinity enabled Adam to make a bold (if inaccurate) statement to the world: "I can handle it. Everything's fine. I am invincible."

⁂ THE GENDER STRAITJACKET

Many years ago, when I began my research into boys, I had assumed that since America was revising its ideas about girls and women, it must have also been reevaluating its traditional ideas about boys, men, and masculinity. But over the years my research findings have shown that as far as boys today are concerned, the old Boy Code—the outdated and constricting assumptions, models, and rules about boys that our society has used since the nineteenth century—is still operating in force. I have been surprised to find that even in the most progressive schools and the most politically correct communities in every part of the country and in families of all types, the Boy Code continues to affect the behavior of all of us—the boys themselves, their parents, their teachers, and society as a whole. None of us is immune—it is so ingrained. I have caught myself behaving in accordance with the code, despite my awareness of its falseness—denying sometimes that I'm emotionally in pain when in fact I am; insisting that everything is all right, when it is not.

The Boy Code puts boys and men into a gender straitjacket that constrains not only them but everyone else, reducing us all as human beings, and eventually making us strangers to ourselves and to one another—or, at least, not as strongly connected to one another as we long to be.

The Boy Code is so strong, yet so subtle, in its influence that boys may not even know they are living their lives in accordance with it. In fact, they may not realize there is such a thing until they violate the code in some way or try to ignore it. When they do, however, society tends to let there know—swiftly and forcefully— in the form of a taunt by a sibling, rebuke by a parent or a teacher, or ostracism by classmates.

But, it doesn't have to be this way. I know that Adam could have been saved a great deal of pain if his parents and the well-meaning school authorities had known how to help him, how to make him feel safe to express his real feelings, beginning with the entirely natural anxiety about starting at a new school. This could have eased the transition from on school to a new one, rather than leaving Adam to tough it out by himself—even though Adam would have said, "Everything's all right."

◊ THE BOY CODE: FOUR INJUNCTIONS

Boys learn the Boy Code in sandboxes, playgrounds, schoolrooms, camps, churches, and hangouts, and are taught by peers, coaches, teachers, and just about everybody else. In the "Listening to Boys' Voices" study, even very young boys reported that they felt they must "keep a stiff upper lip," "not show their feelings," "act real tough," "not act too nice," "be cool," "just laugh and brush it off when someone punches you." These boys were not referring to subtle suggestions about how they "might" comport themselves. Rather, they were invoking strict rules they had absorbed about how they "must" behave, rules that most of them seemed to genuinely fear breaking.

Relying on well-known research, Professors Deborah David and Robert Brannon divided these kinds of do-or-die rules, or "injunctions," boys follow into four basic stereotyped male ideals or models of behavior. These four imperatives are at the heart of the Boy Code.

The "sturdy oak"

Men should be stoic, stable, and independent. A man never shows weakness. Accordingly, boys are not to share pain or grieve openly. Boys are considered to have broken this guideline, for instance, if they whimper, cry, or complain—or sometimes even if they simply ask for an explanation in a confusing or frightening situation. As one boy in the "Voices" study put it: "If somebody slugs you in the face, probably the best thing you could do is just smile and act like it didn't hurt. You definitely shouldn't cry or say anything." The "sturdy oak" requirement drains boys' energy because it calls upon them to perform a constant "acting job"—to pretend to be confident when they may feel afraid, sturdy when they may feel shaky, independent when they may be desperate for love, attention, and support.

"Give 'em hell."

This is the stance of some of our sports coaches, of roles played by John Wayne, Clint Eastwood, and Bruce Lee, a stance based on a false self, of extreme daring, bravado, and attraction to violence. This injunction stems largely from the myth that "boys will be boys," —the misconception that somehow boys are biologically wired to act like macho, high-energy, even violent supermen. This is the Boy Code requirement that leads many boys to "dare" each other to engage in risky behaviors and that causes some parents to simply shrug their shoulders if their sons injure themselves or others.

The "big wheel"

This is the imperative men and boys feel to achieve status, dominance, and power. Or, understood another way, the "big wheel" refers to the way in which boys and men are taught to avoid shame at all costs, to wear the mask of coolness, to act as though everything is going all right, as though everything is under control, even if it isn't. This Boy Code imperative leads many boys and men to push themselves excessively at academic or career-related work, often in an effort to repress feelings of failure or unhappiness.

"No sissy stuff"

Perhaps the most traumatizing and dangerous injunction thrust on boys and men is the literal gender straitjacket that prohibits boys from expressing feelings or urges seen (mistakenly) as "feminine"—dependence, warmth, empathy. According to the ideal of "no sissy stuff," such feelings and behaviors are taboo. Rather than being allowed to explore these emotional states and activities, boys are prematurely forced to shut them out, to become self-reliant. And when boys start to break under the strain, when nonetheless they display "feminine" feelings or behaviors, they are usually greeted not with empathy but with ridicule, with taunts and threats that shame them for their failure to act and feel in stereotypically "masculine" ways. And so boys become determined never to act that way again—they bury those feelings.

And so in several fundamental ways the Boy Code affects the ability of boys and adults to connect.

First, it separates boys from their parents too early, before most boys are actually emotionally prepared for it. When boys encounter some of early childhood's most trying times—when they sleep alone in a crib for the first time, are sent away for two weeks of summer camp, or separate from their parents for the first day of kindergarten—they are often being pushed toward pseudo-independence before they're really ready.

Yet when boys rebel against this push to separate—when they cry, get injured, or tell friends that they'd rather stay at home than go outside and play—society's Boy Code makes them feel ashamed of themselves. Shame haunts many boys all their lives, undermining their core of self-confidence, eroding their fragile self-esteem, leaving them with profound feelings of loneliness, sadness, and disconnection. Moreover, it affects our ability to fully connect with our boys.

Even when boys appear sad or afraid, our culture lets them know in no uncertain terms that they had better toughen up and "tough it out" by themselves. The feelings boys are forced to repress become so troubling that some boys may show the apparent symptoms of attention deficit disorder and serious conduct disorders, become depressed, and—when they're older—turn to alcohol or drugs. Indeed, the same kind of shame that silences adolescent girls from expressing their true voice affects boys at a much younger age—at the age of five or six.

But the good news, I also believe, is that neither boys nor the adults who care for them need to live by these rules. Boys can rebel against them and revise the code for boys and girls so that they can experience a broad range of feelings and behaviors. Parents do not have to resist their deepest feelings for their sons or let myths about boys overwhelm the wisdom of their own instincts. Together we can unlearn the Boy Code. Together we can insist on enjoying close, emotionally rich relationships, based on connection instead of disconnection.

⫸ HELPING BOYS RECONNECT: A PRIMER FOR PARENTS

As powerful as the cultural imperatives of the Boy Code may be in pushing boys of all ages to separate from their parents, toughen themselves up and restrict their emotional lives, there is a lot we can do as adults to help boys overcome these conventional pressures. Here are some basic guidelines I would suggest:

At least once a day, give your boy your undivided attention

This means you're not speaking with someone else, you're not simultaneously trying to cook, clean, read, or do some other task. You're listening closely. He's got your attention. While sometimes he may not want to talk—while he may just want to play a game, get some help on his homework, or complain about having to do chores—showing him this attention, even if he doesn't always soak it up, gives him the message that you're there, that you care, and that he has a daily time and place when he can share things with you. It's not important that he always unload heavy emotions on you. And he may signal that he prefers to talk about things at some later point. He just needs to feel your regular loving presence and know that you're eager to know what's happening in his world.

Encourage the expression of a full range of emotions

From the moment a boy is born and throughout his life, it's important he gets the message that all of his emotions are valid. With an infant, this means we need to mirror back all of the feelings the baby expresses. Rather than forcing him to constantly smile or laugh, we also need to show him we're receptive to his sadness, fear, or other painful emotions. So when a young infant begins to frown, yawn, kick, or cry, rather than trying to "cheer him up" or "smooth things over" by making happy faces at him or ignoring his displays of discomfort, show him your empathy, let him know you understand how he's feeling, and show him with your words, facial expressions, and gestures that you respect and understand his genuine feelings. With toddlers and school-age boys, we need to ask questions—"What happened?" "Are you feeling sad about something?" "Tell me what's making you unhappy"—and, again, express our empathy—"Gee, that sounds unfair!" "I'm sorry it hurts so much." We also need to use a broad range of emotion words—happy, sad, tired, disappointed, scared, nervous rather than limiting our discussion of emotions to words such as "anger" that force boys to channel the gamut of their feelings into one word and one emotion.

In our daily attention-giving time with our sons, we need to pay close attention to what he's saying and how he's acting. If he complains, expresses fears or anxieties, cries, or otherwise shows emotions that reveal he's hurting, ask him what he's going through and let him talk about all that he is experiencing. With an older boy, be sure to ask him questions about his relationships with girls, with other boys, with his siblings, teachers, and other friends and acquaintances. Ask him to share with you not only what's going well in those relationships, but also what's going less well. Ask him what he enjoys about them and what he finds difficult. By probing about both the "positive" and "negative" sides of these relationships, older boys will begin to discuss a broad array of thoughts and feelings.

When a boy expresses vulnerable feelings, avoid teasing or taunting him

While it's natural to want to be playful with our sons, and though showing him a sense of levity and good cheer sometimes helps him to overcome unpleasant feelings or situations, by and large it's important that we not "cut off" his painful emotions by teasing or taunting him. So, for, example, when he comes home and complains that his teacher told him he needs a haircut, rather than teasing that he "sure looks like a real fuzz ball," ask him how his teacher's comments made him feel, hear him out, and tell him that you too don't appreciate what the teacher said. Or if your teenage son announces despondently that his sweetheart just "dumped him," rather than joking that it must have been his bad breath that got to her or that his heart "must just be totally broken," instead ask him if he'd like to talk about it and, if so, listen to what he'd like to share with you and try to mirror back in an empathic way the feelings you sense he's trying to convey. Teasing and taunting rarely heal the boy. Empathy, however, goes miles to help him learn how to express and cope with a broad range of feelings.

Avoid using shaming language in talking with a boy

Research, as well as everyday observation, reveals that parents often—although unintentionally—use shaming language with their male children that they do not use with girls. It's important to find ways to talk with boys that do not shame them, and that they can respond to. If a boy does something that surprises or concerns you, a natural reaction is to ask, "How could you do that?" But that implies that the act, whatever it was, was wrong and casts the boy in the role of the evil perpetrator. Rather, you might ask, "What's going on?" or "What happened?" which suggests that you have not formed a judgment about the situation under discussion.

If a boy comes home with a less than stellar report card, a parent—understandably concerned—may challenge him and deliver an ultimatum, "You're going to have to work harder than this. These grades won't get you into a good college." Undoubtedly, the boy knows he is not performing as well as others or as well as he would like. The better parental response might be "You're still struggling with math, aren't you. What could we do to help?"

Or suppose a boy declines an invitation to visit a friend or go to a party. Rather than say, "It would do you good to get out of the house. Besides, that boy is really nice," you could try to find out why the boy no longer wants to be with his friend— "Has something happened between you two guys?"—or what it is about the party that doesn't appeal to him—"Will somebody be there you don't get along with?"

Such language carries tremendous power to make a boy feel shame and to reinforce his own conception that he is somehow toxic.

Look behind anger, aggression, and rambunctiousness

In so many cases, a boy who seems angry, displays a lot of aggression, or is constantly rambunctious is indirectly asking for our help. If you notice a boy who is acting in such ways, try to create a setting where he'll feel comfortable talking with you and then ask him how things are with him. With a young boy, you might not be able to ask him a lot of direct questions—and he may not yet be able to talk about feelings in a clear way—but try your best to get a sense of what he's feeling. For instance, if you notice that your son has seemed angry a lot lately, you might say, "Gosh, you've seemed upset a lot. Is everything OK? Have things been rough for you lately?" Or, if you're a schoolteacher and you notice a boy who's constantly roughing up and provoking other kids, rather than chastising the boy, ask him how things are at home. Ask him if he's upset about something. Try to get a sense of whether there might be deeper, more vulnerable feelings that are motivating his anger or rowdy behavior. You might even tell him that sometimes when we act irritably or show aggression, we might be feeling sadness or other upset feelings.

Express your love and empathy openly and generously

Despite all the messages you might receive about "letting go" of your son, of not staying too attached to him, of not "babying" him, you simply can never show him too much love or empathy. Cutting off your affection and support, to let him "stand on his own," as we've discussed in this chapter, can actually traumatize him.

Tell your boy that you love him as often as you like. Give him hugs. Tell him you're proud of him and that you care about him. Stay involved in his emotional life. Seek opportunities to connect with him for moments of playful closeness and emotional sharing. If he asks you to let him alone, give him the space he needs, but let him know that you love him very much and that when he's ready to spend time together, you'll be up for it. You cannot "spoil" your son with too much love or attention. You will not make him "girl-like" or "feminine" by maintaining a close relationship. There's simply no such thing as too much love!

Let boys know that they don't need to be "sturdy oaks"

So many boys, even at a very young age, feel that they need to act like a "sturdy oak." When there are problems at home, when he suffers his own failures or disappointments, or when there's a need for somebody who's physically or emotionally "strong" for others to lean on and he feels he has to be that support, the boy is often pushed to "act like a man," to be the one who is confident and unflinching. No boy should be called upon to be the tough one. No boy should be hardened in this way. So through thick and thin, let your boy know that he doesn't have to act like a "sturdy oak." Talk to him honestly about your own fears and vulnerabilities and encourage him to do the same. The more genuine he feels he can be with you, the more he'll be free to express his vulnerability and the stronger he will become.

Create a model of masculinity for him that is broad and inclusive

Despite all the narrow messages about "being a guy" that they may get at school, on television, or elsewhere, you can help boys to create their own model of masculinity. Try to help them develop a model that is broad and inclusive. Try to do for them what we have done for girls by valuing them as people before evaluating them as a distinct (and therefore restricted) gender. This means encouraging boys in all their interests, relationships, and activities. It means letting them know that "big guys *do* cry." It also means exposing boys to people who bend society's strict gender rules—to men who are nurses, women who are plumbers, girls who are "jocks," boys who cook, and so on. Boys especially benefit from getting to know adult male "role models" who exude masculinity in a genuine and expansive way. When you give your son a sense that there's no one single way of being "manly," you're helping him develop confidence about who he really is. You're letting him know that no matter what he enjoys doing, whom he likes spending time with, and what sorts of feelings he experiences, he's a "real boy" on his way to being a "real man."

⟋ DISCUSSION QUESTIONS

1. List three movies or television shows from popular culture that reinforce the boy code.

2. How is the boy code enforced? Regardless of your gender, think of how you might have reinforced some aspect of the boy code in your interactions with others.

3. How do you think boys and girls (or men and women) enforce the boy code differently?

4. How is the boy code related to the epidemic of school shootings across the country?

5. How might the boy code cause particular problems for boys as they grow up and are expected to enter into romantic relationships?

17

Racial Formation

Michael Omi and Howard Winant

In 2008 Barack Obama became the first African American president of the United States. Less than 50 years earlier it was still perfectly legal for public establishments to refuse to serve African Americans, and overt racial discrimination was still a widespread, socially accepted phenomenon in many parts of society. His election represents an important historical milestone, but is also an opportunity to look sociologically at racial identity and how racial categories are created and perceived. Race is usually thought of as a biological category and the most common markers we use to iden-tify race are physical in nature—skin color, hair color and texture, and facial features. But in this article, Omi and Winant demonstrate how race is anything but natural. They argue that racial categories are a reflection of social, economic, and political forces that shape these socially constructed categories, not biology. For example, Barack Obama's father was Black, but his mother was White. While he is usually referred to as an African American (or Black), in terms of biology he has just as much in common with his predecessor George W. Bush as he does with his wife Michelle. This represents what Omi and Winant term hypo-descent, *or the "affiliation with the subordinate rather than the superordinate group in order to avoid the ambiguity of the intermediate identity" (p. 188). The racial categories used on the census are another example of the social basis for racial*

Chapter 4, pp. 57-69 from *Racial Formation in the United States: From the 1960's to the 1990's*, 2nd edition, by Michael Omi and Howard Winant. Copyright © 1994 by Michael Omi and Howard Winant. Reprinted with permission from Routledge.

categories. Rarely have the categories available to people been the same in the census every 10 years. This is reflective of social, not biological, changes in the population.

As you read, pay particular attention to the ways that conflicts in the wider society spill over into the supposedly biological category of race.

I n 1982–83, Susie Guillory Phipps unsuccessfully sued the Louisiana Bureau of Vital Records to change her racial classification from black to white. The descendant of an eighteenth-century white planter and a black slave, Phipps was designated "black" in her birth certificate in accordance with a 1970 state law which declared anyone with at least one-thirty-second "Negro blood" to be black. The legal battle raised intriguing questions about the concept of race, its meaning in contemporary society, and its use (and abuse) in public policy. Assistant Attorney General Ron Davis defended the law by pointing out that some type of racial classification was necessary to comply with federal record-keeping requirements and to facilitate programs for the prevention of genetic diseases. Phipps's attorney, Brian Begue, argued that the assignment of racial categories on birth certificates was unconstitutional and that the one-thirty-second designation was inaccurate. He called on a retired Tulane University professor who cited research indicating that most whites have one-twentieth "Negro" ancestry. In the end, Phipps lost. The court upheld a state law which quantified racial identity, and in so doing affirmed the legality of assigning individuals to specific racial groupings.[1]

The Phipps case illustrates the continuing dilemma of defining race and establishing its meaning in institutional life. Today, to assert that variations in human physiognomy are racially based is to enter a constant and intense debate. Scientific interpretations of race have not been alone in sparking heated controversy; religious perspectives have done so as well.[2]

Most centrally, of course, race has been a matter of political contention. This has been particularly true in the United States, where the concept of race has varied enormously over time without ever leaving the center stage of US history.

〢 WHAT IS RACE?

Race consciousness, and its articulation in theories of race, is largely a modern phenomenon. When European explorers in the New World "discovered" people who looked different than themselves, these "natives" challenged then existing conceptions of the origins of the human species, and raised disturbing questions as to whether all could be considered in the same "family of man."[3] Religious debates flared over the attempt to reconcile the Bible with the existence of "racially distinct" people. Arguments took place over creation itself, as theories of polygenesis questioned whether God had made only one species of humanity ("monogenesis"). Europeans wondered if the natives of the New World were indeed human beings with redeemable souls. At stake were not only the prospects for conversion, but the types of treatment to be accorded them. The expropriation of property, the denial of political rights, the introduction of slavery and other forms of coercive labor, as well as outright extermination, all presupposed a worldview which distinguished Europeans–children of God, human beings, etc.–from "others." Such a worldview was needed to explain why some should be "free" and others enslaved, why some had rights to land and property while others did not. Race, and the interpretation of racial differences, was a central factor in that worldview.

In the colonial epoch science was no less a field of controversy than religion in attempts to comprehend the concept of race and its meaning. Spurred on by the classificatory scheme of living organisms devised by Linnaeus in *Systema Naturae*, many scholars in the eighteenth and nineteenth centuries dedicated themselves to the identification and ranking of variations in humankind. Race was thought of as a *biological* concept, yet its precise definition was the subject of debates which, as we have noted, continue to rage today. Despite efforts ranging from Dr Samuel Morton's studies of cranial capacity[4] to contemporary attempts to base racial classification on shared gene pools, the concept of race has defied biological definition.[5]

Attempts to discern the *scientific meaning* of race continue to the present day. Although most physical anthropologists and biologists have abandoned the quest for a scientific basis to determine racial categories, controversies have recently flared in the area of genetics and educational psychology. For instance, an essay by Arthur Jensen which argued that hereditary factors shape intelligence not only revived the "nature or nurture" controversy, but raised highly volatile questions about racial equality itself.[6] Clearly the attempt to establish a *biological basis* of race has not been swept into the dustbin of history, but is being resurrected in various scientific arenas. All such attempts seek to remove the concept of race from fundamental social, political, or economic determination. They suggest instead that the truth of race lies in the terrain of innate characteristics, of which skin color and other physical attributes provide only the most obvious, and in some respects most superficial, indicators.

⋙ RACE AS A SOCIAL CONCEPT

The social sciences have come to reject biologistic notions of race in favor of an approach which regards race as a social concept. Beginning in the eighteenth century, this trend has been slow and uneven, but its direction clear. In the nineteenth century Max Weber discounted biological explanations for racial conflict and instead highlighted the social and political factors which engendered such conflict.[7] The work of pioneering cultural anthropologist Franz Boas was crucial in refuting the scientific racism of the early twentieth century by rejecting the connection between race and culture, and the assumption of a continuum of "higher" and "lower" cultural groups. Within the contemporary social science literature, race is assumed to be a variable which is shaped by broader societal forces.

Race is indeed a preeminently *sociohistorical* concept. Racial categories and the meaning of race are given concrete expression by the specific social relations and historical context in which they are embedded. Racial meanings have varied tremendously over time and between different societies.

In the United States, the black/white color line has historically been rigidly defined and enforced. White is seen as a "pure" category. Any racial intermixture makes one "nonwhite." In the movie *Raintree County*, Elizabeth Taylor describes the worst of fates to befall whites as "havin' a little Negra blood in ya'–just one little teeny drop and a person's all Negra."[8] This thinking flows from what Marvin Harris has characterized as the principle of *hypo-descen*t:

> By what ingenious computation is the genetic tracery of a million years of evolution unraveled and each man [sic] assigned his proper social box? In the United States, the mechanism employed is the rule of hypo-descent. This descent rule requires Americans to believe that anyone who is known to have had a Negro ancestor is a Negro. We admit nothing in between. "Hypo-descent" means affiliation with the subordinate rather than the superordinate group in order to avoid the ambiguity of intermediate identity. . . . The rule of hypo-descent is, therefore, an invention, which we in the United States have made in order to keep biological facts from intruding into our collective racist fantasies.[9]

The Susie Guillory Phipps case merely represents the contemporary, expression of this racial logic.

By contrast, a striking feature of race relations in the lowland areas of Latin America since the abolition of slavery has been the relative absence of sharply defined racial groupings. No such rigid descent rule characterizes racial identity in many Latin American societies. Brazil, for example, has historically had less rigid conceptions of race, and thus a variety of "intermediate" racial categories exist. Indeed, as Harris notes, "One of the most striking consequences of the Brazilian system of racial identification is that parents and children and even brothers and sisters are frequently accepted as representatives of quite opposite racial types."[10] Such a possibility is incomprehensible within the logic of racial categories in the US.

To suggest another example: the notion of "passing" takes on new meaning if we compare various American cultures' means of assigning racial identity. In the United States, individuals who are actually "black" by the logic of hypo-descent have attempted to skirt the discriminatory barriers imposed by law and custom by attempting to "pass" for white.[11] Ironically, these same individuals would not be able to pass for "black" in many Latin American societies.

The meaning of race is defined and contested throughout society, in both collective action and personal practice. In the process, racial categories themselves are formed, transformed, destroyed and re-formed. We use the term *racial formation* to refer to the process by which social, economic and political forces determine the convent and importance of racial categories, and by which they are in turn shaped by racial meanings. Crucial to this formulation is the treatment of race as a *central axis* of social relations which cannot be subsumed under or reduced to some broader category or conception.

⦚ RACIAL IDEOLOGY AND RACIAL IDENTITY

The seemingly obvious, "natural" and "common sense" qualities which the existing racial order exhibits themselves testify to the effectiveness of the racial formation process in constructing racial meanings and racial identities.

One of the first things we notice about people when we meet them (along with their sex) is their race. We utilize race to provide clues about *who* a person is. This fact is made painfully obvious when we encounter someone whom we cannot conveniently racially categorize—someone who is, for example, racially "mixed" or of an ethnic/racial group with which we are not familiar. Such an encounter becomes a source of discomfort and momentarily a crisis of racial meaning. Without a racial identity, one is in danger of having no identity.

Our compass for navigating race relations depends on preconceived notions of what each specific racial group looks like. Comments such as, "Funny, you don't look black," betray an underlying image of what black should be. We also become disoriented when people do not act "black," "Latino," or indeed "white." The content of such stereotypes reveals a series of unsubstantiated beliefs about who these groups are and what "they" are like.[12]

In US society, then, a kind of "racial etiquette" exists, a set of interpretative codes and racial meanings which operate in the interactions of daily life. Rules shaped by our perception of race in a comprehensively racial society determine the "presentation of self,"[13] distinctions of status, and appropriate modes of conduct. "Etiquette" is not mere universal adherence to the dominant group's rules, but a more dynamic combination of these rules with the values and beliefs of subordinated groupings. This racial "subjection" is quintessentially ideological. Everybody learns some combination, some version, of the rules of racial classification, and of their own racial identity, often without obvious teaching or conscious inculcation. Race becomes "common sense"–a way of comprehending, explaining and acting in the world.

Racial beliefs operate as an "amateur biology," a way of explaining the variations in "human nature."[14] Differences in skin color and other obvious physical characteristics supposedly provide visible clues to differences lurking underneath. Temperament, sexuality, intelligence, athletic ability, aesthetic preferences and so on are presumed to be fixed and discernible from the palpable mark of race. Such diverse questions as our confidence and trust in others (for example, clerks or salespeople, media figures, neighbors), our sexual preferences and romantic images, our tastes in music, films, dance, or sports, and our very ways of talking, walking, eating and dreaming are ineluctably shaped by notions of race. Skin color "differences" are thought to explain perceived differences in intellectual, physical and artistic temperaments, and to justify distinct treatment of racially identified individuals and groups.

The continuing persistence of racial ideology suggests that these racial myths and stereotypes cannot be exposed as such in the popular imagination. They are, we think, too essential, too integral, to the maintenance of the US social order. Of course, particular meanings, stereotypes and myths can change, but the presence of a system of racial meanings and stereotypes, of racial ideology, seems to be a permanent feature of US culture.

≫ RACIALIZATION: THE HISTORICAL DEVELOPMENT OF RACE

In the United States, the racial category of "black" evolved with the consolidation of racial slavery. By the end of the seventeenth century, Africans whose specific identity was Ibo, Yoruba, Fulani, etc., were rendered "black" by an ideology of exploitation based on racial logic—the establishment and maintenance of a "color line." This of course did not occur overnight. A period of indentured servitude which was not rooted in racial logic preceded the consolidation of racial slavery. With slavery, however, a racially based understanding of society was set in motion which resulted in the shaping of a specific *racial* identity not only for the slaves but for the European settlers as well. Winthrop Jordan has observed: "From the initially common term *Christian,* at mid-century there was a marked shift toward the terms *English* and *free.* After about 1680, taking the colonics as a whole, a new term of self-identification appeared–*white.*"[15]

We employ the term *racialization* to signify the extension of racial meaning to a previously racially unclassified relationship, social practice or group. Racialization is an ideological process, an historically specific one. Racial ideology is constructed from preexisting conceptual (or, if one prefers, "discursive") elements and emerges from the struggles of competing political projects and ideas seeking to articulate similar elements differently. An account of racialization processes that avoids the pitfalls of US ethnic history[16] remains to be written.

Particularly during the nineteenth century, the category of "white" was subject to challenges brought about by the influx of diverse groups who were not of the same Anglo-Saxon stock as the founding immigrants. In the nineteenth century, political and ideological struggles emerged over the classification of Southern Europeans, the Irish and Jews, among other "non-white" categories.[17] Nativism was only effectively curbed by the institutionalization of a racial order that drew the color line *around*, rather than *within*, Europe.

By stopping short of racializing immigrants from Europe after the Civil War, and by subsequently allowing their assimilation, the American racial order was reconsolidated in the wake of the tremendous challenge placed before it by the abolition of racial slavery.[18] With the end of Reconstruction in 1877, an effective program for limiting the emergent class struggles of the later nineteenth century was forged: the definition of the working class in racial terms–as "white." This was not accomplished by any legislative decree or capitalist maneuvering to divide the working class, but rather by white workers themselves. Many of them were recent immigrants, who organized on racial lines as much as on traditionally defined class lines.[19] The Irish on the West Coast, for example, engaged in vicious anti-Chinese race-baiting and committed many pogrom-type assaults on Chinese in the course of consolidating the trade union movement in California.

Thus the very political organization of the working class was in important ways a racial project. The legacy of racial conflicts and arrangements shaped the definition of interests and in turn led to the consolidation of institutional patterns (e.g. segregated unions, dual labor markets, exclusionary legislation) which perpetuated the color line within the working class.

⧄ RACIAL FORMATION: THE CREATION OF RACIAL MEANINGS

Much racial theory, we have argued, treats race as a manifestation or epiphenomenon of other supposedly more fundamental categories of sociopolitical identity, notably those of ethnicity, class and nation. In such accounts, race is not regarded as a continually evolving category in its own right; in fact, these approaches have often imagined that race would decline in importance, even disappear, as economic or political "progress" rendered "race thinking" obsolete.[20]

We hope to alter this situation by presenting the outlines of a theory of *racial formation*. In our view, racial meanings pervade US society, extending from the shaping of individual racial identities to the structuring of collective political action on the terrain of the state.

An approach based on the concept of racial formation should treat race in the United States as a fundamental organizing principle of social relationships. To give this notion some concreteness, let us distinguish between the *micro-level* and *macro-level* of social relations.

At the micro-level, race is a matter of individuality, of the formation of identity. The ways in which we understand ourselves and interact with others, the structuring of our practical activity—in work and family, as citizens and as thinkers (or "philosophers")[21]—these are all shaped by racial meanings and racial awareness.

At the macro-level, race is a matter of *collectivity*, of the formation of social structures: economic, political and cultural/ideological. Social structure may be understood as a series of "sites:"

> We conceive of a site as a region of social life with a coherent set of constitutive social relations—the *structure* of the site. Thus in the advanced capitalist social formation, the liberal democratic state, the capitalist economy, and the patriarchal family may be considered sites in that each may be characterized by a distinct set of "rules of the game" for participation in practices.[22]

The racial order is organized and enforced by the continuity and reciprocity between these two "levels" of social relations. The micro- and macro-levels, however, are only analytically distinct. In our lived experience, in politics, in culture, in economic life, they are continuous and reciprocal. Racial discrimination, for example—considered, as a "macro-level" set of economic, political and ideological/cultural practices—has obvious consequences for the experience and identities of individuals. It affects racial meanings, intervenes in "personal life," is interpreted politically, etc.[23] Another example: racial identity—considered as a "micro-level" complex of individual practices and "consciousness"—shapes the universe of collective action. The panoply of individual attributes—from one's patterns of speech or tastes in food or music to the economic, spatial, familial, or citizenship "role" one occupies—provides the essential themes for political organization, the elements of economic self-reliance, etc.[24]

The theory of racial formation, then, suggests that racial phenomena penetrate and link these two "levels" of social relationships. But this is only part of the story;

the concept of race as an organizing principle of social relations provides a description, a classification of racial phenomena in the US, and also explains the continuity of these phenomena,[25] but it does not yet offer a conception of the process of racial formation. To grasp this process we must understand the way in which the meaning of these phenomena is politically contested.

🎐 CONTESTING THE SOCIAL MEANING OF RACE

Once we understand that race overflows the boundaries of skin color, superexploitation, social stratification, discrimination and prejudice, cultural domination and cultural resistance, state policy (or of any other particular social relationship we list), once we recognize the racial dimension present to some degree in every identity, institution and social practice in the United States—once we have done this, it becomes possible to speak of *racial formation*. This recognition is hard-won; there is a continuous temptation to think of race as an *essence*, as something fixed, concrete and objective, as (for example) one of the categories just enumerated. And there is also an opposite temptation: to see it as a mere illusion, which an ideal social order would eliminate.

In our view it is crucial to break with these habits of thought. The effort must be made to understand race as an unstable and "decentered" complex of social meanings constantly being transformed by political struggle. It is imperative that we achieve this understanding for two reasons. First, because today as in the past racial minorities pay a heavy price in human suffering as a result of their categorization as "other" by the dominant racial ideology; this is true not only in the United States, but across the world. Second, because racial politics are emblematic, we believe, of a new stage of US politics as a whole, a new socially based politics.[26]

The crucial task, then, is to suggest how the widely disparate circumstances of individual and group racial identities, and of the racial institutions and social practices with which these identities are intertwined, are formed and transformed over time. This takes place, we argue, through *political contestation over racial meanings*. Such contestation occurs today throughout American society: it takes place at the level of "personal" relationships (indeed it arises within individuals whose very identities and racial "beliefs" are necessarily contradictory); it exists in "objective" relationships such as work or political activity; and it occurs in cultural representation.

The racial dimensions of a particular relationship or social practice are never given automatically. If they appear obvious, this only means that they are already contextualized in racial ideologies familiar to their subjects. Of course, it is often the case that the racial dynamics of a given relationship go unnoticed: far from being sources of conflict or of difficult decisions, they are "nonevents," giving rise to "nondecisions."[27]

Frequently, though, especially in recent decades, racial dynamics are quite visible in social life. They cause uncertainty in the minds of individuals subject to them ("Is this 'fair'?" "Am 'I' being recognized?" "How do I 'work' this?"). They confront institutions, local communities and families with deep-seated conflicts and agonizing dilemmas. They structure large-scale policy debates. They inspire movements. These individuals, groups, institutions and movements are moved— in our view by the efforts of "intellectuals"—to make new interpretations of racial meanings, to understand the meaning of race and racial identity in new ways. Once reinterpreted, *rearticulated,* racial meanings are disrupted and space for political contestation is opened.

DISCUSSION QUESTIONS

1. What does the term *racial formation* mean? How might the sudden appearance of *Arab* as a racial designation after 9/11 be explained by this concept?

2. Omi and Winant state that racial beliefs "operate as an 'amateur biology, a way of explaining the variations in 'human nature'" (p. 190). How is this similar to how gender operates in social interactions?

3. What are some examples of the macrolevel and microlevel types of discrimination that the authors describe on page 192?

NOTES

1. *San Francisco Chronicle*, 14 September 1982, 19 May 1983. Ironically, the 1970 Louisiana law was enacted to supersede an old Jim Crow statute which relied on the idea of "common report" in determining an infant's race. Following Phipps's unsuccessful attempt to change her classification and have the law declared unconstitutional, a legislative effort arose which culminated on the repeal of the law. *See San Francisco Chronicle.* 23 June 1983.

2. The Mormon Church, for example, has been heavily criticized for its doctrine of Black Inferiority.

3. Thomas F. Gossett notes:

> Race theory . . . had up until fairly modern times no firm hold on European thought. On the other hand, race theory and race prejudice were by no means unknown at the time when the English colonists came to North America. Undoubtedly, the age of exploration led many to speculate on race differences at a period when neither Europeans nor Englishmen were prepared to make allowances for vast cultural diversities. Even though race theories had not then secured wide acceptance or even sophisticated formulation, the first contacts of the Spanish with the Indians in the Americas can now be recognized as the beginning of a struggle between conceptions of the nature of primitive peoples which has not yet been wholly settled. (Thomas F. Gossett, *Race: The History of an Idea in America* (New York: Schocken Books, 1965), p. 16.)

Winthrop Jordan provides a detailed account of early European colonialists' attitudes about color and race in White *over Black: American Attitudes Toward the Negro*, 1550-1812 (New York: Norton, 1977 [1968]), pp. 3-43.

4. Pro-slavery physician Samuel George Morton (1799-1851) compiled a collection of 800 crania from all parts of the world which formed the sample for his studies of race. Assuming that the larger the size of the cranium translated into greater intelligence, Morton established a relationship between race and skull capacity. Gossett reports that:

> In 1849, one of his studies included the following results: The English skulls in his collection proved to be the largest, with an average cranial capacity of 96 cubic inches. The Americans and Germans were rather poor seconds, both with cranial capacities of 90 cubic inches. At the bottom of the list were the Negroes with 83 cubic inches, the Chinese with 82, and the Indians with 79. (Ibid., p. 74.)

On Morton's methods, see Stephen J. Gould, "The Finagle Factor," *Human Nature (July* 1978).

5. Definitions of race founded upon a common pool of genes have not held up when confronted by scientific research which suggests that the differences *within* a given human population are greater than those between populations. See L. L. Cavalli-Sforza, "The Genetics of Human Populations," *Scientific American,* September 1974, pp. 81-89.

6. Arthur Jensen, "How Much Can We Boost IQ and Scholastic Achievement?", *Harvard Educational Review* 39 (1969):1-123.

7. Ernst Moritz Manasse, "Max Weber on Race," *Social Research* 14 (1947):191-221.

8. Quoted in Edward D. C. Campbell, Jr., *The Celluloid South: Hollywood and the Southern Myth* (Knoxville: University of Tennessee Press, 1981), pp. 168-70.

9. Marvin Harris, *Patterns of Race in the Americas* (New York: Norton, 1964), p. 56.

10. Ibid., p. 57.

11. After James Meredith had been admitted as the first black student at the University of Mississippi, Harry S. Murphy announced that he, and not Meredith, was the first black student to attend "Ole Miss." Murphy described himself as black but was able to pass for white and spent nine months at the institution without attracting any notice (ibid., p. 56).

12. Gordon W. Allport, *The Nature of Prejudice* (Garden City, NY: Doubleday,1958), pp. 184-200.

13. We wish to use this phrase loosely, without committing ourselves to a particular position on such social psychological approaches as symbolic interactionism, which are outside the scope of this study. An interesting study on this subject is S. M. Lyman and W. A. Douglass, "Ethnicity: Strategies of Individual and Collective Impression Management," *Social Research* 40(2) (1973).

14. Michael Billig, "Patterns of Racism: Interviews with National Front Members," *Race and Class* 20(2) (Autumn 1978):161-79.

15. Jordan, *White Over Black, p.* 95; emphasis added.

16. Historical focus has been placed either on particular racially defined groups or on immigration and the "incorporation" of ethnic groups. In the former case the characteristic ethnicity theory pitfalls and apologetics such as functionalism and cultural pluralism may be avoided, but only by sacrificing much of the focus on race. In the latter case, race is considered a manifestation of ethnicity.

17. The degree of antipathy for these groups should not be minimized. A northern commentator observed in the 1850s: "An Irish Catholic seldom attempts to rise to a higher condition than that in which he is placed, while the Negro often makes the attempt with success." Quoted in Gossett, op. cit., p. 288.

18. This analysis, as will perhaps be obvious, is essentially DuBoisian. Its main source will be found in the monumental (and still largely unappreciated) *Black Reconstruction in the United States, 1860-1880* (New York: Atheneum,1977 [1935]).

19. Alexander Saxton argues that:

> North Americans of European background have experienced three great racial confrontations: with the Indian, with the African, and with the Oriental. Central to each transaction has been a totally one-sided preponderance of power, exerted for the exploitation of nonwhites by the dominant white society. In each case (but especially in the two that began with systems of enforced labor), white workingmen have played a crucial, yet ambivalent, role. They have been both exploited and exploiters. On the

one hand, thrown into competition with nonwhites as enslaved or "cheap" labor they suffered economically; on the other hand, being white, they benefited by that very exploitation which was compelling the nonwhites to work for low wages or for nothing. Ideologically they were drawn in opposite directions. *Racial identification cut at right angles to class consciousness.* (Alexander Saxton, *The Indispensable Enemy: Labor and the Anti-Chinese Movement in California* (Berkeley and Los Angeles: University of California Press, 1971), p. 1; emphasis added.)

20. Milton Gordon describes this belief as "the liberal expectancy," in a treatment particularly relevant to ethnicity theory; see his *Human Nature, Class, and Ethnicity* (New York: Oxford University Press, 1964), pp. 69-70. Nathan Glazer has argued repeatedly that racial classification is but a temporary manifestation of hostility toward new immigrants whose eventual incorporation into the "American ethnic pattern" lays to rest the use of racial categories; see his "Government and the American Ethnic Pattern," in W. A. Van Horne and T. A. Tonneson, eds, *Ethnicity and Public Policy* (Madison: University of Wisconsin Press, 1982) p. 30; *idem, Affirmative Discrimination* (New York: Basic Books 1975), chapter 1. Many other examples could be cited.

21. It is essential to destroy the widespread prejudice that philosophy is a strange and difficult thing just because it is the specific intellectual activity of a particular category of specialists or of professional and systemic philosophers. It must first be shown that all men [sic] are philosophers, be defining the limits and characteristics of the "spontaneous philosophy" which is proper to everybody. This philosophy is contained in: 1. Language itself, which is a totality of determined notions, and concepts and not just words grammatically devoid of content; 2. "common sense" ...; 3. Popular religion and, therefore, also in the entire system of beliefs, superstitions, opinions, ways of seeing things and of acting, which are collectively bundled together under the name of 'folklore.' (Antonio Gramsci, "The Study of Philosophy," *Selections from ethe Prison Notebooks*, Quentin Hoare and Geoffrey Nowell Smith, eds (New York: International Publishers, 1971) p. 323)

22. Samuel Bowles and Herbert Gintis, "On the Heterogeneity of Power" (unpublished MS, 1983), p. 17, emphasis original. In another paper, Bowles and Gintis define a "site" as "an area of social activity with a characteristic set of social relations defining its specificity.... A site is defined not by what is *done* there, but by what imparts *regularity* to what is done there, its characteristic 'rules of the game'" (Herbert Gintis and Samuel Bowles, "Structure of Practice in the Labor Theory of Value," *Review of Radical Political Economics*, vol. 12, no. 4 (Winter 1981; emphasis original). "Sites" such as families, state institutions, or realms of the economy obviously require further theorization as to their general characteristics. They are of interest here because they suggest the comprehensive character of racial meanings.

23. Thus discrimination brings about a whole range of shifts in racial identities, not only of its victims but also of its perpetrators, a subject far too vast to address properly

here. It may occasion family discord, guilt, or feelings of inferiority or superiority. It may structure attempts to "pass" or to deny racial belonging, or become generalized as a symbol of individual indignity; conversely, discrimination may generate individual or collective resentment or opposition.

24. We describe how traditional elements of Black identity provided the basis for political mobilization in the early civil rights movement.

25. This continuity might be described—to borrow a phrase from Foucault—as "regularity in dispersion." By this we mean that racial phenomena vary widely: among different racially defined groups, regionally, in respect to other variables such as class and gender, etc., but that they exhibit crucial equivalences and isomorphisms as well. The continuity of "micro-" and "macro-level" racial dynamics, for example, which holds true across all racial groups, illustrates this point. See Michel Foucault, *The Archaeology of Knowledge* (New York: Pantheon, 1972), pp. 37-8.

26. We argue that throughout the postwar period an expanded *social* politics based on movement forms or mobilization has been supplanting the economically based politics characteristic of the early twentieth century and institutionalized in the political alignment of the New Deal.

27. Power structure Theory and policy analysis have recognized for some years now that in certain situations power imbalances are so uneven that opposition is useless, and a conflictual "mobilization of bias" (Schatt-schneider) cannot be achieved. It follows that the very absence of conflict may indicate the presence of such an imbalance. See Peter Bachrach and Morton Baratz, *Power and Poverty* (New York: Oxford, 1970); Matthew Crensen, *The Unpoltics of Air Pollution* (Baltimore: John Hopkins University Press, 1971).

18

How to Talk Nasty about Blacks without Sounding "Racist"

Eduardo Bonilla-Silva

The dominant racial ideology in contemporary America is color blindness. Marked by an aversion to overt, individual level racism and a cultural belief that any remaining discrimination can best be remedied by ignoring race all together, color-blindness shapes both public and private discussions of race.

In this article, Eduardo Bonilla-Silva argues that contrary to fostering equality, color blindness merely locks the systems of privilege enjoyed by Whites even more firmly in place and functions to silence the kinds of conversations about racism that might result in genuine, productive change. The quintessential example of this is when someone is accused of "playing the race card," a phrase that implies one is unfairly blaming race or racism in the context of a problem or event. It's a way of shutting out any criticism or commentary that might suggest that any type of racism might be at work.

Even in casual, private conversations, the ideology of color blindness pervades, especially among Whites. In this article, Bonilla-Silva catalogs some of the linguistic and rhetorical strategies used by White college students that allow them to

Bonilla-Silva, E. (2002). The linguistics of color blind racism: How to talk nasty about blacks without sounding "racist." Critical Sociology, 28(1-2), 41-64. doi: 10.1177/08969205020280010501.

express attitudes and opinions that indicate negative attitudes toward minorities yet do not sound overtly racist. As you read, think about your own discussion about race and whether your linguistic strategies differ depending on whom you are talking to.

"I am a little bit for affirmative action, but . . ." "Yes and no, I mean . . ." "I am not prejudiced, but . . ." "Some of my best friends are black" "I sort of agree and disagree" All these phrases have become standard linguistic fare of whites' contemporary racetalk. But what do these phrases mean? For some analysts, they are expressions of whites' racial ambivalence (Hass et al. 1992; Katz and Hass 1988). For others, they are expressions of progress and resistance in racial matters (Schuman et al. 1997). Yet for a smaller group of analysts,[1] they represent whites' careful consideration of all sides on racial matters (Lipset 1996; Sniderman and Carmines 1997; Sniderman and Piazza 1993).

In contrast to these mainstream explanations, I contend that these phrases, as well as the ideas expressed after these phrases are interjected, are part of the style[2] of color blind racism, the dominant racial ideology of the post–civil rights era. This ideology emerged as part of the great racial transformation that occurred in the late sixties and early seventies in the United States. As the Jim Crow overt style of maintaining white supremacy was replaced with "now you see it, now you don't" practices that were subtle, apparently non-racial, and institutionalized, an ideology fitting to this era emerged (Brooks 1990, 1996; Smith 1995; Bonilla-Silva and Lewis 1999). In contrast with Jim Crow, color blind racism major themes are (1) the extension of the principles of liberalism to racial matters in an abstract manner, (2) cultural rather than biological explanation of minorities' inferior standing and performance in labor and educational markets, (3) naturalization of racial phenomena such as residential and school segregation, and (4) the claim that discrimination has all but disappeared (Bonilla-Silva 2001; Bonilla-Silva and Forman 2000; c.f., Jackman (1994), Essed (1996), and Bobo, Kluegel, and Smith (1997)). I offer as much data on each case I cite in an effort to clarify the muddy waters of color blindness.

The data for the analysis comes from interviews gathered as part of ... the 1997 Survey of College Students' Social Attitudes. The study was conducted among 600 students (451 whites) taking social science courses in three Universities (Southern University or SU, Midwestern University or MU, and Western University or WU). The interviews were gathered from a random sample of the 90 percent (406) of the white students who included information on how to contact them. Altogether there are 41 interviews with college students (10 percent sub-sample).

╲╲ RACISM WITHOUT RACIAL EPITHETS: COLOR BLINDNESS AND THE AVOIDANCE OF RACIAL TERMINOLOGY

Today using words such as "Nigger" and "Spic" is seen as an immoral act. More significantly, saying things that sound or can be perceived as racist is disallowed. And because the dominant racial ideology portends to be color blind, there is little space for socially sanctioned speech about race-related matters. Does this mean that whites do not talk in public[3] about nonwhites? As many researchers have shown, they do but they do so in a very careful, indirect, hesitant manner and, occasionally, even through code language (Edsall and Edsall 1992). Not surprisingly, very few white respondents in these studies used traditional Jim Crow terminology to refer to blacks. Only one college student used terms such as "colored" or "Negroes" to refer to blacks and not a single one used the term "nigger" as a legitimate term. The student who used the term "colored" was Rachel, a MU student with very conservative racial views. However, it is not clear if she used the term as part of her normal repertoire or if it was a slip of her tongue. She used the term in her answer to a question about her college friends.

> Um . . . I wouldn't say mostly white. I'd say, it's probably a mix. Um, 'cause I have like a lot of Asian friends. I have a lot of, um . . . colored friends, ya' know, but . . . ya' know, it wasn't . . . maybe not even the same, like, background either, I don't know. It's hard to tell, ya' know? From looking at somebody, so . . . [4]

It is important to point out that the fact that young whites do not use racial slurs as legitimate terms in *public* discussions does not mean that they do not use these terms or derogate blacks in other forms in *private* discussions. For example, most college students acknowledged listening or telling racist jokes with friends and six even told the jokes in the interviews.[5] Below I provide two examples of these jokes.

Lynn, a MU student, told the following crude racist joke she heard back home.

> Lynn: Okay [**laughing**] It was, it's terrible, but, um, what do you call . . . a car full of niggers driving off a cliff?
>
> Interviewer: What?
>
> Lynn: A good beginning

Eric, another MU student, told the following joke:

> It was, uh, what do you call a black man . . . a black man in a, in a coat and a tie? And it was, uh, the defendant or something. Yeah, it was the defendant. And that was, that was probably a couple of weeks ago or something that I heard that.

In addition, racist terminology is current in the life of students as illustrated by the fact that over half of them acknowledged having friends or close relatives who are "racist." For example, John, an older student at WU, revealed that his father used to use racist terminology to refer to blacks. When asked about his family's involvement in politics, John said the following:

> Well, I'd say not real involvement, but uh . . . I did notice that my father referred to black people as . . . niggers. He'd also call them colored people. Uh. . . . but uh, that was mainly just the environment that he grew up in and I don't think he really wanted to hurt anyone's feelings.

John also confessed that his father had influenced his views and that he struggled over this fact. His confession came in the middle of a discussion about how often he talks about racial issues now. After pointing out that "a cousin of mine . . . married a black" and that he attends "church regularly and I have friends that are interracially married," John stated the following:

> You got to admit it, you know, this is prejudiced country, I mean, uh . . . I really got to bury a lot of uh . . . stinkin' thinking uh, I was taught as I was growing up uh, I have to really look at things because sometimes unconsciously I may discriminate against somebody and I try not to . . .

\\\\ READING THROUGH THE RHETORICAL MAZE OF COLOR BLINDNESS

Because post-civil rights racial norms disallow the open expression of *direct* racial views and positions, whites have developed a concealed way of voicing them. In this section I examine the most common verbal strategies used by whites in post-civil rights' racetalk.

A) "I am not prejudiced, but . . ." and "Some of my best friends are"

Among the interviewees I found four college students who used the, phrase "I'm not prejudiced, but" in their answers. I cite one example from the students to illustrate how respondents used this semantic move. Lee, a WU student, inserted a version of the move to soften his opposition to affirmative action. In a back-and-forth between Lee and the interviewer, the interviewer asked him point blank, "So, so, are you saying now that you would, you oppose it more so, or . . . ?"

> Yeah . . . I would say. I don't know if that's racist or what, but I don't know. I don't really talk about that much with people, you know. So, I really haven't developed such a strong, a really strong opinion about it, but I guess I do oppose it now.

The "Some of my best friends are . . ." phrase was used by eight students to signify that they could not possibly be "racist." For example, Carol, a student at SU, described the racial makeup of her school as follows:

> We of course had white and black, Hispanic, Oriental, um, one of my best friends was considered Pacific Islander so um, it was a very good mix, I mean, very . . . I didn't, there were no distinct um, lines between white people and the minorities, as far as the people *I* hung out with and the classes I was in.

Later on, when asked to specify the proportion minority in her class, Carol said,

> Um, it was pretty good half and half. I mean, there were, there was a good half of my gifted friends in my class was minority [**Interviwer: OK. And that's like what kind?**] Um, all. We had um, black, Spanish, um, my two best friends in high school were Oriental, well one was half Vietnamese and one was Japanese.

Carol went on to repeat two more times that these two Asians were her "best friends." Elsewhere (Bonilla-Silva 2001) I examine in some detail the nature of these interracial friendships, I just point out for now the strategic nature of some of these claims. For instance, because Carol said four times that some of her best friends were "Oriental," it was easier for her to state all sorts of anti-minority positions that included even her preference for white mates.

B) "I am not black, so I don't know"

Since these two moves have become cliché (and hence less effective), whites have developed other moves to accomplish the same goal. One such move is stating that "I am not black, so I don't know." After this phrase is inserted, respondents usually proceed with statements betraying a strong stance on the matter in question. About one quarter of the white college students used the phrase "I am not black, so I don't know." For example, Brian, a student at SU, inserted the statement in response to the direct question on discrimination.

> Uh, I don't know. I believe them. I don't know, I'm not a black person living so I don't hang out with a lot of black people, so I don't see it happen. But I do watch TV and we were watching the stupid talk shows there's nothing else on and there's people out there. And uh, I don't know, just that and just hearing the news and stuff. I'm sure it's less than it used to be, at least that's what everybody keeps saying so . . . But, uh, *I* think it's less. But uh, I can't say. But I can't speak for like a black person who says they're being harassed or being uh, prejudice or uh, discriminated against.

Brian's carefully worded statement allows him to safely state his belief that discrimination "it's less than it used to be." Later on in the interview Brian stated that although discrimination happens in "corporations like Texaco," that he assumes "there's also corporations where it doesn't happen that way . . . so, there's really both sides to the coin."

The second example is Liz, a student at MU. She also used the phrase in her answer to the direct question on discrimination.

> Um, just because I'm not black, I'm not Hispanic, I don't really, don't understand. I don't go through it I guess. But then again, I've seen like racism on, you know, towards whites, scholarships and as far as school goes, which, I mean, which bothers me too. So I guess I can kind of understand.

In a specific question on whether or not blacks experience discrimination in jobs and promotions, Liz answered by avoiding the issue by making a statement of her belief in abstract liberalism.

> Um, I just think that the best qualified should probably get the job and that . . . you know, like I wouldn't see why someone black wouldn't get a job over someone white who was more qualified or better suited for the job.

Since Liz hinted that blacks lie when they make claims of discrimination, the interviewer asked her the following question: "Mmhm. So when they say that that happens to them, do you think they're . . . lying, or . . . ?" Liz then proceeded to make a quick reversal to restore her image of neutrality.

I mean, I don't think they're lying, but I wouldn't, I mean, I guess in my little world, that everything is perfect, I wouldn't see why that would happen. But I guess that there are people who are, you know, racist who do, you know, would not promote someone black just because they're black, which I don't really understand, you know.

C) "Yes and no, but . . ."

A common way of stating racial views without opening yourself to the charge of racism is apparently taking all sides on an issue. The following two examples illustrate how college students used this stylistic tool. First is Mark, a MU student, expressed his view on affirmative action as follows:

Yes and no. This is probably the toughest thing I have deciding. I really . . . 'cause I've thought about this a lot, but . . . I can make a pro–con list and I still wouldn't like. I've heard most of the issues on this subject and I honestly couldn't give a definite answer.

Mark, who was taking a sociology course at the time of the interview, recognized that minorities "don't have the same starting points and, if you are starting from so much lower, they should definitely be granted *some* additional opportunities to at least have an equal . . . playing ground." However, Mark added, "I'm gonna be going out for a job next year, and I'll be honest, I'd be upset if I'm just as qualified as someone else, and individually, I'd be upset if a company takes, you know, like an African American over me just because he is an African American." Mark repeated this point when discussing three affirmative action-based hiring scenarios. When asked if he would personally support the hypothetical company's decisions, Mark said: "I, I? If I'm that person, I'm not gonna support it. If I'm that majority getting rejected just because I'm a different race." Mark also used a similar argument to explain what he thinks happens in college admissions. Thus Mark's support for affirmative action is theoretical rather than practical.

Emily, a student at SU, answer to a question on providing minorities special opportunities to be admitted into universities was,

. . . Unique opportunities . . . um . . . I don't know? There might be, I guess, some minorities do get uh schools aren't as well-funded as others. So, I would have to say yes and no. I think they should get an opportunity to come, but I also don't thin they should allow other people to come. 'Cause that's sort of like a double-edged sword, maybe because you are discriminating against one group any way, any way you do it uh, and I don't believe in that, and I don't think you should discriminate against one group to give another a better chance. And I don't believe that's fair at all. But I also don't believe that it's fair they have to (attend a) school that's not uh, can't teach as well or don't have the facilities to teach them like they should. Um, I don't know. I'm kinda wishy-washy on that.

In Emily's answer to the direct question on discrimination, her position an affirmative action became clearer.

. . . I just have a problem with the discrimination, you're gonna discriminate against a group, umm, and what happened in the past is horrible and it should never happen again, but I also think that to move forward you have to let go of the past and let go of what happened. Um, you know, and it should really start equaling out um, 'cause I feel that some of, some of it will go too far and it will swing the other way. Umm, one group is going to be discriminated against, I don't, I don't believe in that. I don't think one group should have an advantage over another, um, regardless of what happened in the past.

Thus, Emily opposes affirmative action as it is practiced because she believes it is reverse discrimination and hence favors programs that are not in place (expanding educational opportunities for minorities before college) or that would not change minorities' status at all (perfect equal opportunity without changing the group-level inequalities).

D) Anything but race

Another rhetorical move typical of color blind racism is the "Anything but race" strategy.[6] This strategy involves interjecting comments such as "Is not a prejudiced thing" to dismiss the fact that race affects an aspect of the respondent's life. Hence, this tool allows whites to smooth out racial fractures in their otherwise color blind story. This strategy was used by over half of the students. Sonny, a student at MU, used this tool to explain why she did not have minority friends while growing up. Sonny revealed in the interview that she had Italian friends but suggested that "race never came into play" and that "most of my friends were . . . just normal kids." After revealing that "one of my best friends is Indian (Asian Indian)," she pondered why she and her friends did not have blacks in their crowd.

. . . I mean, there was so many kids. I don't think we had any black friends. I don't know why. It kid of stuck together and . . . I don't know, it wasn't that we, it wasn't that we wouldn't be *like* . . . *allowing* to black people. It's just that . . . there was never, like, an opportunity. There's no . . . population like that around where we lived.

Rick, a Mormon student at WU who opposed affirmative action, argued that blacks read "too much" when they do not get jobs. Rick's answered the question, "How would you counter those who believe that this company (a company described as 97% white in the process of making a hiring decision between a black and a white applicant) has a serious diversity company?,"

Um . . . I would probably say to them um . . . I'd say, "Do you know for sure? Do you know the manager, the person that hires them? Do you know them to be racist? Do you know that they are that way?" Um . . . I'd probably say, "If I knew the guy, I'd say he just got hired based on how well his score is. Or maybe is just whites in that neighborhood or mostly whites or not as many blacks percentage wise. And . . . I would claim that I think that they are looking too much into the situation . . . reading too much . . . reading too much racism into the situation . . . while there probably isn't any at all.

Rick, as most of the students who were asked to explain why the company was 97% white, could not concede that discrimination had anything to do with this situation. Thus, Rick's position and way of stating it clearly amount to "anything but race."

≫ "THEY ARE THE RACIST ONES . . .": PROJECTION AS A RHETORICAL TOOL

Projection is part of our normal equipment to defend our selves. It is also an essential tool in the creation of a corporate identity (Us versus Them) (Bartra 1994). More pertinent to this section, paranoid projection helps us "escape from guilt and responsibility and affix blame elsewhere" (Keen 1986: 21). College students projected racial motivations onto blacks as a way of avoiding responsibility and feeling good about themselves. Their projections appeared on a variety of issues (e.g., affirmative action, school and residential segregation, interracial friendship and marriage, and blacks' work ethic), but most often on the hot issue of so-called black self-segregation. For example, Janet, a student at SU, answered a question on whether or not blacks self-segregate as follows:

> I think they segregate themselves. Or, I mean, I don't know how everybody else is, but I would have no problem with talking with or being friends with a black person or any other type of minority. I think they've just got into their heads that they are different and, as a result, they're pulling themselves away.

The interviewer followed-up Janet's answer with a question trying to ascertain if Janet had tried to mingle with blacks, but Janet cut her off quickly with the following statement: "They're off to their own kind of little own world."

Janet projected once more in her answer to the interracial marriage question onto people who marry across the color line.

> I would feel that in most situations they're not really thinking of the, the child. I mean, they might not really think anything of it, *but* in reality I think most of the time when the child is growing up, he's going to be picked on because he has parents from different races and it's gonna ultimately affect the child and, and the end result is they're only thinking of them, of their own happiness, not the happiness of, of the kid.

By projecting selfishness onto people who intermarry, Janet was able voice safely her otherwise racially problematic stance on intermarriage. Nevertheless, she admitted that if she or a member of her family ever became involved wit someone from a different race, her family, "would *not* like it *at all!* [**laughs**].

Kim, another SU student, projected segregationist attitudes onto blacks.

> Um, mainly I think they segregate themselves. I think that, you know, they have um, you know, I guess they probably feel they don't fit in, but I don't know if they really try. I don't know, you know, like they have their own Unions and I don't know how hard they try to fit into, you know, like ours, and we can't really fit into theirs 'cause we are not really allowed. I mean, I don't think all of them, like a lot of them are. I have several, you know, people that are in my classes that are minorities and they're just fine. I mean, for me, it's not like they don't want to talk to me 'cause I'm white or anything [**laughs**], they just, I don't know . . .

Although all projections are exculpatory (Memmi 2000), most accomplish this task implicitly. However, Kim not only projects racial motivations onto blacks but *openly* exonerates whites (and herself) for not mingling with blacks.

⦚ "IT MAKES ME A LITTLE ANGRY . . .": THE ROLE OF DIMINUTIVES IN COLOR BLIND RACETALK

Because maintaining a non-racial, color blind stance is key, whites use diminutives to soften their racial blows. Hence, when they oppose affirmative action, few say, "I against affirmative action." Instead, they say something such as, "I am just a little bit against affirmative action." Similarly, few whites who oppose interracial marriage flatly state, "I am against interracial marriage." Instead, they say something such as, "I am just a bit concerned about the welfare of the children." About half of the college students used diminutives to cushion their views on issues such as interracial marriage and affirmative action.

For instance, Andy, a student at WU, answered the question on interracial marriage as follows:

> I would say I have a little bit of the same concern about the children just because it's more, I mean, would be more difficult on them. But, I mean, I definitely [**nervous laugh**] have no problem with any form of interracial marriage . . . Um, that's just, just an extra hurdle that they would have to over, overcome with the children, but, but I? it wouldn't be a detriment to the kids, I don't think. That just makes it a little more difficult for them.

Mickey, a student at MU, used diminutives to make the claim that people at MU were oversensitive about matters regarding race or sexual orientation. Andy made his comments in response to a question about whether on not he participated in political activities in campus. After stating in no uncertain terms that he did not, the interviewer, curious by the tone of his answer, commented "You sounded pretty staunch in your no." Andy replied:

> Yeah, I just, I don't know. I think . . . everybody, everybody here just seems like really uptight about that kind of stuff and, I mean, maybe it's just because I never had to deal with that kind of stuff at home, but, ya' know, it seems like you have to watch everything you say because if you slip a little bit, and you never know, there's a protest the next day . . .

When asked to explain what kind of "slips" he was referring to, Andy said,

> Like, I mean, if you hear a professor say something, like a racial slur, or something just like a little bit, ya' know, a little bit outta hand, ya' know. I mean . . . I mean, I would just see it as like . . . ya' know, he was just, you took it out of context or something, but, ya' know, is just little things like

that. It's just, it's so touchy. Everything is so touchy it seems like around here. And I don't, like . . . I don't like to get into debates about stuff and, ya' know, about cultures and stuff like that. 'Cause I've seen it, I've seen it around here, ya' know, plenty, ya know, about like, with religious stuff and gay stuff and minority stuff. And it's just nothin' of that, I just don't like to get into that stuff.

Thus, Mickey uses the diminutives to state that people at MU are hypersensitive because they protest when a professor does "little things" like saying "a racial slur" in class. Brian, the SU student cited above, after stating in a half-hearted way that he supported government intervention to increase the level of school integration in the country, commented the following on busing:

That works as long as—I think it's stupid, like I'm no sure the way things are going, but I heard things like people taking three hour bus rides just to be integrated into school, I mean, that's ridiculous. If there's a school closer by, you know, that just seems like, you know, going a little bit extreme on this integration thing, you know.

〈〈 "I, I, I, I DON'T MEAN, YOU KNOW, BUT . . .": RHETORICAL INCOHERENCE AND COLOR BLINDNESS

Rhetorical incoherence (e.g., grammatical mistakes, lengthy pauses, repetition, etc.) is part of all natural speech. Nevertheless, the degree of incoherence increases noticeably when people discuss sensitive subjects. And because the new racial climate in America forbids the open expression of racially-based feelings, views, and positions, when whites discuss issues that make them feel uncomfortable, they become almost incomprehensible. Almost all the college student became incoherent when discussing various racial issues, particularly when discussing their personal relationships with blacks. For example, Ray, a MU who was very articulate throughout the interview, became almost incomprehensible when answering the question about whether he had been involved with minorities while in college.

Um well, she's really my first girlfriend, to be quite honest with you [**laughs**]. Um . . . uh, so to answer that question, no. Um, but I would not . . . I mean, I would not ever . . . preclude, ub, a black woman from being my girlfriend on the basis that she was black. Ya' know, I mean, ya' know what I mean? If you're looking about it from, ya' know, the standpoint of just attraction, I mean, I think that, ya' know . . . I think, ya' know, I think, ya' know, all women are, I mean, all women have a sort of different type of beauty, if you will. And I think that, ya' know, for black women, it's somewhat different than white women. Um, but I don't think it's, ya know, I mean, it's, it's . . . it's nothing that would ever stop me from like, uh . . . I mean, I don't know, I mean, I don't if that's . . . I mean, that's just sort of been my impression. I mean, it's not like! would ever say, "No, I'll never have a black girlfriend," but it just seems to me like I'm not as attracted to black women as I am to white women, for whatever reason. It's not about prejudice, it's just sort of like, ya' know, whatever. Just sort of the way, way . . . like I see white women as compared to black women, ya' know?

The interviewer followed-up Ray's answer with the question, "Do you have any idea why that would be?," to which he replied the following: "I, I, I [*sighs*] don't really know. It's just sort of hard to describe. It's just like, ya' know, who you're more drawn to, ya' know, for whatever reason, ya' know?"

Another issue that made some students feel seemingly uncomfortable was the matter of self-segregation. For example, Ann, a WU student, became very hesitant in her answer to the question of whether blacks self-segregate or are not made to feel welcome.

Um, no, I don't think they segregate themselves, they just probably just, um, I guess probably they're . . . I don't know. Let's see . . . let's uh, try to ? Like um, we were trying? Like um, mutual friends, I suppose, maybe . . . and probably maybe it's just your peers that you know, or maybe that they, they have more, um, more like activities, or classes and clubs, I don't really know, but I don't think it's necessarily conscious, un, I don't . . . I wouldn't say that uh, I would feel uh, uncomfortable going and talking to a whole group.

⁂ CONCLUSION

If the myth of color blind racism is going to stick, whites need to have tools to repair mistakes (or the appearance of mistakes) rhetorically. In this article I documented the numerous tools available to whites to restore a color blind image when whiteness seeps through discursive cracks. Color blind racism's racetalk avoids racist terminology and preserves its myth through semantic moves such as "I am not a racist, but," "Some of my best friends are . . . ," "I am not black, but," and "Yes and no." Additionally, when something could be interpreted as racially motivated, whites can use the "Anything but race" strategy. Thus, if a school or neighborhood is completely white, they can say "It's not a racial thing" or "It's economics, not race." They can also project the matter onto blacks by saying things such as "They don't want to live with us" or "Blacks are the really prejudiced ones."

But how can whites protect themselves against the charge of racism when they state positions that may be interpreted as racist? They can use diminutives as racial shock absorbers and utter statements such as "I am a little bit against affirmative action because it is terribly unfair to whites" or "I am a bit concerned about interracial marriage because the children suffer so much." And these tools can be mixed-up as the interlocutor sees fit (Wetherell and Potter 1992). Hence, respondents could use a diminutive ("I am a little bit upset with blacks . . ."), followed by a projection (". . . because they cry racism for everything even though they are the ones who are racist . . ."), and balanced out their statement with semantic moves at the end to land safely (". . . and I am not being racial about this, is just that, I don't know").

These interviews also revealed that talking about race in America is a highly emotional matter. Almost all the respondents exhibited a degree of incoherence at some point or other in the interview. Digressions, long pauses, repetition, and self corrections were the order of the day. This incoherent talk is the result of talking about race in a world that insists race does not matter rather than a tool of color blindness. However, since it is so preeminent, it must be included as part of the linguistic modalities of color blind racism.

Finally, I end with a methodological observation that has policy implications. If there is a new racial ideology that has an arsenal of rhetorical tools to avoid the appearance of racism, analysts must be fully aware of its existence and develop the analytical and interpretive know-how to dissect color blind nonsense. Analysts unaware of these developments (or unwilling to accept them) will continue producing research suggesting that racial matters in the United States have improved dramatically and, like color blinders, urge for race-neutral social policies. It is the task of progressive social scientists to expose color blindness, show the continuing significance of race, and wake-up color blind researchers to the color of the facts of race in contemporary United States.

\\\ DISCUSSION QUESTIONS

1. What are the strategies used by the students? Can you think of ways that these strategies are used in discussing issues that are uncomfortable other than race?

2. Why do you think the students Bonilla-Silva interviewed rely on these strategies? If the underlying implications of what they are saying are negative, why don't they just express those opinions outright?

3. Do your parents or grandparents talk about race differently than the students described in the article? If so, what do you think accounts for this difference?

∭ REFERENCES

Bartra, Roger 1994 *Wild Men in the Looking Glass: The Mythic Origins of European Otherness.* Ann Arbor, MI: The University of Michigan Press.

Bobo, Lawrence, James Kluegel and Ryan Smith 1997 "Laissez faire Racism: The Crystallization of a Kinder, Gentler, Antiblack Ideology," in Steven A. Tuch and Jack Martin (eds.), *Racial Attitudes in the 1990s,* pp. 15–42. Westport, CT: Praeger.

Bonilla-Silva, Eduardo 2001 *White Supremacy and Racism in the Post-Civil Rights Era.* Boulder, CO: Lynne Rienner Publishers.

Bonilla-Silva, Eduardo and Tyrone A. Forman 2000 "I'm not a racist, but . . . : Mapping white college students' racial ideology in the USA," (with Bonilla-Silva), in *Discourse ξ Society* 11(1): 50–85.

Bonilla-Silva, Eduardo and Amanda E. Lewis 1999 "The New Racism: Racial Structure in the United States, 1960s–1990s." *Race, Nation, and Citizenship,* pp. 55–100, edited by Paul Wong. Boulder, Colorado: Westview Press.

Brooks, Roy L. 1990 *Rethinking the American Race Problem.* Berkeley: University of California Press.

Brooks, Roy L. 1996 *Integration or Separation: A Strategy for Racial Equality.* Cambridge, MA and London: Harvard University Press.

Essed, Philomena 1996 *Diversity: Gender, Color, and Culture.* Amherst, MA: University of Massachusetts Press.

Edsall, Thomas B. and M.D. Edsall 1992 *Chain Reaction.* New York: W.W. Norton.

Grier, Peter and James N. Thurman 1999 "Youths' Shifting Attitudes on Race." *Christian Science Monitor,* August 18.

Hass, R. Glen, I. Katz, N. Rizzo, J. Bailey and L. Moore 1992 "When racial ambivalence evokes negative affect, using a disguised measure of mood." *Personality and Social Psychology Bulletin* 18: 786–797.

Jackman, Mary 1994 *The Velvet Glove.* Berkeley: University of California Press.

Katz, Irwin and R.G. Hass 1988 "Racial ambivalence and American value conflict: Correlational and priming studies of dual cognitive structures." *Journal of Personality and Social Psychology* 55: 893–905.

Keen, Sam 1986 *Faces of the Enemy: Reflections of the Hostile Imagination.* New York: Harper and Row.

Lipset, Seymour Martin 1996 *American Exceptionalism.* New York and London: W.W. Norton.

Memmi, Albert 2000 *Racism.* Minneapolis and London: University of Minnesota Press.

Otis-Graham, Lawrence 1995 *Member of the Club.* New York: Harper Collins.

Sears, David, Jim Sidanius and Lawrence Bobo 2000 *Racialized Politics.* Chicago and London: The University of Chicago Press.

Schuman, Howard et al. 1997 *Racial Attitudes in America.* Cambridge, MA: Harvard University Press.

Smith, Robert C. 1995 *Racism in the Post-Civil Rights Era: Now You See It, Now You Don't.* New York: State University of New York Press.

Smith, Tom W. 1999 "Measuring Inter-Racial Friendships: Experimental Comparisons." GSS Methodological Report No. 91.

Sniderman, Paul M. and Edward G. Carmines 1997 *Reaching Beyond Race.* Cambridge, MA, and London: Harvard University Press.

Sniderman, Paul and Thomas Piazza 1993 *The Scar of Race.* Cambridge, MA: Harvard University Press.

Thomas, Melvin 2000 "Anything But Race: The Social Science Retreat from Racism," *African American Research Perspectives* Winter 79: 96.

Wetherell, Margaret and Jonathan Potter 1992 *Mapping the Language of Racism.* New York: Columbia University Press.

⚜ NOTES

1. See the new consensus among survey researchers on racial attitudes in David O. Sears, Jim Sidanius, and Lawrence Bobo, *Racialized Boundaries (2000).* See especially Michael Dawson's piece. "Slowly Coming to Grips with the Effects of the American Racial Order on American Policy Preferences," in the same volume.

2. The style of an ideology refers to its peculiar *linguistic manners and rhetorical strategies* (or *racetalk*), to the technical tools that allow users to articulate its frames and storylines. For a full elaboration of the racial ideology paradigm, see Chapter 3 in Eduardo Bonilla-Silva, *White Supremacy and Racism in the Post-Civil Rights Era* (Boulder: Lynne Rienner Publishers, 2001).

3. Many analysts have observed that private racetalk by whites about non-whites is more direct and clearly racist. For example, Lawrence Otis-Graham, in *Member of the Club* (1995), shows how when whites feel free to talk about race they do and in the nastiest fashion.

4. The following are the basic conventions I used in the transcriptions. Respondent's emphasis (*italics*), comments on respondent's demeanor − tone, etc.−or by the interviewer (**bold print**), and pauses (. . .).

5. A survey conducted by Zogby International at the request of Philip Klinkner, Director of Arthur Levitt Public Affairs Center at Hamilton College, of randomly selected people ages 18 to 29 in 1999 found that 90 percent of the respondents had heard racist jokes occasionally. Grier Peter and James N. Thurman, "Youths' Shifting Attitudes on Race," *Christian Science Monitor*, August 18, 1999.

6. Melvin Thomas has found that this perspective affects deeply social science research on racial matters. Melvin Thomas, "Anything But Race: The Social Science Retreat from Racism," *African American Research Perspectives* Winter 79:96 (2000).

19

The Code of the Streets

By Elijah Anderson

In this article, Elijah Anderson explains the code of the streets, *a set of norms that govern interactions in public spaces in poor, inner-city African American neighborhoods. His insightful analysis sheds light on the social context of the interpersonal violence that plagues many of these neighborhoods. Homicide is the leading cause of death for young African American men, but what is often reported in the news as random or senseless violence likely has its basis in the logic of the code of the streets. Anderson points out that the majority of the residents in these neighborhoods are law-abiding citizens with mainstream values, what he and other residents call* decent families. *But a small portion of* street families *also live in these neighborhoods. Street families are marked by more extreme poverty, a lack of consideration for others, less involved parenting, and a belief in the values of the code of the streets.*

The main feature of the code of the streets is to display a willingness to use violence to get or maintain respect in interpersonal interactions. Respect is a scarce commodity in communities that lack good job prospects and educational opportunities, so public interactions become an important locale for getting and maintaining respect. Because decent and street families must coexist in the same neighborhood, those from decent families must also adhere to and use the code in order to safely navigate public space. As Anderson insightfully explains, there is much more to the stereotypical image of swaggering, violence-prone, inner city minorities than there appears on the surface.

"The Code of the Streets" by Elijah Anderson, The *Atlantic,* May 1, 1994. Reprinted by permission of the author.

Of all the problems besetting the poor inner-city black community, none is more pressing than that of interpersonal violence and aggression. It wreaks havoc daily with the lives of community residents and increasingly spills over into downtown and residential middle-class areas. Muggings, burglaries, carjackings, and drug-related shootings, all of which may leave their victims or innocent bystanders dead, are now common enough to concern all urban and many suburban residents. The inclination to violence springs from the circumstances of life among the ghetto poor—the lack of jobs that pay a living wage, the stigma of race, the fallout from rampant drug use and drug trafficking, and the resulting alienation and lack of hope for the future.

Simply living in such an environment places young people at special risk of falling victim to aggressive behavior. Although there are often forces in the community which can counteract the negative influences, by far the most powerful being a strong, loving, "decent" (as inner-city residents put it) family committed to middle-class values, the despair is pervasive enough to have spawned an oppositional culture, that of "the streets," whose norms are often consciously opposed to those of mainstream society. These two orientations—decent and street—socially organize the community, and their coexistence has important consequences for residents, particularly children growing up in the inner city. Above all, this environment means that even youngsters whose home lives reflect mainstream values—and the majority of homes in the community do—must be able to handle themselves in a street-oriented environment.

This is because the street culture has evolved what may be called a code of the streets, which amounts to a set of informal rules governing interpersonal public behavior, including violence. The rules prescribe both a proper comportment and a proper way to respond if challenged. They regulate the use of violence and so allow those who are inclined to aggression to precipitate violent encounters in an approved way. The rules have been established and are enforced mainly by the street-oriented, but on the streets the distinction between street and decent is often irrelevant; everybody knows that if the rules are violated, there are penalties. Knowledge of the code is thus largely defensive; it is literally necessary for operating in public. Therefore, even though families with a decency orientation are usually opposed to the values of the code, they often reluctantly encourage their children's familiarity with it to enable them to negotiate the inner-city environment.

At the heart of the code is the issue of respect—loosely defined as being treated "right," or granted the deference one deserves. However, in the troublesome public environment of the inner city, as people increasingly feel buffeted by forces beyond their control, what one deserves in the way of respect becomes more and more problematic and uncertain. This in turn further opens the issue of respect to sometimes intense interpersonal negotiation. In the street culture, especially among young people, respect is viewed as almost an external entity that is hard-won but easily lost, and so must constantly be guarded. The rules of the code in fact provide a framework for negotiating respect. The person whose very appearance—including his clothing, demeanor, and way of moving—deters transgressions feels that he possesses, and may be considered by others to possess, a measure of respect. With the right amount of respect, for instance, he can avoid "being bothered" in public. If he is bothered, not only may he be in physical danger but he has been disgraced or "dissed" (disrespected). Many of the forms that dissing can take might seem petty to middle-class people (maintaining eye contact for too long, for example), but to those invested in the street code, these actions become serious indications of the other person's intentions. Consequently, such people become very sensitive to advances and slights, which could well serve as warnings of imminent physical confrontation.

This hard reality can be traced to the profound sense of alienation from mainstream society and its institutions felt by many poor inner-city black people, particularly the young. The code of the streets is actually a cultural adaptation to a profound lack of faith in the police and the judicial system. The police are most often seen as representing the dominant white society and not caring to protect inner-city residents. When called, they may not respond, which is one reason many residents feel they must be prepared to take extraordinary measures to defend themselves and their loved ones against those who are inclined to aggression. Lack of police accountability has in fact been incorporated into the status system: the person who is believed capable of "taking care of himself" is accorded a certain deference, which translates into a sense of physical and psychological control. Thus the street code emerges where the influence of the police ends and personal responsibility for one's safety is felt to begin. Exacerbated by the proliferation of drugs and easy access to guns, this volatile situation results in the ability of the street oriented minority (or those who effectively "go for bad") to dominate the public spaces.

⫸ DECENT AND STREET FAMILIES

Although almost everyone in poor inner-city neighborhoods is struggling financially and therefore feels a certain distance from the rest of America, the decent and the street family in a real sense represent two poles of value orientation, two contrasting conceptual categories. The labels "decent" and "street," which the residents themselves use, amount to evaluative judgments that confer status on local residents. The labeling is often the result of a social contest among individuals and families of the neighborhood. Individuals of the two orientations often coexist in the same extended family. Decent residents judge themselves to be so while judging others to be of the street, and street individuals often present themselves as decent, drawing distinctions between themselves and other people. In addition, there is quite a bit of circumstantial behavior—that is, one person may at different times exhibit both decent and street orientations, depending on the circumstances. Although these designations result from so much social jockeying, there do exist concrete features that define each conceptual category.

Generally, so-called decent families tend to accept mainstream values more fully and attempt to instill them in their children. Whether married couples with children or single-parent (usually female) households, they are generally "working poor" and so tend to be better off financially than their street-oriented neighbors. They value hard work and self-reliance and are willing to sacrifice for their children. Because they have a certain amount of faith in mainstream society, they harbor hopes for a better future for their children, if not for themselves. Many of them go to church and take a strong interest in their children's schooling. Rather than dwelling on the real hardships and inequities facing them, many such decent people, particularly the increasing number of grandmothers raising grandchildren, see their difficult situation as a test from God and derive great support from their faith and from the church community.

Extremely aware of the problematic and often dangerous environment in which they reside, decent parents tend to be strict in their child-rearing practices, encouraging children to respect authority and walk a straight moral line. They have an almost obsessive concern about trouble of any kind and remind their children to be on the lookout for people and situations that might lead to it. At the same time, they are themselves polite and considerate of others, and teach their children to be the same way. At home, at work, and in church, they strive hard to maintain a positive mental attitude and a spirit of cooperation.

So-called street parents, in contrast, often show a lack of consideration for other people and have a rather superficial sense of family and community. Though they may love their children, many of them are unable to cope with the physical and emotional demands of parenthood, and find it difficult to reconcile their needs with those of their children. These families, who are more fully invested in the code of the streets than the decent people are, may aggressively socialize their children into it in a normative way. They believe in the code and judge themselves and others according to its values.

In fact the overwhelming majority of families in the inner-city community try to approximate the decent-family model, but there are many others who clearly represent the worst fears of the decent family. Not only are their financial resources extremely limited, but what little they have may easily be misused. The lives of the street-oriented are often marked by disorganization. In the most desperate circumstances people frequently have a limited understanding of priorities and consequences, and so frustrations mount over bills, food, and, at times, drink, cigarettes, and drugs. Some tend toward self-destructive behavior; many street-oriented women are crack-addicted ("on the pipe"), alcoholic, or involved in complicated relationships with men who abuse them. In addition, the seeming intractability of their situation, caused in large part by the lack of well-paying jobs and the persistence of racial discrimination, has engendered deep-seated bitterness and anger in many of the most desperate and poorest blacks, especially young people. The need both to exercise a measure of control and to lash out at somebody is often reflected in the adults' relations with their children. At the least, the frustrations of persistent poverty shorten the fuse in such people—contributing to a lack of patience with anyone, child or adult, who irritates them.

In these circumstances a woman—or a man, although men are less consistently present in children's lives—can be quite aggressive with children, yelling at and striking them for the least little infraction of the rules she has set down. Often little if any serious explanation follows the verbal and physical punishment. This response teaches children a particular lesson. They learn that to solve any kind of interpersonal problem one must quickly resort to hitting or other violent behavior. Actual peace and quiet, and also the appearance of calm, respectful children conveyed to her neighbors and friends, are often what the young mother most desires, but at times she will be very aggressive in trying to get them. Thus she may be quick to beat her children, especially if they defy her law, not because she hates them but because this is the way she knows to control them. In fact, many street-oriented women love their children dearly. Many mothers in the community subscribe to the notion that there is a "devil in the boy" that must be beaten out of him or that socially "fast girls need to be whupped." Thus much of what borders on child abuse in the view of social authorities is acceptable parental punishment in the view of these mothers.

Many street-oriented women are sporadic mothers whose children learn to fend for themselves when necessary, foraging for food and money any way they can get it. The children are sometimes employed by drug dealers or become addicted themselves. These children of the street, growing up with little supervision, are said to "come up hard." They often learn to fight at an early age, sometimes using short-tempered adults around them as role models. The street-oriented home may be fraught with anger, verbal disputes, physical aggression, and even mayhem. The children observe these goings-on, learning the lesson that might make right. They quickly learn to hit those who cross them, and the dog-eat-dog mentality prevails.

In order to survive, to protect oneself, it is necessary to marshal inner resources and be ready to deal with adversity in a hands-on way. In these circumstances physical prowess takes on great significance.

In some of the most desperate cases, a street-oriented mother may simply leave her young children alone and unattended while she goes out. The most irresponsible women can be found at local bars and crack houses, getting high and socializing with other adults. Sometimes a troubled woman will leave very young children alone for days at a time. Reports of crack addicts abandoning their children have become common in drug infested inner-city communities. Neighbors or relatives discover the abandoned children, often hungry and distraught over the absence of their mother. After repeated absences, a friend or relative, particularly a grandmother, will often step in to care for the young children, sometimes petitioning the authorities to send her, as guardian of the children, the mother's welfare check, if the mother gets one. By this time, however, the children may well have learned the first lesson of the streets: survival itself, let alone respect, cannot be taken for granted; you have to fight for your place in the world.

⦚⦚ CAMPAIGNING FOR RESPECT

These realities of inner-city life are largely absorbed on the streets. At an early age, often even before they start school, children from street oriented homes gravitate to the streets, where they "hang"—socialize with their peers. Children from these generally permissive homes have a great deal of latitude and are allowed to "rip and run" up and down the street. They often come home from school, put their books down, and go right back out the door. On school nights eight- and nine-year-olds remain out until nine or ten o'clock (and teenagers typically come in whenever they want to). On the streets they play in groups that often become the source of their primary social bonds. Children from decent homes tend to be more carefully supervised and are thus likely to have curfews and to be taught how to stay out of trouble.

When decent and street kids come together, a kind of social shuffle occurs in which children have a chance to go either way. Tension builds as a child comes to realize that he must choose an orientation. The kind of home he comes from influences but does not determine the way he will ultimately turn out—although it is unlikely that a child from a thoroughly street oriented family will easily absorb decent values on the streets. Youths who emerge from street-oriented families but develop a decency orientation almost always learn those values in another setting— in school, in a youth group, in church. Often it is the result of their involvement with a caring "old head" (adult role model).

In the street, through their play, children pour their individual life experiences into a common knowledge pool, affirming, confirming, and elaborating on what they have observed in the home and matching their skills against those of others. And they learn to fight. Even small children test one another, pushing and shoving, and are ready to hit other children over circumstances not to their liking. In turn, they are readily hit by other children, and the child who is toughest prevails. Thus the violent resolution of disputes, the hitting and cursing, gains social reinforcement. The child in effect is initiated into a system that is really a way of campaigning for respect.

In addition, younger children witness the disputes of older children, which are often resolved through cursing and abusive talk, if not aggression or outright violence. They see that one child succumbs to the greater physical and mental abilities of the other. They are also alert and attentive witnesses to the verbal and physical fights of adults, after which they compare notes and share their interpretations of the event. In almost every case the victor is the person who physically won the altercation, and this person often enjoys the esteem and respect of onlookers. These experiences reinforce the lessons the children have learned at home: might makes right, and toughness is a virtue, while humility is not. In effect they learn the social meaning of fighting. When it is left virtually unchallenged, this understanding becomes an ever more important part of the child's working conception of the world. Over time the code of the streets becomes refined.

Those street-oriented adults with whom children come in contact—including mothers, fathers, brothers, sisters, boyfriends, cousins, neighbors, and friends— help them along in forming this understanding by verbalizing the messages they are getting through experience: "Watch your back." "Protect yourself." "Don't punk out." "If somebody messes with you, you got to pay them back." "If someone disses you, you got to straighten them out." Many parents actually impose sanctions if a child is not sufficiently aggressive. For example, if a child loses a fight and comes home upset, the parent might respond, "Don't you come in here crying that somebody beat you up; you better get back out there and whup his ass. I didn't raise no punks! Get back out there and whup his ass. If you don't whup his ass, I'll whup your ass when you come home." Thus the child obtains reinforcement for being tough and showing nerve.

While fighting, some children cry as though they are doing something they are ambivalent about. The fight may be against their wishes, yet they may feel constrained to fight or face the consequences—not just from peers but also from caretakers or parents, who may administer another beating if they back down. Some adults recall receiving such lessons from their own parents and justify repeating them to their children as a way to toughen them up. Looking capable of taking care of oneself as a form of self-defense is a dominant theme among both street-oriented and decent adults who worry about the safety of their children. There is thus at times a convergence in their child-rearing practices, although the rationales behind them may differ.

\\ SELF-IMAGE BASED ON "JUICE"

By the time they are teenagers, most youths have either internalized the code of the streets or at least learned the need to comport themselves in accordance with its rules, which chiefly have to do with interpersonal communication. The code revolves around the presentation of self. Its basic requirement is the display of a certain predisposition to violence. Accordingly, one's bearing must send the unmistakable if sometimes subtle message to "the next person" in public that one is capable of violence and mayhem when the situation requires it, that one can take care of oneself. The nature of this communication is largely determined by the demands of the circumstances but can include facial expressions, gait, and verbal expressions—all of which are geared mainly to deterring aggression. Physical appearance, including clothes, jewelry, and grooming, also plays an important part in how a person is viewed; to be respected, it is important to have the right look.

Even so, there are no guarantees against challenges, because there are always people around looking for a fight to increase their share of respect—or "juice," as it is sometimes called on the street. Moreover, if a person is assaulted, it is important, not only in the eyes of his opponent but also in the eyes of his "running buddies," for him to avenge himself. Otherwise he risks being "tried" (challenged) or "moved on" by any number of others. To maintain his honor he must show he is not someone to be "messed with" or "dissed." In general, the person must "keep himself straight" by managing his position of respect among others; this involves in part his self-image, which is shaped by what he thinks others are thinking of him in relation to his peers.

Objects play an important and complicated role in establishing self-image. Jackets, sneakers, gold jewelry, reflect not just a person's taste, which tends to be tightly regulated among adolescents of all social classes, but also a willingness to possess things that may require defending. A boy wearing a fashionable, expensive jacket, for example, is vulnerable to attack by another who covets the jacket and either cannot afford to buy one or wants the added satisfaction of depriving someone else of his. However, if the boy forgoes the desirable jacket and wears one that isn't "hip," he runs the risk of being teased and possibly even assaulted as an unworthy person. To be allowed to hang with certain prestigious crowds, a boy must wear a different set of expensive clothes—sneakers and athletic suit—every day. Not to be able to do so might make him appear socially deficient. The youth comes to covet such items—especially when he sees easy prey wearing them.

In acquiring valued things, therefore, a person shores up his identity—but since it is an identity based on having things, it is highly precarious. This very precariousness gives a heightened sense of urgency to staying even with peers, with whom the person is actually competing. Young men and women who are able to command respect through their presentation of self—by allowing their possessions and their body language to speak for them—may not have to campaign for regard but may, rather, gain it by the force of their manner. Those who are unable to command respect in this way must actively campaign for it—and are thus particularly alive to slights.

One way of campaigning for status is by taking the possessions of others. In this context, seemingly ordinary objects can become trophies imbued with symbolic value that far exceeds their monetary worth. Possession of the trophy can symbolize the ability to violate somebody—to "get in his face," to take something of value from him, to "dis" him, and thus to enhance one's own worth by stealing someone else's. The trophy does not have to be something material. It can be another person's sense of honor, snatched away with a derogatory remark. It can be the outcome of a fight. It can be the imposition of a certain standard, such as a girl's getting herself recognized as the most beautiful. Material things, however, fit easily into the pattern. Sneakers, a pistol, even somebody else's girlfriend, can become a trophy. When a person can take something from another and then flaunt it, he gains a certain regard by being the owner, or the controller, of that thing. But this display of ownership can then provoke other people to challenge him. This game of who controls what is thus constantly being played out on inner-city streets, and the trophy—extrinsic or intrinsic, tangible or intangible—identifies the current winner.

An important aspect of this often violent give-and-take is its zero-sum quality. That is, the extent to which one person can raise himself up depends on his ability to put another person down. This underscores the alienation that permeates the inner-city ghetto community. There is a generalized sense that very little respect is to be had, and therefore everyone competes to get what affirmation he can of the little that is available. The craving for respect that results gives people thin skins. Shows of deference by others can be highly soothing, contributing to a sense of security, comfort, self-confidence, and self-respect. Transgressions by others which go unanswered diminish these feelings and are believed to encourage further transgressions. Hence one must be ever vigilant against the transgressions of others or even appearing as if transgressions will be tolerated. Among young people, whose sense of self-esteem is particularly vulnerable, there is an especially heightened concern with being disrespected. Many inner-city young men in particular crave respect to such a degree that they will risk their lives to attain and maintain it.

The issue of respect is thus closely tied to whether a person has an inclination to be violent, even as a victim. In the wider society people may not feel required to retaliate physically after an attack, even though they are aware that they have been degraded or taken advantage of. They may feel a great need to defend themselves during an attack, or to behave in such a way as to deter aggression (middle-class people certainly can and do become victims of street-oriented youths), but they are much more likely than street-oriented people to feel that they can walk away from a possible altercation with their self-esteem intact. Some people may even have the strength of character to flee, without any thought that their self-respect or esteem will be diminished.

In impoverished inner-city black communities, however, particularly among young males and perhaps increasingly among females, such flight would be extremely difficult. To run away would likely leave one's self-esteem in tatters. Hence people often feel constrained not only to stand up and at least attempt to resist during an assault but also to "pay back"—to seek revenge—after a successful assault on their person. This may include going to get a weapon or even getting relatives involved. Their very identity and self-respect, their honor, is often intricately tied up with the way they perform on the streets during and after such encounters. This outlook reflects the circumscribed opportunities of the inner-city poor. Generally people outside the ghetto have other ways of gaining status and regard, and thus do not feel so dependent on such physical displays.

⟋⟍ BY TRIAL OF MANHOOD

On the street, among males these concerns about things and identity have come to be expressed in the concept of "manhood." Manhood in the inner city means taking the prerogatives of men with respect to strangers, other men, and women— being distinguished as a man. It implies physicality and a certain ruthlessness. Regard and respect are associated with this concept in large part because of its practical application: if others have little or no regard for a person's manhood, his very life and those of his loved ones could be in jeopardy. But there is a chicken-and-egg aspect to this situation: one's physical safety is more likely to be jeopardized in public because manhood is associated with respect. In other words, an existential link has been created between the idea of manhood and one's self-esteem, so that it has become hard to say which is primary. For many inner-city youths, manhood and respect are flip sides of the same coin; physical and psychological well-being are inseparable, and both require a sense of control, of being in charge.

The operating assumption is that a man, especially a real man, knows what other men know—the code of the streets. And if one is not a real man, one is somehow diminished as a person, and there are certain valued things one simply does not deserve. There is thus believed to be a certain justice to the code, since it is considered that everyone has the opportunity to know it. Implicit in this is that everybody is held responsible for being familiar with the code. If the victim of a mugging, for example, does not know the code and so responds "wrong," the perpetrator may feel justified even in killing him and may feel no remorse. He may think, "Too bad, but it's his fault. He should have known better."

So when a person ventures outside, he must adopt the code—kind of shield, really—to prevent others from "messing with" him. In these circumstances it is easy for people to think they are being tried or tested by others even when this is not the case. For it is sensed that something extremely valuable is at stake in every interaction, and people are encouraged to rise to the occasion, particularly with strangers. For people who are unfamiliar with the code—generally people who live outside the inner city—the concern with respect in the most ordinary interactions can be frightening and incomprehensible. But for those who are invested in the code, the clear object of their demeanor is to discourage strangers from even thinking about testing their manhood. And the sense of power that attends the ability to deter others can be alluring even to those who know the code without being heavily invested in it—the decent inner-city youths. Thus a boy who has been leading a basically decent life can, in trying circumstances, suddenly resort to deadly force.

Central to the issue of manhood is the widespread belief that one of the most effective ways of gaining respect is to manifest "nerve." Nerve is shown when one takes another person's possessions (the more valuable the better), "messes with" someone's woman, throws the first punch, "gets in someone's face," or pulls a trigger. Its proper display helps on the spot to check others who would violate one's person and also helps to build a reputation that works to prevent future challenges. But since such a show of nerve is a forceful expression of disrespect toward the person on the receiving end, the victim may be greatly offended and seek to retaliate with equal or greater force. A display of nerve, therefore, can easily provoke a life-threatening response, and the background knowledge of that possibility has often been incorporated into the concept of nerve.

True nerve exposes a lack of fear of dying. Many feel that it is acceptable to risk dying over the principle of respect. In fact, among the hard-core street-oriented, the clear risk of violent death may be preferable to being "dissed" by another. The youths who have internalized this attitude and convincingly display it in their public bearing are among the most threatening people of all, for it is commonly assumed that they fear no man. As the people of the community say, "They are the baddest dudes on the street." They often lead an existential life that may acquire meaning only when they are faced with the possibility of imminent death. Not to be afraid to die is by implication to have few compunctions about taking another's life. Not to be afraid to die is the quid pro quo of being able to take somebody else's life—for the right reasons, if the situation demands it. When others believe this is one's position, it gives one a real sense of power on the streets. Such credibility is what many inner-city youths strive to achieve, whether they are decent or street-oriented, both because of its practical defensive value and because of the positive way it makes them feel about themselves. The difference between the decent and the street-oriented youth is often that the decent youth makes a conscious decision to appear tough and manly; in another setting—with teachers, say, or at his part-time job—he can be polite and deferential. The street-oriented youth, on the other hand, has made the concept of manhood a part of his very identity; he has difficulty manipulating it—it often controls him.

⦚ GIRLS AND BOYS

Increasingly, teenage girls are mimicking the boys and trying to have their own version of "manhood." Their goal is the same—to get respect, to be recognized as capable of setting or maintaining a certain standard. They try to achieve this end in the ways that have been established by the boys, including posturing, abusive language, and the use of violence to resolve disputes, but the issues for the girls are different. Although conflicts over turf and status exist among the girls, the majority of disputes seem rooted in assessments of beauty (which girl in a group is "the cutest"), competition over boyfriends, and attempts to regulate other people's knowledge of and opinions about a girl's behavior or that of someone close to her, especially her mother.

A major cause of conflicts among girls is "he say, she say." This practice begins in the early school years and continues through high school. It occurs when "people," particularly girls, talk about others, thus putting their "business in the streets." Usually one girl will say something negative about another in the group, most often behind the person's back. The remark will then get back to the person talked about. She may retaliate or her friends may feel required to "take up for" her. In essence this is a form of group gossiping in which individuals are negatively assessed and evaluated. As with much gossip, the things said may or may not be true, but the point is that such imputations can cast aspersions on a person's good name. The accused is required to defend herself against the slander, which can result in arguments and fights, often over little of real substance. Here again is the problem of low self-esteem, which encourages youngsters to be highly sensitive to slights and to be vulnerable to feeling easily "dissed." To avenge the dissing, a fight is usually necessary.

Because boys are believed to control violence, girls tend to defer to them in situations of conflict. Often if a girl is attacked or feels slighted, she will get a brother, uncle, or cousin to do her fighting for her. Increasingly, however, girls are doing their own fighting and are even asking their male relatives to teach them how to fight. Some girls form groups that attack other girls or take things from them. A hard-core segment of inner-city girls inclined toward violence seems to be developing. As one thirteen year-old girl in a detention center for youths who have committed violent acts told me, "To get people to leave you alone, you gotta fight. Talking don't always get you out of stuff." One major difference between girls and boys: girls rarely use guns. Their fights are therefore not life-or-death struggles. Girls are not often willing to put their lives on the line for "manhood." The ultimate form of respect on the male-dominated inner-city street is thus reserved for men.

⩔ "GOING FOR BAD"

In the most fearsome youths such a cavalier attitude toward death grows out of a very limited view of life. Many are uncertain about how long they are going to live and believe they could die violently at any time. They accept this fate; they live on the edge. Their manner conveys the message that nothing intimidates them; whatever turn the encounter takes, they maintain their attack—rather like a pit bull, whose spirit many such boys admire. The demonstration of such tenacity "shows heart" and earns their respect.

This fearlessness has implications for law enforcement. Many street oriented boys are much more concerned about the threat of "justice" at the hands of a peer than at the hands of the police. Moreover, many feel not only that they have little to lose by going to prison but that they have something to gain. The toughening-up one experiences in prison can actually enhance one's reputation on the streets. Hence the system loses influence over the hard core who are without jobs, with little perceptible stake in the system. If mainstream society has done nothing for them, they counter by making sure it can do nothing to them.

At the same time, however, a competing view maintains that true nerve consists in backing down, walking away from a fight, and going on with one's business. One fights only in self-defense. This view emerges from the decent philosophy that life is precious, and it is an important part of the socialization process common in decent homes. It discourages violence as the primary means of resolving disputes and encourages youngsters to accept nonviolence and talk as confrontational strategies. But "if the deal goes down," self-defense is greatly encouraged. When there is enough positive support for this orientation, either in the home or among one's peers, then nonviolence has a chance to prevail. But it prevails at the cost of relinquishing a claim to being bad and tough, and therefore sets a young person up as at the very least alienated from street-oriented peers and quite possibly a target of derision or even violence.

Although the nonviolent orientation rarely overcomes the impulse to strike back in an encounter, it does introduce a certain confusion and so can prompt a measure of soul-searching, or even profound ambivalence. Did the person back down with his respect intact or did he back down only to be judged a "punk"—a poison lacking manhood? Should he or she have acted? Should he or she have hit the other person in the mouth? These questions beset many young men and women during public confrontations. What is the "right" thing to do? In the quest for honor, respect, and local status—which few young people are uninterested in—common sense most often prevails, which leads many to opt for the tough approach, enacting their own particular versions of the display of nerve. The presentation of oneself as rough and tough is very often quite acceptable until one is rested. And then that presentation may help the person pass the test, because it will cause fewer questions to be asked about what he did and why. It is hard for a person to explain why he lost the fight or why he backed down. Hence many will strive to appear to "go for bad," while hoping they will never be tested. But when they are tested, the outcome of the situation may quickly be out of their hands, as they become wrapped up in the circumstances of the moment.

〜 AN OPPOSITIONAL CULTURE

The attitudes of the wider society are deeply implicated in the code of the streets. Most people in inner-city communities are not totally invested in the code, but the significant minority of hard-core street youths who are have to maintain the code in order to establish reputations, because they have—or feel they have—few other ways to assert themselves. For these young people the standards of the street code are the only game in town. The extent to which some children—particularly those who through upbringing have become most alienated and those lacking in strong and conventional social support—experience, feel, and internalize racist rejection and contempt from mainstream society may strongly encourage them to express contempt for the more conventional society in turn. In dealing with this contempt and rejection, some youngsters will consciously invest themselves and their considerable mental resources in what amounts to an oppositional culture to preserve themselves and their self-respect. Once they do, any respect they might be able to garner in the wider system pales in comparison with the respect available in the local system; thus they often lose interest in even attempting to negotiate the mainstream system.

At the same time, many less alienated young blacks have assumed a street-oriented demeanor as a way of expressing their blackness while really embracing a much more moderate way of life; they, too, want a nonviolent setting in which to live and raise a family. These decent people are trying hard to be part of the mainstream culture, but the racism, real and perceived, that they encounter helps to legitimate the oppositional culture. And so on occasion they adopt street behavior. In fact, depending on the demands of the situation, many people in the community slip back and forth between decent and street behavior.

A vicious cycle has thus been formed. The hopelessness and alienation many young inner-city black men and women feel, largely as a result of endemic joblessness and persistent racism, fuels the violence they engage in. This violence serves to confirm the negative feelings many whites and some middle-class blacks harbor toward the ghetto poor, further legitimating the oppositional culture and the code of the streets in the eyes of many poor young blacks. Unless this cycle is broken, attitudes on both sides will become increasingly entrenched, and the violence, which claims victims black and white, poor and affluent, will only escalate.

⟩⟩ DISCUSSION QUESTIONS

1. Why does use of the code by those from "decent" families make perfect sense according to Anderson?

2. How does enactment of the code of the streets relate to Goffman's ideas from *The Presentation of Self*?

3. If you had to write a code of the campus for your school, what would the rules be? What are the norms and expectations that govern interactions in public spaces where you go to school?

4. What does the code of the streets have in common with bullying that happens in middle-class, mostly White communities?

20

The Uses of Poverty: The Poor Pay All

Herbert J. Gans

Efforts to significantly reduce or eliminate the number of people living in poverty have been underway for decades. While the approach has varied, from Roosevelt's New Deal in the 1930s to the welfare reforms enacted by Bill Clinton in 1996, poverty has remained stubbornly on the American landscape. In 2013, over 46 million Americans, about 15% of the population, lived below the poverty line. In this article, Herbert Gans proposes a very different explanation of why poverty is so hard to get rid of. Relying on the functionalist perspective, he argues that having a group of people who are poor serves many useful social functions. These functions benefit and stabilize society at large in many ways. It's important to note that he isn't arguing that poverty is good or enjoyable for those who live in it. Rather, he is arguing that because having people who are poor has benefits for those who are not poor, it's unlikely to disappear anytime soon. As you read, think about how Gans' perspective differs from how the causes of poverty is typically discussed on the news or among your family and friends.

Some twenty years ago Robert K. Merton applied the notion of functional analysis to explain the continuing though maligned existence of the urban political machine: if it continued to exist, perhaps it fulfilled latent - unintended or unrecognized - positive functions. Clearly it did. Merton pointed out how

"The Uses of Poverty: The Poor Pay All," by Herbert J. Gans from *Social Policy*, July/August 1971. Reprinted with permission from Social Policy Magazine.

the political machine provided central authority to get things done when a decentralized local government could not act, humanized the services of the impersonal bureaucracy for fearful citizens, offered concrete help (rather than abstract law or justice) to the poor, and otherwise performed services needed or demanded by many people but considered unconventional or even illegal by formal public agencies.

Today, poverty is more maligned than the political machine ever was; yet it, too, is a persistent social phenomenon. Consequently, there may be some merit in applying functional analysis to poverty, in asking whether it also has positive functions that explain its persistence.

Merton defined functions as "those observed consequences [of a phenomenon] which make for the adaptation or adjustment of a given [social] system." I shall use a slightly different definition; instead of identifying functions for an entire social system, I shall identify them for the interest groups, socio-economic classes, and other population aggregates with shared values that 'inhabit' a social system. I suspect that in a modern heterogeneous society, few phenomena are functional or dysfunctional for the society as a whole, and that most result in benefits to some groups and costs to others. Nor are any phenomena indispensable; in most instances, one can suggest what Merton calls "functional alternatives" or equivalents for them, i.e., other social patterns or policies that achieve the same positive functions but avoid the dysfunctions.

Associating poverty with positive functions seems at first glance to be unimaginable. Of course, the slumlord and the loan shark are commonly known to profit from the existence of poverty, but they are viewed as evil men, so their activities are classified among the dysfunctions of poverty. However, what is less often recognized, at least by the conventional wisdom, is that poverty also makes possible the existence or expansion of respectable professions and occupations, for example, penology, criminology, social work, and public health. More recently, the poor have provided jobs for professional and para-professional "poverty warriors," and for journalists and social scientists, this author included, who have supplied the information demanded by the revival of public interest in poverty.

Clearly, then, poverty and the poor may well satisfy a number of positive functions for many nonpoor groups in American society. I shall describe thirteen such functions - economic, social and political - that seem to me most significant.

\\\ THE FUNCTIONS OF POVERTY

First, the existence of poverty ensures that society's "dirty work" will be done. Every society has such work: physically dirty or dangerous, temporary, dead-end and underpaid, undignified and menial jobs. Society can fill these jobs by paying higher wages than for "clean" work, or it can force people who have no other choice to do the dirty work - and at low wages. In America, poverty functions to provide a low-wage labor pool that is willing - or rather, unable to be unwilling - to perform dirty work at low cost. Indeed, this function of the poor is so important that in some Southern states, welfare payments have been cut off during the summer months when the poor are needed to work in the fields. Moreover, much of the debate about the Negative Income Tax and the Family Assistance Plan [welfare programs] has concerned their impact on the work incentive, by which is actually meant the incentive of the poor to do the needed dirty work if the wages therefrom are no larger than the income grant. Many economic activities that involve dirty work depend on the poor for their existence: restaurants, hospitals, parts of the garment industry, and "truck farming," among others, could not persist in their present form without the poor.

Second, because the poor are required to work at low wages, they subsidize a variety of economic activities that benefit the affluent. For example, domestics subsidize the upper middle and upper classes, making life easier for their employers and freeing affluent women for a variety of professional, cultural, civic and partying activities. Similarly, because the poor pay a higher proportion of their income in property and sales taxes, among others, they subsidize many state and local governmental services that benefit more affluent groups. In addition, the poor support innovation in medical practice as patients in teaching and research hospitals and as guinea pigs in medical experiments.

Third, poverty creates jobs for a number of occupations and professions that serve or "service" the poor, or protect the rest of society from them. As already noted, penology would be minuscule without the poor, as would the police. Other activities and groups that flourish because of the existence of poverty are the numbers game, the sale of heroin and cheap wines and liquors, Pentecostal ministers, faith healers, prostitutes, pawn shops, and the peacetime army, which recruits its enlisted men mainly from among the poor.

Fourth, the poor buy goods others do not want and thus prolong the economic usefulness of such goods - day-old bread, fruit and vegetables that otherwise would have to be thrown out, secondhand clothes, and deteriorating automobiles and buildings. They also provide incomes for doctors, lawyers, teachers, and others who are too old, poorly trained or incompetent to attract more affluent clients.

In addition to economic functions, the poor perform a number of social functions: Fifth, the poor can be identified and punished as alleged or real deviants in order to uphold the legitimacy of conventional norms. To justify the desirability of hard work, thrift, honesty, and monogamy, for example, the defenders of these norms must be able to find people who can be accused of being lazy, spendthrift, dishonest, and promiscuous. Although there is some evidence that the poor are about as moral and law-abiding as anyone else, they are more likely than middle-class transgressors to be caught and punished when they participate in deviant acts. Moreover, they lack the political and cultural power to correct the stereotypes that other people hold of them and thus continue to be thought of as lazy, spendthrift, etc., by those who need living proof that moral deviance does not pay.

Sixth, and conversely, the poor offer vicarious participation to the rest of the population in the uninhibited sexual, alcoholic, and narcotic behavior in which they are alleged to participate and which, being freed from the constraints of affluence, they are often thought to enjoy more than the middle classes. Thus many people, some social scientists included, believe that the poor not only are more given to uninhibited behavior (which may be true, although it is often motivated by despair more than by lack of inhibition) but derive more pleasure from it than affluent people (which research by Lee Rainwater, Walter Miller and others shows to be patently untrue). However, whether the poor actually have more sex and enjoy it more is irrelevant; so long as middle-class people believe this to be true, they can participate in it vicariously when instances are reported in factual or fictional form.

Seventh, the poor also serve a direct cultural function when culture created by or for them is adopted by the more affluent. The rich often collect artifacts from extinct folk cultures of poor people; and almost all Americans listen to the blues, Negro spirituals, and country music, which originated among the Southern poor. Recently they have enjoyed the rock styles that were born, like the Beatles, in the slums, and in the last year, poetry written by ghetto children has become popular in literary circles. The poor also serve as culture heroes, particularly, of course, to the Left; but the hobo, the cowboy, the hipster, and the mythical prostitute with a heart of gold have performed this function for a variety of groups.

Eighth, poverty helps to guarantee the status of those who are not poor. In every hierarchical society, someone has to be at the bottom; but in American society, in which social mobility is an important goal for many and people need to know where they stand, the poor function as a reliable and relatively permanent measuring rod for status comparisons. This is particularly true for the working class, whose politics is influenced by the need to maintain status distinctions between themselves and the poor, much as the aristocracy must find ways of distinguishing itself from the nouveaux riches.

Ninth, the poor also aid the upward mobility of groups just above them in the class hierarchy. Thus a goodly number of Americans have entered the middle class through the profits earned from the provision of goods and services in the slums, including illegal or nonrespectable ones that upper-class and upper-middle-class businessmen shun because of their low prestige. As a result, members of almost every immigrant group have financed their upward mobility by providing slum housing, entertainment, gambling, narcotics, etc., to later arrivals - most recently to Blacks and Puerto Ricans.

Tenth, the poor help to keep the aristocracy busy, thus justifying its continued existence. "Society" uses the poor as clients of settlement houses and beneficiaries of charity affairs; indeed, the aristocracy must have the poor to demonstrate its superiority over other elites who devote themselves to earning money.

Eleventh, the poor, being powerless, can be made to absorb the costs of change and growth in American society. During the nineteenth century, they did the backbreaking work that built the cities; today, they are pushed out of their neighborhoods to make room for "progress." Urban renewal projects to hold middle-class taxpayers in the city and expressways to enable suburbanites to commute downtown have typically been located in poor neighborhoods, since no other group will allow itself to be displaced. For the same reason, universities, hospitals, and civic centers also expand into land occupied by the poor. The major costs of the industrialization of agriculture have been borne by the poor, who are pushed off the land without recompense; and they have paid a large share of the human cost of the growth of American power overseas, for they have provided many of the foot soldiers for Vietnam and other wars.

Twelfth, the poor facilitate and stabilize the American political process. Because they vote and participate in politics less than other groups, the political system is often free to ignore them. Moreover, since they can rarely support Republicans, they often provide the Democrats with a captive constituency that has no other place to go. As a result, the Democrats can count on their votes, and be more responsive to voters - for example, the white working class - who might otherwise switch to the Republicans.

Thirteenth, the role of the poor in upholding conventional norms (see the fifth point, above) also has a significant political function. An economy based on the ideology of laissez faire requires a deprived population that is allegedly unwilling to work or that can be considered inferior because it must accept charity or welfare in order to survive. Not only does the alleged moral deviancy of the poor reduce the moral pressure on the present political economy to eliminate poverty but socialist alternatives can be made to look quite unattractive if those who will benefit most from them can be described as lazy, spendthrift, dishonest and promiscuous.

《 THE ALTERNATIVES

I have described thirteen of the more important functions poverty and the poor satisfy in American society, enough to support the functionalist thesis that poverty, like any other social phenomenon, survives in part because it is useful to society or some of its parts. This analysis is not intended to suggest that because it is often functional, poverty should exist, or that it must exist. For one thing, poverty has many more dysfunctions that functions; for another, it is possible to suggest functional alternatives.

For example, society's dirty work could be done without poverty, either by automation or by paying "dirty workers" decent wages. Nor is it necessary for the poor to subsidize the many activities they support through their low-wage jobs. This would, however, drive up the costs of these activities, which would result in higher prices to their customers and clients. Similarly, many of the professionals who flourish because of the poor could be given other roles. Social workers could provide counseling to the affluent, as they prefer to do anyway; and the police could devote themselves to traffic and organized crime. Other roles would have to be found for badly trained or incompetent professionals now relegated to serving the poor, and someone else would have to pay their salaries. Fewer penologists would be employable, however. And Pentecostal religion probably could not survive without the poor - nor would parts of the second- and third-hand goods market. And in many cities, "used" housing that no one else wants would then have to be torn down at public expense.

Alternatives for the cultural functions of the poor could be found more easily and cheaply. Indeed, entertainers, hippies, and adolescents are already serving as the deviants needed to uphold traditional morality and as devotees of orgies to "staff" the fantasies of vicarious participation. The status functions of the poor are another matter. In a hierarchical society, some people must be defined as inferior to everyone else with respect to a variety of attributes, but they need not be poor in the absolute sense. One could conceive of a society in which the "lower class," though last in the pecking order, received 75 percent of the median income, rather than 15-40 percent, as is now the case. Needless to say, this would require considerable income redistribution.

The contribution the poor make to the upward mobility of the groups that provide them with goods and services could also be maintained without the poor's having such low incomes. However, it is true that if the poor were more affluent, they would have access to enough capital to take over the provider role, thus competing with and perhaps rejecting the "outsiders." (Indeed, owing in part to antipoverty programs, this is already happening in a number of ghettos, where white storeowners are being replaced by Blacks.) Similarly, if the poor were more affluent, they would make less willing clients for upper-class philanthropy, although some would still use settlement houses to achieve upward mobility, as they do now. Thus "Society" could continue to run its philanthropic activities.

The political functions of the poor would be more difficult to replace. With increased affluence the poor would probably obtain more political power and be more active politically. With higher incomes and more political power, the poor would be likely to resist paying the costs of growth and change. Of course, it is possible to imagine urban renewal and highway projects that properly reimbursed the displaced people, but such projects would then become considerably more expensive, and many might never be built. This, in turn, would reduce the comfort and convenience of those who now benefit from urban renewal and expressways. Finally, hippies could serve also as more deviants to justify the existing political economy - as they already do. Presumably, however, if poverty were eliminated, there would be fewer attacks on that economy. In sum, then, many of the functions served by the poor could be replaced if poverty were eliminated, but almost always at higher costs to others, particularly more affluent others. Consequently, a functional analysis must conclude that poverty persists not only because it fulfills a number of positive functions but also because many of the functional alternatives to poverty would be quite dysfunctional for the affluent members of society. A functional analysis thus ultimately arrives at much the same conclusion as radical sociology, except that radical thinkers treat as manifest what I describe as latent: that social phenomena that are functional for affluent or powerful groups and dysfunctional for poor or powerless ones persist; that when the elimination of such phenomena through functional alternatives would generate dysfunctions for the affluent or powerful, they will continue to persist; and that phenomena like poverty can be eliminated only when they become dysfunctional for the affluent or powerful, or when the powerless can obtain enough power to change society.

﹘ DISCUSSION QUESTIONS

1. What are some of the useful functions of poverty Gans lists? Do you benefit from any of these functions?

2. Does Gans think that it is impossible to get rid of poverty or just that it is unlikely it will happen? What is his reasoning?

3. How might Gans's argument about the role of poverty in society be related to the difficulty of stemming illegal immigration into the United States?

21

Unequal Childhoods

Class, Race, and Family Life

Annette Lareau

Much attention has been paid to how experiences in childhood shape us as adults. A great deal of this research focuses on how formative experiences affect our personalities and the types of relationships we have as adults. While it is well established that the social class of your parents is an excellent predictor of your future social class, exactly how *this happens isn't as straightforward as it seems. Certainly the amount of wealth a family has contributes to things like quality of education (via neighborhood), social contacts, and formative experiences (attending sailing camp as opposed to playing in the neighborhood vacant lot for example). But there are even more subtle ways that social class influences our life chances. In this article, Annette Lareau uses a sociological approach to examine how social class is reproduced through different parenting styles. The results of her careful ethnographic study reveal general differences in the approach and philosophy of parenting by working-class versus middle-class parents, what she terms the* natural growth *approach and the* concerted cultivation *approach. Each has clear benefits and drawbacks for kids, but it is the concerted cultivation approach that middle-class parents use that implicitly teaches children how to negotiate and navigate in social interactions in a way that opens more doors of opportunity and leads to greater rewards.*

As you read, think about your own childhood experience. Which approach most closely describes your experience? How do you think you would have benefited if you had grown up in a family that used the other approach?

L aughing and yelling, a white fourth-grader named Garrett Tallinger splashes around in the swimming pool in the backyard of his four-bedroom home in the suburbs on a late spring afternoon. As on most evenings, after a quick dinner his father drives him to soccer practice. This is only one of Garrett's many activities. His brother has a baseball game at a different location. There are evenings when the boys' parents relax, sipping a glass of wine. Tonight is not one of them. As they rush to change out of their work clothes and get the children ready for practice, Mr. and Mrs. Tallinger are harried.

Only ten minutes away, a Black fourth-grader, Alexander Williams, is riding home from a school open house.[1] His mother is driving their beige, leather-upholstered Lexus. It is 9:00 P.M. on a Wednesday evening. Ms. Williams is tired from work and has a long Thursday ahead of her. She will get up at 4:45 A.M. to go out of town on business and will not return before 9:00 P.M. On Saturday morning, she will chauffeur Alexander to a private piano lesson at 8:15 A.M., which will be followed by a choir rehearsal and then a soccer game. As they ride in the dark, Alexander's mother, in a quiet voice, talks with her son, asking him questions and eliciting his opinions. In interactions with professionals, the Williamses, like some other middle-class parents in the study, seem relaxed and communicative. They want Alex to feel this way too, so they teach him how to be an informed, assertive client. On one hot summer afternoon, Ms. Williams uses a doctor visit as an opportunity for this kind of instruction. During the drive to the doctor's office, the field-worker listens as Ms. Williams prepares Alexander to be assertive during his regular checkup: As we enter Park Lane, [Christina] says quietly to Alex, "Alexander you should be thinking of questions you might want to ask the doctor. You can ask him anything you want. Don't be shy. You can ask anything." Alex thinks for a minute, then says, "I have some bumps under my arms from my deodorant."Christina: "Really? You mean from your new deodorant?" Alex: "Yes." Christina: "Well, you should ask the doctor."

Alex's mother is teaching him that he has the right to speak up (e.g., "don't be shy"; "you can ask anything"). Most important, she is role modeling the idea that he should prepare for an encounter with a person in a position of authority by gathering his thoughts ahead of time

Discussions between parents and children are a hallmark of middle-class child rearing. Like many middle-class parents, Ms. Williams and her husband see themselves as "developing" Alexander to cultivate his talents in a concerted fashion. Organized activities, established and controlled by mothers and fathers, dominate the lives of middle-class children such as Garrett and Alexander. By making certain their children have these and other experiences, middle-class parents engage in a process of *concerted cultivation*. From this, a robust sense of entitlement takes root in the children: This sense of entitlement plays an especially important role in institutional settings, where middle-class children learn to question adults and address them as relative equals.

Only twenty minutes away, in blue-collar neighborhoods, and slightly farther away, in public housing projects, childhood looks different. Mr. Yanelji, a white working-class father, picks up his son Little Billy, a fourth-grader, from an after-school program. They come home and Mr. Yanelli drinks a beer while Little Billy first watches television, then rides his bike and plays in the street. Other nights, he and his Dad sit on the sidewalk outside their house and play cards. At about 5:30 P.M. Billy's mother gets home from her job as a house cleaner. She fixes dinner and the entire family sits down to eat together. Extended family are a prominent part of their lives. Ms. Yanelli touches base with her "entire family every day" by phone. Many nights Little Billy's uncle stops by, sometimes bringing Little Billy's youngest cousin. In the spring, Little Billy plays baseball on a local team. Unlike for Garrett and Alexander, who have at least four activities a week, for Little Billy, baseball is his only organized activity outside of school during the entire year. Down the road, a white working-class girl, Wendy Driver, also spends the evening with her girl cousins, as they watch a video and eat popcorn, crowded together on the living room floor.

Farther away, a Black fourth-grade boy, Harold McAllister, plays outside on a summer evening in the public housing project in which he lives. His two male cousins are there that night, as they often are. After an afternoon spent unsuccessfully searching for a ball so they could play basketball, the boys had resorted to watching sports on television. Now they head outdoors for a twilight water balloon fight. Harold tries to get his neighbor, Miss Latifa, wet. People sit in white plastic lawn chairs outside the row of apartments. Music and television sounds waft through the open windows and doors.

The adults in the lives of Billy, Wendy, and Harold want the best for them. Formidable economic constraints make it a major life task for these parents to put food on the table, arrange for housing, negotiate unsafe neighborhoods, take children to the doctor (often waiting for city buses that do not come), clean children's clothes, and get children to bed and have them ready for school the next morning. But unlike middle-class parents, these adults do not consider the concerted development of children, particularly through organized leisure activities, an essential aspect of good parenting. Unlike the Tallingers and Williamses, these mothers and fathers do not focus on concerted cultivation. For them, the crucial responsibilities of parenthood do not lie in eliciting their children's feelings, opinions, and thoughts. Rather, they see a clear boundary between adults and children. Parents tend to use directives: they tell their children what to do rather than persuading them with reasoning. Unlike their middle-class counterparts, who have a steady diet of adult organized activities, the working-class and poor children have more control over the character of their leisure activities. Most children are free to go out and play with friends and relatives who typically live close by. Their parents and guardians facilitate the *accomplishment of natural growth.*[2] Yet these children and their parents interact with central institutions in the society, such as schools, which firmly and decisively promote strategies of concerted cultivation in child rearing. For working-class and poor families, the cultural logic of child rearing at home is out of synch with the standards of institutions. As a result, while children whose parents adopt strategies of concerted cultivation appear to gain a sense of entitlement, children such as Billy Yanelli, Wendy Driver, and Harold McAllister appear to gain an emerging sense of distance, distrust, and constraint in their institutional experiences.

Table 1. Typology of Differences in Child Rearing

| | **Child-Rearing Approach** | |
	Concerted Cultivation	*Accomplishment of Natural Growth*
Key Elements	Parent actively fosters and assesses child's talents opinions, and skills	Parent cares for child and allows child to grow
Organization of Daily Life	Multiple child leisure activities orchestrated by adults	"Hanging out," particularly with kin, by child
Language Use	Reasoning/directives; child contestation of adult statements; Extended negotiations between parents and child	Directives; rare questioning or challenging of adults by child; general acceptance by child of directives
Interventions in Institutions	Criticisms and interventions on behalf of child; training of child to take on this role	Dependence on institutions; sense of powerlessness and frustration; conflict between child-rearing practices at home and at school
Consequences	Emerging sense of entitlement on the part of the child	Emerging sense of constraint on the part of the child

What is the outcome of these different philosophies and approaches to child rearing? Quite simply, they appear to lead to the transmission of differential advantages to children. In this study, there was quite a bit more talking in middle-class homes than in working-class and poor homes, leading to the development of greater verbal agility, larger vocabularies, more comfort with authority figures, and more familiarity with abstract concepts. Importantly, children also developed skill differences in interacting with authority figures in institutions and at home. Middle-class children such as Garrett Tallinger and Alexander Williams learn, as young boys, to shake the hands of adults and look them in the eye. In studies of job interviews, investigators have found that potential employees have less than one minute to make a good impression. Researchers stress the importance of eye contact, firm handshakes, and displaying comfort with bosses during the interview. In poor families like Harold McAllister's, however, family members usually do not look each other in the eye when conversing. In addition, as Elijah Anderson points out, they live in neighborhoods where it can be dangerous to look people in the eye too long.[3] The types of social competence transmitted in the McAllister family are valuable, but they are potentially less valuable (in employment interviews, for example) than those learned by Garrett Tallinger and Alexander Williams.

The white and Black middle-class children in this study also exhibited an emergent version of the sense of entitlement characteristic of the middle-class. They acted as though they had a right to pursue their own individual preferences and to actively manage interactions in institutional settings. They appeared comfortable in these settings; they were open to sharing information and asking for attention. Although some children were more outgoing than others, it was common practice among middle-class children to shift interactions to suit their preferences. Alexander Williams knew how to get the doctor to listen to his concerns (about the bumps under his arm from his new deodorant). His mother explicitly trained and encouraged him to speak up with the doctor. Similarly, a Black middle-class girl, Stacey Marshall, was taught by her mother to expect the gymnastics teacher to accommodate her individual learning style. Thus, middle-class children were trained in "the rules of the game" that govern interactions with institutional representatives. They were not conversant in other important social skills, however, such as organizing their time for hours on end during weekends and summers, spending long periods of time away from adults, or hanging out with adults in a nonobtrusive, subordinate fashion. Middle-class children also learned (by imitation and by direct training) how to make the rules work in their favor. Here, the enormous stress on reasoning and negotiation in the home also has a potential advantage for future institutional negotiations. Additionally, those in authority responded positively to such interactions. Even in fourth grade, middle-class children appeared to be acting on their own behalf to gain advantages. They made special requests of teachers and doctors to adjust procedures to accommodate their desires.

The working-class and poor children, by contrast, showed an emerging sense of constraint in their interactions in institutional settings. They were less likely to try to customize interactions to suit their own preferences. Like their parents, the children accepted the actions of persons in authority (although at times they also covertly resisted them). Working-class and poor parents sometimes were not as aware of their children's school situation (as when their children were not doing homework). Other times, they dismissed the school rules as unreasonable. For example, Wendy Driver's mother told her to "punch" a boy who was pestering her in class; Billy Yanelli's parents were proud of him when he "beat up" another boy on the playground, even though Billy was then suspended from school. Parents also had trouble getting "the school" to respond to their concerns. When Ms. Yanelli complained that she "hates" the school, she gave her son a lesson in powerlessness and frustration in the face of an important institution. Middle-class children such as Stacey Marshall learned to make demands on professionals, and when they succeeded in making the rules work in their favor they augmented their "cultural capital" (i.e., skills individuals inherit that can then be translated into different forms of value as they move through various institutions) for the future.[4] When working-class and poor children confronted institutions, however, they generally were unable to make the rules work in their favor nor did they obtain capital for adulthood. Because of these patterns of legitimization, children raised according to the logic of concerted cultivation can gain advantages, in the form of an emerging sense of entitlement, while children raised according to the logic of natural growth tend to develop an emerging sense of constraint.[5]

How Does It Matter?

Both concerted cultivation and the accomplishment of natural growth offer intrinsic benefits (and burdens) for parents and their children. Nevertheless, these practices are accorded different social values by important social institutions. There are signs that some family cultural practices, notably those associated with concerted cultivation, give children advantages that other cultural practices do not.

In terms of the rhythms of daily life, both concerted cultivation and the accomplishment of natural growth have advantages and disadvantages. Middle-class children learn to develop and value an individualized sense of self. Middle-class children are allowed to participate in a variety of coveted activities: gymnastics, soccer, summer camps, and so on. These activities improve their skills and teach them, as Mr. Tallinger noted, to be better athletes than their parents were at comparable ages. They learn to handle moments of humiliation on the field as well as moments of glory. Middle-class children learn, as Mr. Williams noted, the difference between baroque and classical music. They learn to perform. They learn to present themselves. But this cultivation has a cost. Family schedules are disrupted. Dinner hours are very hard to arrange. Siblings such as Spencer and Sam Tallinger spend dreary hours waiting at athletic fields and riding in the car going from one event to another. Family life, despite quiet interludes, is frequently frenetic. Parents, especially mothers, must reconcile conflicting priorities, juggling events whose deadlines are much tighter than the deadlines connected to serving meals or getting children ready for bed. The domination of children's activities can take a toll on families. At times, everyone in the middle-class families—including ten-year-old children—seemed exhausted. Thus, there are formidable costs, as well as benefits to this child-rearing approach.

Working-class and poor children also had advantages, as well as costs, from the cultural logic of child rearing they experienced. Working-class and poor children learned to entertain themselves. They played outside, creating their own games, as Tyrec Taylor did with his friends. They did not complain of being bored. Working-class and poor children also appeared to have boundless energy. They did not have the exhaustion that we saw in middle-class children the same age. Some working-class and poor children longed to be in organized activities—Katie Brindle wanted to take ballet and Harold McAllister wanted to play football. When finances, a lack of transportation, and limited availability of programs conspired to prevent or limit their participation, they were disappointed. Many were also deeply aware of the economic constraints and the limited consumption permitted by their family's budget. Living spaces were small, and often there was not much privacy. The television was almost always on and, like many middle-class children growing up in the 1950s, working-class and poor children watched unrestricted amounts of television. As a result, family members spent more time together in shared space than occurred in middle-class homes. Indeed, family ties were very strong, particularly among siblings. Working-class and poor children also developed very close ties with their cousins and other extended family members.

Within the home, these two approaches to child rearing each have identifiable strengths and weaknesses. When we turn to examining institutional dynamics outside the home, however, the unequal benefits of middle-class children's lives compared to working-class and poor children's lives become clearer. In crucial ways, middle-class family members appeared reasonably comfortable and entitled, while working-class and poor family members appeared uncomfortable and constrained. For example, neither Harold nor his mother seemed as comfortable as Alexander and his mother had been as they interacted with their physician. Alexander was used to extensive conversation at home; with the doctor, he was at ease initiating questions. Harold, who was used to responding to directives at home, primarily answered questions from the doctor, rather than posing his own. Unlike Ms. Williams, Ms. McAllister did not see the enthusiastic efforts of her daughter Alexis to share information about her birthmark as appropriate behavior. Ms. Williams not only permitted Alexander to hop up and down on the stool to express his enthusiasm; she explicitly trained him to be assertive and well prepared for his encounter with the doctor. Harold was reserved. He did not show an emerging sense of entitlement, as Alexander and other middle-class children did. Absorbing his mother's apparent need to conceal the truth about the range of foods in his diet, Harold appeared cautious, displaying an emerging sense of constraint.

This pattern occurred in school interactions, as well. Some working-class and poor parents had warm and friendly relations with educators. Overall, however, working-class and poor parents in this study had much more distance or separation from the school than did middle-class mothers. At home, Ms. McAllister could be quite assertive, but at school she was subdued. The parent-teacher conference yielded Ms. McAllister few insights into her son's educational experience.[6]

Other working-class and poor parents also appeared baffled, intimidated, and subdued in parent-teacher conferences. Ms. Driver, frantically worried because Wendy, a fourth-grader, was not yet able to read, resisted intervening, saying, "I don't want to jump into anything and find it is the wrong thing." When working-class and poor parents did try to intervene in their children's educational experiences, they often felt ineffectual. Billy Yanelli's mother appeared relaxed and chatty when she interacted with service personnel, such as the person who sold her lottery tickets on Saturday morning. With "the school," however, she was very apprehensive. She distrusted school personnel. She felt bullied and powerless.

There were also moments in which parents encouraged children to outwardly comply with school officials but, at the same time, urged them to resist school authority. Although well aware of school rules prohibiting fighting, the Yanellis directly trained their son to "beat up" a boy who was bothering him. Similarly, when Wendy Driver complained about a boy who pestered her and pulled her ponytail, and the teacher did not respond, her mother advised her to "punch him." Ms. Driver's boyfriend added, "Hit him when the teacher isn't looking."[7]

The unequal level of trust, as well as differences in the amount and quality of information divulged, can yield unequal profits during a historical period such as ours, when professionals applaud assertiveness and reject passivity as an inappropriate parenting strategy.[8] Middle-class children and parents often (but not always) accrued advantages or profits from their efforts. Alexander Williams succeeded in having the doctor take his medical concerns seriously. The Marshall children ended up in the gifted program, even though they did not qualify.

Overall, the routine rituals of family life are not equally legitimized in the broader society. Parents' efforts to reason with children (even two-year-olds) are seen as more educationally valuable than parents' use of directives. Spending time playing soccer or baseball is deemed by professionals as more valuable than time spent watching television. Moreover, differences in the cultural logic of child rearing are attached to unequal currency in the broader society. The middle-class strategy of concerted cultivation appears to have greater promise of being capitalized into social profits than does the strategy of the accomplishment of natural growth found in working-class and poor homes. Alexander Williams's vocabulary grew at home, in the evenings, as he bantered with his parents about plagiarism and copyright as well as about the X-Men. Harold McAllister, Billy Yanelli, and Wendy Driver learned how to manage their own time, play without the direction of adults, and occupy themselves for long periods of time without being bored. Although these are important life skills, they do not have the same payoff on standardized achievement tests as the experiences of Alexander Williams.

These potential benefits for middle-class children, and costs for working-class and poor children, are necessarily speculative, since at the end of the study, the children were still in elementary school. Still, there are important signs of hidden advantages being sown at early ages. The middle-class children have extensive experience with adults in their lives with whom they have a relatively contained, bureaucratically regulated, and somewhat superficial relationship. As children spend eight weeks playing soccer, baseball, basketball, and other activities, they meet and interact with adults acting as coaches, assistant coaches, car pool drivers, and so on. This contact with relative strangers, although of a different quality than contact with cousins, aunts, and uncles, provides work-related skills. For instance, as Garrett shakes the hand of a stranger and looks him or her in the eye, he is being groomed, in an effortless fashion, for job interviews he will have as an adult (employment experts stress the importance of good eye contact). In the McAllister home, family members have great affection and warmth toward one another, but they do not generally look each other in the eye when they speak; this training is likely to be a liability in job interviews. In settings as varied as health care and gymnastics, middle-class children learn at a young age to be assertive and demanding. They expect, as did Stacey Marshall, for institutions to be responsive to them and to accommodate their individual needs. By contrast, when Wendy Driver is told to hit the boy who is pestering her (when the teacher isn't looking) or Billy Yanelli is told to physically defend himself, despite school rules, they are not learning how to make bureaucratic institutions work to their advantage. Instead, they are being given lesson in frustration and powerlessness.

⫷⫸ DISCUSSION QUESTIONS

1. Which of these styles was closest to your own childhood experience? Do you think there is perhaps a third or fourth model of parenting that should be examined?

2. How does concerted cultivation prepare middle-class and upper-class children for success later in life?

3. What are the advantages of the natural growth approach? What are the downsides of concerted cultivation?

4. In recent years the "helicopter parent" phenomenon has gotten a fair bit of attention. Which parenting style is this associated with? What do you think motivates parents to engage in this behavior?

5. How can parents try to balance both of these approaches to child rearing to maximize the benefits of each? What about the way our social institutions are set up would have to change in order to accommodate parents who wish to use both approaches?

⫷⫸ NOTES

1. Choosing words to describe social groups also becomes a source of worry, especially over the possibility of reinforcing negative stereotypes. I found the available terms to describe members of racial and ethnic groups to be problematic in one way or another. The families I visited uniformly described themselves as "Black." Recognizing that some readers have strong views that Black should be capitalized, I have followed that convention, despite the lack of symmetry with the term white. In sum, this book alternates among the terms "Black," "Black American," "African American," and "white," with the understanding that "white" here refers to the subgroup of non-Hispanic whites.

2. Some readers have expressed concern that this phrase, "the accomplishment of natural growth," underemphasizes all the labor that mothers and fathers do to take care of children. They correctly note that working-class and poor parents themselves would be unlikely to use such a term to describe the process of caring for children. These concerns are important. As I stress in the text (especially in the chapter on Katie Brindle, Chapter 5) it does take an enormous amount of work for parents, especially mothers, of all classes to take care of children. But poor and working-class mothers

have fewer resources with which to negotiate these demands. Those whose lives the research assistants and I studied approached the task somewhat differently than did middle-class parents. They did not seem to view children's leisure time as their responsibility; nor did they see themselves as responsible for assertively intervening in their children's school experiences. Rather, the working-class and poor parents carried out their chores, drew boundaries and restrictions around their children, and then, within these limits, allowed their children to carry out their lives. It is in this sense that I use the term "the accomplishment of natural growth."

3. Elijah Anderson, *Code of the Street;* see especially Chapter 2.

4. For a more extensive discussion of the work of Pierre Bourdieu see the theoretical appendix; see also David Swartz's excellent book *Culture and Power*

5. I did not study the full range of families in American society, including elite families of tremendous wealth, nor, at the other end of the spectrum, homeless families. In addition, I have a purposively drawn sample. Thus, I cannot state whether there are other forms of child rearing corresponding to other cultural logics. Still, data from quantitative studies based on nationally representative data support the patterns I observed. For differences by parents' social class position and children's time use, see especially Sandra Hofferth and John Sandberg, "Changes in American Children's Time, 1981–1997." Patterns of language use with children are harder to capture in national surveys, but the work of Melvin Kohn and Carmi Schooler, especially *Work and Personality,* shows differences in parents' child-rearing values. Duane Alwin's studies of parents' desires are generally consistent with the results reported here. See Duane Alwin, "Trends in Parental Socialization Values." For differences in interventions in institutions, there is extensive work showing social class differences in parent involvement in education. See the U. S. Department of Education, *The Condition of Education, 2001,* p.175.

6. Of course, some middle-class parents also appeared slightly anxious during parent-teacher meetings. But overall, middle-class parents spoke more, and they asked educators more questions, including more critical and penetrating ones, than did working-class and poor parents.

7. Working-class and poor children often resisted and tested school rules, but they did not seem to be engaged in the same process of seeking an accommodation by educators to their own *individual* preferences that I witnessed among middle-class children. Working-class and poor children tended to react to adults' offers or, at times, plead with educators to repeat previous experiences, such as reading a particular story, watching a movie, or going to the computer room. In these interactions, the boundaries between adults and children were firmer and clearer than those with middle-class children.

8. Carol Heimer and Lisa Staffen, *For the Sake of the Children.*

22

Preparing for Power: Curriculum and Cultural Capital

Peter W. Cookson, Jr. and Caroline Persell

This article highlights the role of education in creating and reproducing class divisions by examining the curriculum at elite boarding schools. Here, high school-aged young adults live and study in an environment very similar to elite colleges, with lush campuses, vast and varied curriculum, and many extracurricular activities. While the expensive price tag of these private schools is one obvious way that social class is reproduced, there are other more subtle ways that these schools keep and maintain the social class structure. Students at these schools have ample opportunity to learn and practice socially valued cultural capital: *the tastes, styles, habits, dispositions, hobbies, and language of elites. Cookson and Persell document how students at these schools have experiences and gain skills that put them at significant advantage not just to succeed in college but to successfully negotiate the upper echelons of power in the wider society. As you read, think about how your own experience in high school compares to those at the elite schools they describe.*

B orrowing from the British, early American headmasters and teachers advocated a boarding school curriculum that was classical, conservative, and disciplined. It wasn't until the latter part of the nineteenth century that such "soft" subjects as English, history, and mathematics were given a place beside Latin, Greek, rhetoric, and logic in the syllabus. It was the early schoolmasters' belief that young minds, especially boys' minds, if left to their own devices, were undisciplined, even anarchic. The only reliable antidote to mental flabbiness was a rigorous, regular regime of mental calisthenics. A boy who could not flawlessly recite long Latin passages was required to increase his mental workouts. Classical languages were to the mind what cold showers were to the body: tonics against waywardness.

Girls, with some exceptions, were not thought of as needing much mental preparation for their future roles as wives and mothers. Their heads were best left uncluttered by thought; too much book learning could give a girl ideas about independence. Besides, the great majority of them were not going on to college, where even more classical languages were required.

As an intellectual status symbol, the classical curriculum helped distinguish gentlemen from virtually everyone else and thus defined the difference between an "educated" man and an untutored one, as well as the difference between high culture and popular culture. Such a division is critical to exclude nonmembers from groups seeking status. For a long time a classical curriculum was the only path to admission to a university, as Harvard and many others required candidates to demonstrate proficiency in Latin and Greek (Levine 1980). Thus, the curriculum of boarding schools has long served both social and practical functions.

Culture, much like real estate or stocks, can be considered a form of capital. As the French scholars Pierre Bourdieu and Jean-Claude Passeron (1977) have indicated, the accumulation of cultural capital can be used to reinforce class differences. Cultural capital is socially created: what constitutes the "best in western civilization" is not arrived at by happenstance, nor was it decided upon by public election. The more deeply embedded the values, the more likely they will be perceived as value free and universal.

Thus curriculum is the nursery of culture and the classical curriculum is the cradle of high culture. The definition of what is a classical course of study has evolved, of course, since the nineteenth century. Greek and Latin are no longer required subjects in most schools—electives abound. But the disciplined and trained mind is still the major objective of the boarding school curriculum.

The contrast between the relatively lean curricula of many public schools and the abundant courses offered by boarding schools is apparent. In catalogues of the boarding school's academic requirements, courses are usually grouped by subject matter, and at the larger schools course listings and descriptions can go on for several dozen pages. Far from sounding dreary, the courses described in most catalogues are designed to whet the intellectual appetite. Elective subjects in particular have intriguing titles such as "Hemingway: The Man and His Work," "Varieties of the Poetic Experience," "Effecting Political Change," "Rendezvous with Armageddon," and for those with a scientific bent, "Vertebrate Zoology" and "Mammalian Anatomy and Physiology."

Boarding school students are urged to read deeply and widely. A term course on modern American literature may include works from as many as ten authors, ranging from William Faulkner to Jack Kerouac. Almost all schools offer a course in Shakespeare in which six or seven plays will be read.

In history, original works are far more likely to be assigned than excerpts from a textbook. A course on the Presidency at one school included the following required readings: Rossiter, *The American Presidency;* Hofstadter, *The American Political Tradition;* Hargrove, *Presidential Leadership;* Schlesinger, *A Thousand Days;* Kearns, *Lyndon Johnson and the American Dream;* and White, *Breach of Faith.* Courses often use a college-level text, such as Garraty's *The American Nation* or Palmer's *A History of the Modern World.* Economic history is taught as well—in one school we observed a discussion of the interplay between politics and the depression of 1837—and the idea that there are multiple viewpoints in history is stressed. It is little wonder that many prep school graduates find their first year of college relatively easy.

An advanced-placement English class uses a collection of *The Canterbury Tales* by Geoffrey Chaucer that includes the original middle English on the left page and a modern English translation on the right. An advanced third-year French course includes three or four novels as well as two books of grammar and readings. Even social science courses require a great deal of reading. In a course called "An Introduction to Human Behavior" students are assigned eleven texts including works from B. F. Skinner, Sigmund Freud, Erich Fromm, Jean Piaget, and Rollo May.

Diploma requirements usually include: 4 years of English, 3 years of math, 3 years in one foreign language, 2 years of history or social science, 2 years of laboratory science, and 1 year of art. Many schools require a year of philosophy or religion and also may have such noncredit diploma requirements as: 4 years of physical education, a library skills course, introduction to computers, and a seminar on human sexuality. On average, American public high-school seniors take one year less English and math, and more than a year less foreign language than boarding school students (Coleman, Hoffer, and Kilgore 1982, 90). Moreover, in the past two decades there has been a historical decline in the number of academic subjects taken by students in the public schools (Adelman 1983).

Because success on the Scholastic Aptitude Test is so critical for admission to a selective college, it is not uncommon for schools to offer English review classes that are specifically designed to help students prepare for the tests. Most schools also offer tutorials and remedial opportunities for students who are weak in a particular subject. For foreign students there is often a course in English as a second language.

As the arts will be part of the future roles of boarding school students, the music, art, and theater programs at many schools are enriching, with special courses such as "The Sound and Sense of Music," "Advanced Drawing," and "The Creative Eye in Film." Student art work is usually on display, and almost every school will produce several full-length plays each year, for example, *Arsenic and Old Lace, A Thurber Carnival, Dracula,* and *The Mousetrap.*

Music is a cherished tradition in many boarding schools, in keeping with their British ancestry. The long-standing "Songs" at Harrow, made famous because Winston Churchill liked to return to them for solace during World War II, are a remarkable display of school solidarity. All 750 boys participate, wearing identical morning coats with tails. Every seat is filled in the circular, sharply tiered replica of Shakespeare's Globe Theater as the boys rise in unison, their voices resonating in the rotunda.

The belief that a well-rounded education includes some "hands-on" experience and travel runs deep in the prep view of learning. Virtually every boarding school provides opportunities for their students to study and work off campus. As volunteers, Taft students, for instance, can "tutor on a one-to-one basis in inner-city schools in Waterbury, act as teachers' helpers in Waterbury Public Schools and work with retarded children at Southbury Training School." They can also work in convalescent homes, hospitals, and day-care centers, and act as "apprentices to veterinarians and help with Girl Scout troops" (*Taft* 1981–82, 21). At the Ethel Walker School in Connecticut, girls can go on whale watches, trips to the theater, or work in the office of a local politician. The Madeira School in Virginia has a co-curriculum program requiring students to spend every Wednesday participating in volunteer or internship situations.

Generally speaking, the schools that take the position that manual labor and firsthand experience are good for the soul as well as the mind and body are more progressive in orientation than other schools. At the Putney School every student has to take a tour of duty at the cow barn, starting at 5:30 A.M. In their own words, "Putney's work program is ambitious. We grow much of our own food, mill our own lumber, pick up our own trash, and have a large part in building our buildings. . . .Stoves won't heat until wood is cut and split" (*The Putney School* 1982, 3).

Various styles of student-built structures dot the campus of the Colorado Rocky Mountain School, and at the tiny Midland School in California, there is no service staff, except for one cook. When the water pump breaks, faculty and students fix it, and when buildings are to be built, faculty and students pitch in. "We choose to live simply, to distinguish between our needs and our wants, to do without many of the comforts which often obscure the significant things in life" (*Midland School* 1983, 1). The creed of self-reliance is reenacted every day at Midland. When a trustee offered to buy the school a swimming pool, he was turned down. Lounging around a pool is not part of the Midland philosophy.

Travel is very much part of the prep way of life and is continued right through the school year. Not only are semesters or a year abroad (usually in France or Spain) offered, but at some of the smaller schools, everyone goes on an extensive field trip. Every March at the Verde Valley School in Arizona the students travel to "Hopi, Navajo and Zuni reservations, to small villages in northern Mexico, to isolated Spanish-American communities in northern New Mexico and to ethnic neighborhoods of Southwestern cities. They live with native families, attend and teach in schools, work on ranches, and participate in the lives of the host families and their communities" (*Verde Valley School* 1982–83, 9). Not all boarding schools, of course, place such a high value on rubbing shoulders with the outside world. At most of the academies, entrepreneurial, and girls schools the emphasis is on service rather than sharing.

While boarding schools may vary in their general philosophy, the actual curricula do not widely differ. The pressures exerted on prep schools to get their students into good colleges means that virtually all students must study the same core subjects. Although not quick to embrace educational innovation, many boarding schools have added computers to their curricula. This has no doubt been encouraged by announcements by a number of Ivy League and other elite colleges that they want their future applicants to be "computer literate." While people at most boarding schools, or anywhere else for that matter, are not quite sure what is meant by computer literate, they are trying to provide well-equipped computer rooms and teachers who can move their students toward computer proficiency.

For students who have particular interests that cannot be met by the formal curriculum, almost all schools offer independent study, which gives students and teachers at boarding schools a great deal of intellectual flexibility. At Groton, for example, independent study can cover a diverse set of topics including listening to the works of Wagner, conducting a scientific experiment, or studying a special aspect of history.

The boarding school curriculum offers students an abundant buffet of regular course work, electives, volunteer opportunities, travel, and independent study, from which to choose a course of study. By encouraging students to treat academic work as an exciting challenge rather than just a job to be done, the prep schools not only pass on culture but increase their students' competitive edge in the scramble for admission to selective colleges.

THE IMPORTANCE OF SPORTS

Even the most diligent student cannot sit in classrooms all day, and because the prep philosophy emphasizes the whole person, boarding schools offer an impressive array of extracurricular activities, the most important of which is athletics. At progressive schools, the competitive nature of sport is deemphasized. The "afternoon out-of-door program" at Putney, for example, allows for a wide variety of outdoor activities that are noncompetitive; in fact, "skiing is the ideal sport for Putney as one may ski chiefly to enjoy himself, the air, the show" (*The Putney School* 1982, 15).

Putney's sense that sport should be part of a communion with nature is not shared by most other schools, however. At most prep schools sport is about competition, and even more important, about winning. An athletically powerful prep school will field varsity, junior varsity, and third-string teams in most major sports. A typical coed or boys school will offer football, soccer, cross-country, water polo, ice hockey, swimming, squash, basketball, wrestling, winter track, gymnastics, tennis, golf, baseball, track, and lacrosse. For the faint-hearted there are alternative activities such as modern dance, cycling, tai chi, yoga, ballet, and for the hopelessly unathletic, a "fitness" class. A truly traditional prep school will also have crew like their English forbears at Eton and Harrow. Certain schools have retained such British games as "Fives," but most stop short of the mayhem masquerading as a game called rugby.

Prep teams compete with college freshmen teams, other prep teams, and occasionally with public schools, although public school competitors are picked with care. Not only is there the possible problem of humiliation on the field, there is the even more explosive problem of fraternization in the stands when prep meets townie. Some schools, known as "jock" schools, act essentially as farm teams for Ivy League colleges, consistently providing them with athletes who have been polished by the prep experience. Many prep schools take public high-school graduates for a post-graduate year, as a way of adding some size and weight to their football teams.

Prep girls also love sports; they participate as much as the boys, often in the same sports, and with as much vigor. A girls' field hockey game between Exeter and Andover is as intense as when the varsity football teams clash. Horseback riding at girls schools is still popular; a number of the girls go on to ride in the show or hunt circuit. Unlike many of the girls in public schools, the boarding-school girl is discouraged from being a spectator. Loafing is considered to be almost as bad for girls as it is for boys.

During the school year the halls of nearly all prep schools are decorated with either bulletins of sporting outcomes or posters urging victory in some upcoming game. Pep rallies are common, as are assemblies when awards are given and the competitive spirit is eulogized. Often the whole school will be bussed to an opponent's campus if the game is considered to be crucial or if the rivalry is long-standing.

Alumni return to see games, and there are frequent contests between alumni and varsity teams. Because preps retain the love of fitness and sports, it is not uncommon for the old warriors to give the young warriors a thrashing. Similarly, the prep life also invariably includes ritual competitions between, say, the girls field hockey team and a pick-up faculty team.

Nowhere is the spirit of victory more pronounced than on the ice of the hockey rink. Few public schools can afford a hockey rink so prep schools can attract the best players without much competition. Some prep schools import a few Canadians each year to fill out the roster. Speed, strength, endurance, and fearlessness are the qualities that produce winning hockey and more than one freshman team from an Ivy League college has found itself out-skated by a prep team. Whatever else may be, in Holden Caulfield's term, "phony" about prep schools, sports are for real. This emphasis on sport is not without its critics. At the Harrow School in London, the new headmaster, who was an all-England rugby player, has begun a program to reward artistic and musical prowess as well as athletic and academic skills.

The athletic facilities at prep schools are impressive, and at the larger schools, lavish. Acres and acres of playing fields, scores of tennis courts, one or more gyms, a hockey rink, a golf course, swimming pools, squash courts, workout rooms—all can be found on many prep school campuses. Generally, the facilities are extremely well maintained. The equipment most preps use is the best, as are the uniforms. One boy described how "when your gym clothes get dirty, you simply turn them in at the locker room for a fresh set." The cost of all this, of course, is extraordinary, but considered necessary, because excellence in sport is part of the definition of a gentleman or a gentlewoman.

The pressure for athletic success is intense on many campuses, and a student's, as well as a school's, social standing can ride on the narrow margin between victory and defeat. Perhaps because of this, schools generally take great pains to play schools of their own size and social eliteness. A study of who plays whom among prep schools reveals that schools will travel great distances, at considerable expense, to play other prep schools whose students and traditions are similar to their own.

\\\ EXTRACURRICULARS AND PREPARATION FOR LIFE

Not all prep school extracurricular activities require sweating, however. Like public school students, preps can work on the school newspaper, yearbook, help to organize a dance, or be part of a blood donor drive, and are much more likely than their public school counterparts to be involved in such activities. For example, one in three boarding school students is involved in student government compared to one in five public school students, and two in five are involved in the school newspaper or yearbook compared to one in five. This evidence is consistent with other research. Coleman, Hoffer, and Kilgore (1982) found that private school students participate more in extracurricular activities than do public school students. The fact that more boarding school students than public school students are involved in activities provides additional opportunities for them to practice their verbal, interpersonal, and leadership skills.

The catalogue of clubs at prep schools is nearly endless. The opportunity for students to develop special nonacademic interests is one of the qualities of life at prep schools that distinguishes them from many public schools. Special interest clubs for chess, sailing, bowling, or gun clubs are popular at boys schools. One elite boys school has a "war games" club. As the boys at this school are feverishly calculating their country's next strategic arms move, the girls in a Connecticut school are attending a meeting of Amnesty International. Girls, in general, tend to spend their off hours studying the gentler arts such as gourmet cooking and art history. One girls school has a club with a permanent service mission to the governor's office.

At some schools students can learn printing, metalwork, or woodworking. The shop for the latter at Groton is amply equipped and much of the work turned out by the students is of professional quality. The less traditional schools offer clubs for vegetarian cooking, weaving, quilting, folk music, and—in subtle juxtaposition to the Connecticut girls school—international cooking. At western schools, the horse still reigns supreme and many students spend endless hours riding, training, cleaning, and loving their own horse, or a horse they have leased from the school.

With the prep emphasis on music, choirs, glee clubs, madrigals, chamber music groups, as well as informal ensembles are all given places to practice. Most schools also have individual practice rooms, and like athletic teams, many prep musicians travel to other schools for concerts and performances.

Some schools offer a five week "Winterim," during which students and faculty propose and organize a variety of off- and on-campus activities and studies. Such a program breaks the monotony of the usual class routine in the middle of winter, a season teachers repeatedly told us was the worst time at boarding school. It also enables students and faculty to explore new areas or interests in a safe way, that is, without grades.

In prep schools there is a perceived need for students to exercise authority as apprentice leaders early in their educational careers. The tradition of delegating real authority to students has British roots, where head boys and prefects have real power within the public schools. Head boys can discipline other boys by setting punishments and are treated by headmaster and housemasters alike as a part of the administration. In the United States, student power is generally more limited, although at the progressive schools students can be quite involved in the administrative decision-making process.

Virtually all prep schools have a student government. The formal structure of government usually includes a student body president, vice president, treasurer, secretary, class presidents, and dorm prefects, representatives, or "whips," as they are called at one school. Clubs also have presidents and there are always committees to be headed. Some schools have student-faculty senates and in schools like Wooster, in Connecticut, students are expected to play a major part in the disciplinary system. An ambitious student can obtain a great deal of experience in committee work, developing transferable skills for later leadership positions in finance, law, management, or politics.

The office of student body president or head prefect is used by the administration primarily as an extension of the official school culture, and most of the students who fill these offices are quite good at advancing the school's best public relations face. A successful student body president, like a good head, is artful in developing an easy leadership style, which is useful because he or she is in a structural political dilemma. Elected by the students but responsible to the school administration, the student politician is a classic go-between, always running the danger of being seen as "selling out" by students and as "uncooperative" by the administration. Occasionally students rebel against too much pandering to the administration and elect a rebel leader, who makes it his or her business to be a thorn in the side of the administration. A number of heads and deans of students watch elections closely, because if elections go "badly" it could mean a difficult year for them.

The actual content of real power varies by school. At some, authority is more apparent than real; at others, student power can affect important school decisions. At Putney, the "Big Committee" is composed of the school director, student leaders, and teachers. The powers of the Big Committee are laid out in the school's constitution, and students at Putney have real input into the decision-making process. At the Thacher School in California, the Student Leadership Council, which is composed of the school chairman, presidents of the three lower classes, and head prefects, is not only responsible for student activities and events, but also grants funds to groups who petition for special allocations. The power of the purse is learned early in the life of a prep school student. At the Westtown School in Pennsylvania, the student council arrives at decisions not by voting yea or nay, "but by following the Quaker custom of arriving at a 'sense of the meeting'" (*Westtown School* 1982–83, 25).

Not all students, of course, participate in school politics; it may well be that many of the students most admired by their peers never run, or never would run, for a political position. The guerrilla leaders who emerge and flourish in the student underlife—or counterculture—may have far greater real power than the "superschoolies" that tend to get elected to public office.

In most coeducational schools boys tend to monopolize positions of power. The highest offices are generally held by boys; girls are found in the vice presidential and secretarial positions. Politics can be important to prep families and we suspect that a number of prep boys arrive at boarding school with a good supply of political ambition. One of the reasons advanced in support of all-girls schools is that girls can gain important leadership experience there.

Some schools try to capture what they see as the best aspects of single-sex and coed schools. They do this by having boys and girls elect distinct school leaders, by having certain customs, places, and events that they share only with members of their own sex, and by having classes, certain other activities, and social events be coeducational. These schools, often called coordinate schools, see themselves as offering the chance to form strong single-sex bonds, to build self-confidence in adolescents, and to provide experience in working and relating to members of both sexes. Girls at coed schools more generally are likely to say they think in ten years they will find the social skills they learned to be the most valuable part of their boarding-school experience.

\\\\ LEARNING BY EXAMPLE

Part of the social learning students obtain is exposure to significant public personalities. Virtually all the schools have guest speaker programs in which well-known people can be seen and heard. Some of the speakers that have appeared at Miss

Porter's School in the last several years include Alex Haley, author; Russell Baker, humorist; Arthur Miller, playwright; and Dick Gregory, comedian. At the boys schools there is a tendency to invite men who are successful in politics and journalism. Recent speakers at the Hill School include: James A. Baker III, Secretary of the Treasury (Hill class of 1948); James Reston, columnist; Frank Borman, astronaut and president of Eastern Airlines; and William Proxmire, United States senator (Hill class of 1934).

Inviting successful alumni to return for talks is one of the ways boarding schools can pass on a sense of the school's efficacy. Throughout the year panels, assemblies, and forums are organized for these occasions. Often the alumni speakers will also have informal sessions with students, visit classrooms, and stay for lunch, tea, or supper.

In keeping with cultural environments of prep schools, especially the select 16 schools, professional musicians, actors, and dancers are regularly invited to perform. Art and sculpture exhibits are common and some schools, such as Andover and Exeter, have permanent art galleries. The art at prep schools is generally either original works by artists such as Toulouse-Lautrec, Matisse, or Daumier, or the work of established contemporary artists such as Frank Stella, who graduated from Andover. At a large school there may be so much cultural activity that it is unnecessary to leave campus for any kind of high cultural event.

Those who come to elite boarding schools to talk or perform are the makers of culture. For adolescents seeking to be the best, these successful individuals give them a sense of importance and enpowerment. All around them are the symbols of their special importance—in Groton's main hallway hangs a personal letter from Ronald Reagan to the headmaster, reminding the students that Groton "boasts a former President of the United States and some of America's finest statesmen." Five or six books a year will be published by a school's alumni; Exeter in particular has many alumni authors, including James Agee, Nathaniel G. Benchley, John Knowles, Dwight Macdonald, Jr., Arthur M. Schlesinger, Jr., Sloan Wilson, and Gore Vidal. Roger L. Stevens, Alan Jay Lerner, and Edward Albee are all Choate-Rosemary Hall alumni, adding luster to a theater program that trains many professional actresses and actors. A student at an elite school is part of a world where success is expected, and celebrity and power are part of the unfolding of life. Not every school is as culturally rich as the elite eastern prep schools, but in the main, most schools work hard to develop an appreciation for high culture. At the Orme School in Arizona, a week is set aside each year in which the whole school participates in looking at art, watching art being made, and making art.

Nowhere is the drive for athletic, cultural, and academic excellence more apparent than in the awards, honors, and prizes that are given to outstanding teams or students at the end of each year. Sporting trophies are often large silver cups with the names of annual champions engraved on several sides. At some schools the triumphs have come with enough regularity to warrant building several hundred yards of glass casing to hold the dozens of medals, trophies, and other mementos that are the victors' spoils. Pictures of past winning teams, looking directly into the camera, seem frozen in time.

Academic prizes tend to be slightly less flashy but no less important. Much like British schoolmasters, American schoolmasters believe in rewarding excellence, so most schools give a number of cultural, service, and academic prizes at the end of each year. There is usually at least one prize in each academic discipline, as well as prizes for overall achievement and effort. There are service prizes for dedicated volunteers, as well as debating and creative writing prizes. Almost all schools have cum laude and other honor societies.

Sitting through a graduation ceremony at a boarding school can be an endurance test—some schools give so many prizes that one could fly from New York to Boston and back in the time it takes to go from the classics prize to the prize for the best woodworking or weaving project. But of course, the greatest prize of all is graduation, and more than a few schools chisel, paint, etch, or carve the names of the graduates into wood, stone, or metal to immortalize their passage from the total institution into the world.

\\\\ REFERENCES

Adelman, Clifford. "Devaluation, Diffusion, and the College Connection: A Study of High School Transcripts, 1964-1981." Washington, D.C.: National Commission on Excellence in Education, 1983.

Bourdieu, Pierre, and Passerson, Jean-Claude. *Reproduction: In Education, Society, and Culture.* Beverly Hills, Calif." Sage, 1977.

Coleman, James S.; Hoffer, Thomas; and Kilgore, Sally. *High School Acheivement.* New York: Basic Books, 1982.

Levine, Steven B. "The Rise of American Boarding Schools and the Development of a National Upper Class." *Social Problems* 28 (October 1980):63-94.

\\\\ DISCUSSION QUESTIONS

1. Visit the website for any one of the following schools: Blair Academy (www.blair.edu), Groton School (www.groton.org), or Phillips Exeter (www.exeter.edu). How do these schools compare to your college in terms of costs and curriculum offerings?

2. Why do you think that these schools offer so many extracurricular activities like the arts, sports, community service, and travel abroad? What is the logic of also emphasizing out of class experiences? Failing public schools are often encouraged to first cut exactly these types of extracurricular programs. Why do you think these important extracurricular activities are not seen as essential at struggling private schools? Is it just a question of money or do you think there may be other reasons?

3. College education is generally presented as a meritocracy, where the most talented and motivated students get into the best colleges and then in turn are rewarded by the most success after they graduate. How much do you think individual talent and motivation plays a role in what type of college people get into and how well they do in school? What, if any, social forces do you think shape someone's likelihood of being successful in school?

⑤SAGE research**methods**

The essential online tool for researchers from the world's leading methods publisher

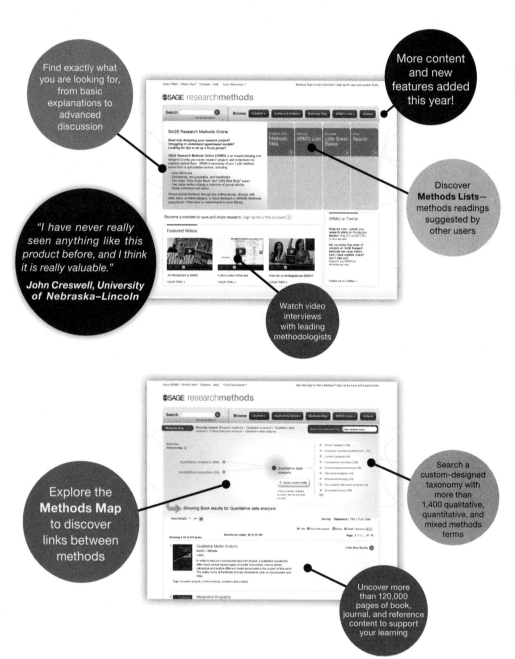

Find exactly what you are looking for, from basic explanations to advanced discussion

More content and new features added this year!

"I have never really seen anything like this product before, and I think it is really valuable."

John Creswell, University of Nebraska–Lincoln

Discover **Methods Lists**— methods readings suggested by other users

Watch video interviews with leading methodologists

Explore the **Methods Map** to discover links between methods

Search a custom-designed taxonomy with more than 1,400 qualitative, quantitative, and mixed methods terms

Uncover more than 120,000 pages of book, journal, and reference content to support your learning

Find out more at
www.sageresearchmethods.com